CLOSE COMPANIONS

CLOSE COMPANIONS

The
Marriage Enrichment
Handbook

DAVID R. MACE

Continuum · New York

To Martha Jane Starr
of Kansas City
And to all who have supported her.

They saw the vision.
They made the venture.

1982

The Continuum Publishing Company
575 Lexington Avenue
New York, New York 10022

Printed in the United States of America

Library of Congress Cataloging in Publication Data

Mace, David Robert.
Close companions.

Bibliography: p. 251
Includes index.
1. Marriage. I. Title.
HQ734.M1838   646.7'8   82-13104
ISBN 0-8264-0206-2   0-8264-0227-5 pbk.

"To this day I believe that there is as much love as hostility in the world. . . . Even in the small circle of my acquaintances, I have found a surprising number of happy marriages and so much incidental kindness that I have quite lost my faith in the wickedness of mankind. . . . I believe that there is a creative spirit in the universe . . . in every man and woman . . . a spirit evident in history, despite every setback and disaster. I believe that the human heritage . . . is greater than ever before, is better protected, and more widely spread, than ever."

—WILL DURANT IN THE *Saturday Review*

"There is no doubt that the conception of the man-woman relationship has never been as complex and ambitious. . . . When the expectation is that marriage will meet all the personality needs of the two partners . . . then a greater number of marriage failures is one of the inevitable results of a much richer, infinitely more fulfilling and indisputably harder concept of marriage. The man-woman relationship is the most personal, deepest and potentially most beautiful relationship two human beings can have. The fact that the Western view of marriage has recognized this and has made this relationship, rather than the procreative or social function of marriage, the central one, is a very marked advance."

—ARIANNA STASSINOPOULOS IN *The Female Woman*

CONTENTS

Part Four—Enriching Marital Therapy and Education

Part Five—Implications for Social Action

DIAGRAMS

TABLES

PREFACE

T HE American family is falling apart." So spoke Urie Bronfenbrenner, of Cornell University, a highly respected family specialist, in an interview reported in *Psychology Today*.

It is a startling statement. Yet there are many who would be inclined to agree. The evidence is constantly before us in the form of increasing divorce rates; broken homes; reports of battered wives and children; undisciplined, disturbed, and delinquent youth; and many other external signs of internal disruption in our homes. We read about these events in our newspapers and magazines; see and hear them reported on radio and television; encounter them in the social circles in which we move; confront them even among our own friends and relatives. Whether we view what is happening as impending disaster, as cultural change, or as emancipation, something is happening to what has throughout recorded history been viewed as the foundation stone of human society.

While this process of disintegration is broad and deep, it has a focal point. The foundation stone of family life has always been marriage, in some shape or form. In all human communities, the marriage customs or laws have been the means of maintaining stable families, which in turn have been the means of maintaining social order. The widespread breakdown of marriage, therefore, has something like a domino effect, sending reverberations far and wide throughout the entire fabric that holds our community life together. It is hard to think of any other event that could happen in civilized society that could have such far-reaching consequences.

There are those among us, of course, who say that marriage is an obsolete institution, which can no longer be expected to survive in the open culture we are creating today, and that the *débâcle* is a signal to us to face impending fundamental changes in the entire structure of human society. There are others who point out that, since most divorced persons remarry within a few years, we are actually freeing marriage from repressive restraints that in the past bound many couples for life to the consequences of immature or unwise choices. There are many interpretations, many opinions, and they are all being freely propagated.

My purpose in this book is to examine what is happening to marriage from these various viewpoints and to focus particularly on an aspect of the subject that has been given little attention and is poorly understood, yet seems to lead to a much more positive assessment of the situation than any others I have encountered: the marriage and family enrichment movement. It is rooted in the conviction that most of the troubles afflicting family life today stem from our failure to see clearly what is happening to marriage as a result of the vast social changes that are taking place, and from our consequent inability to provide the kinds of new services that contemporary marriages and families need to guide them through an era of major cultural transition. I have reached the strong conviction that, if we will only do what is necessary, we now have the opportunity to enable increasing numbers of marriages, and of families, to be happier, healthier, and more creative than ever before in the entire sweep of human history; and this can in time build the foundations of a new and better human society, which is now a real possibility.

I write as a behavioral scientist. Mine is a relatively new field of inquiry, which up to now has been struggling to justify itself, but is at last coming of age. We are on the threshold of a new era in human evolution. The technological sciences have worked wonders in enabling us to tap the vast resources of the world around us. The biological sciences have likewise explored the physical world within us and enabled us to offer longer life and better health to multitudes of people. Neither of these, however, has as yet made human life itself significantly richer or happier. That task depends upon a much deeper understanding of human personality, and especially of human relationships, which the flowering of the behavioral sciences now promises. And it seems to me that there is no human situation where this new promise can be claimed, that could be more significant than when a man and a woman venture to embark on an intimate sharing of their lives, as a means of promoting by mutual cooperation the individual growth of each and the expansion of their relationship into a fundamental unit of world society—a human family.

In the writing of this book, I have drawn on the learnings of a lifetime. My debt to the many who have been my teachers, my colleagues, and my friends is incalculable. Where I have borrowed directly from others, and from known written sources, I have of course identified these. But I have deliberately taken the decision not to provide long lists of references to others who have developed parallel ideas. I prefer to state what I have learned so far, to take full responsibility for it, and to make it clear that my mind is ever open to the illumination of new truth.

Two further points. First, throughout the volume a small amount of repetition will be found. I believe that in a book, as in a musical composition, some repetition gives emphasis to the basic concepts and creates a sense of the unity of the whole. Second, lest any grammatical purist finds fault, let me explain that I deliberately choose to treat the word *couple* as a plural noun.

In conclusion, it is my pleasure to acknowledge very gratefully the help I have received from others in bringing this book into existence. Among friends and colleagues who have read the unpublished manuscript and commented on it, I would especially mention Sarah Catron, Anne Compere, Charles Cole, Ronald Cromwell, Preston Dyer, John Earl, Robert Elfers, Hugh Fielder (in England), Bernard Guerney, Michael Hale, Eldor Kaiser, Sherod Miller, John Robson (in Australia), Antoinette and Leon Smith, Jerry Thompson, and of course my wife, Vera. For help in typing various drafts of the manuscript, I am grateful to Pat Beshears, Anne Compere, Betty Huff, and Connie Rhoads.

PART ONE

Marriage: Old and New

The following chapters explain how a dramatic and fundamental change in our concept of the marriage relationship—from the traditional hierarchical pattern to the new companionship pattern—is taking place in our society. The reasoning is that this change calls for new services to give men and women the equipment they need to appropriate and use their potential for close relationships. Only by doing this can we enable the transition from the traditional marriage pattern to the new companionship pattern to take place successfully.

PROLOGUE

FRANK and Sally are in their middle thirties. He is in business, she is a teacher. They have been married for sixteen years and have two children—Bobby, now fourteen, and Rachel, twelve. Five years ago the parents went to their first marriage-enrichment retreat, and they have been members of the Association of Couples for Marriage Enrichment (ACME)* ever since.

I explained to them that I was going to write this book and asked if I might interview them about what marriage enrichment had meant to them. I am not disclosing their names, and the interview, which was recorded, has been condensed. However, I believe they could be described as typical of couples involved in the marriage-enrichment movement. What follows are the questions I asked and their answers.

Q: Could you sum up, in a few sentences, what marriage enrichment has meant to you?

SALLY: It was a turning point in our life together. Before, we would have said that we had a fairly good marriage. But now we know that we were really far short of our potential. Marriage enrichment opened our eyes to possibilities we had dreamed about, but had failed almost completely to achieve.

FRANK: I agree. I wouldn't say we have come from darkness into light. But it was like coming out of a fog into the sunshine.

Q: Could you interpret this more specifically in terms of contrasts—before and after?

FRANK: I'll try. Before, we didn't communicate very well. Now we do. Before, we had no clear commitment to growth and change in our relationship. Now we do. Before, we avoided conflicts, but when we couldn't avoid them, we got into fights. Now we work through our conflicts and try to use our anger

* See Appendix I.

3

as a guideline for further growth. Before, we just drifted along with no clear goals. Now, we have an intentional marriage, and a growth plan for our future.

SALLY: To me, the big change is summed up in the word *intimacy*. We have moved from a fairly distant relationship to a very close relationship. We have both learned to be much more affectionate, warm, and tender. I think all the other benefits have been based on that fundamental change.

Q: Could you describe just how all this started? How did you get involved in marriage enrichment?

FRANK: It was through another couple in our church. They had been to a marriage-enrichment retreat and told us about it. They encouraged us to sign up. We avoided this at first; but after a big fight we had, we agreed that we needed some new insights. So we went.

SALLY: The retreat turned out to be just what we needed. Of course we were scared at first—most couples are. But the whole experience was so positive, and all the couples were so friendly, that we soon relaxed. And then things began to happen. It seemed like we saw our whole relationship in a new way. You might say it revived dreams we had had on our wedding day and showed us that they could really come true.

FRANK: We ought to add, though, that it was the practical things we learned— the new skills and the new tools—that really gave us new hope.

Q: And what happened after that?

SALLY: Well, we had a feeling of letdown when we settled back into the old routines. But we had been warned about that. And of course we had made a growth plan at the retreat. There it was, all written out, with our signatures and the date! So we knew that if our marriage didn't grow, there would be only one reason—we had failed to do what we both knew we wanted to do.

FRANK: Even so, we could easily have drifted back to the old routines. It isn't easy for a couple to change their behavior.

Q: What was it, then, that kept you on course?

FRANK: It was a lot of things. One was that we had made some short-term contracts, and we found that we felt good when we carried them out. One was to have a daily sharing time, which we had never had before. It helped a lot to keep clearing up misunderstandings before they could develop into a state of alienation.

SALLY: And we gradually learned to affirm each other much more often. That made us both feel good. I was very touched, too, when you freely forgave me for things you would have judged me for before. It meant that I really tried now to change my ways of acting, instead of stubbornly digging in my heels.

FRANK: That was part of my learning to communicate better—to give up Style 2 and use Style 4 instead!

Q: Were you in touch with other ACME couples at this time?

SALLY: Not at first, but it would have been better if we had been. We were raised to feel so private about our marriage. At the retreat, the sense of open-ness to others was so refreshing. But then, back home again, it didn't continue. We felt so isolated.

FRANK: And that was when we got into a support group, organized by the local ACME chapter. Those monthly meetings were both a joy and a challenge. By making ourselves accountable to the group for our continuing growth, we felt a tremendous sense of support. And the friendships we made with those other couples were much closer and deeper than any we had ever experienced before. It was like those people who climb in the Alps, all roped together. If one slips and falls into a crevasse, all the others pull him up again.

Q: What about your relationship to your children? Did that change in any way?

SALLY: It sure did. Not at first, though. We made the mistake of not telling them what had happened to us after the retreat. But when we joined the support group, and learned how other couples were open with their children about their new goals, we talked to ours and asked for their help and support. That was a great experience for all of us.

FRANK: I was to blame for not doing this at first. I was afraid that we would lose our authority over the children if we were open and made ourselves vul-nerable. Now I know how completely wrong I was! In fact, a couple of years later, we joined a family cluster for a year, and that was another great experi-ence.

Q: Can you think of some areas of your relationship that have changed for the better—things like money management, friendships, sex, in-laws?

FRANK: I guess the changes have come gradually, so we've taken them for granted. But yes, I can think of many changes. We used to fight over money, but now we have full agreement on a plan that works. The in-laws? Yes, things go much more smoothly now—we've told them about our marriage-enrichment experiences. They don't discuss this with us—it seems that the privacy attitude toward marriage is much stronger in the older generation.

SALLY: But my mother and I have talked this over very freely. She'd like to go to a marriage-enrichment retreat, but so far my father avoids the issue.

FRANK: Our sex life is much more rewarding, too. We had a big session on this at one meeting of our first support group, and it was a great help to us to be able to share our experiences with the other couples. You mentioned friend-ships. We are much more free about that; we used to have some jealous reac-tions, but now our trust level is much deeper, and that doesn't happen any-more.

Q: The main emphasis in this book is on the idea of the new companionship marriage. Would you like to comment on that?

SALLY: Surely. When we married, we accepted the new concepts of chang-ing women's roles; so in a sense we wanted a companionship marriage. But it was really hard to make it work. I gave up my teaching when the children were small, and I stayed home. But Frank just didn't seem to understand my conflicts, and I couldn't seem to get through to him.

FRANK: I think I see now that the companionship idea can't be imposed on a marriage from outside—we have too many traditional attitudes carried over from the past that we can't give up. So I'd say that the companionship concept must grow from *inside*. It has its roots in the feelings of unity that grow out of a relationship of openness to each other and loving intimacy. Its roots lie deep down.

SALLY: That's well said, Frank. I heartily agree. And until many modern couples really understand this, and put it into practice, they're just not going to know what they're missing.

1
TRADITIONAL MARRIAGE
IN DECLINE

FRANK and Sally are an average twentieth-century married couple. Confronted with the need to improve their relationship, they were ready to respond when the opportunity to be involved in marriage enrichment offered them a chance to do so. This book will have much more to say about the issues they touched on in the brief interview recorded in the Prologue.

However, we cannot understand where marriage is today unless we go back and ask some fundamental questions. What *is* marriage, and how did it develop in the first place? No serious attempt to understand what is happening in our own time can afford to ignore the long process of evolution that has brought us to where we now are. We must, therefore, devote this first chapter to a broad, though brief, historical survey.

The Evolution of Marriage

It is not difficult to conjecture how, in the long process of evolution, marriage could have come into being. Edward Westermarck, in his *History of Human Marriage*, first published in 1891, provides the vital clue in his often-quoted statement, "Marriage is rooted in the family rather than the family in marriage" (1925, vol. 1, p. 72).

Among comparatively simple creatures, there is no need for parental care. The young either start life "fighting fit" and well able to fend for themselves, or they are propagated in such vast numbers that enough of them survive to insure the continuity of the species. Insects, for example, are endowed with a set of instincts that provide them with all they need to cope with life. Young herrings are less able to take care of themselves and are gobbled up in fantastic

7

numbers by waiting predators; but there are always enough of them left to propagate the next generation.

When we move to higher levels, and organisms become more complex, fewer and fewer young are reproduced, and they take longer and longer to mature. Consequently, they need more and more specialized care during their very vulnerable early life. We reach a point at which the mother's eggs can no longer be allowed to hatch outside her body; and when the young do arrive, they need a period of protection. Further up the scale, the young are born so helpless that they require first weeks, then months, then years before they are mature enough to take responsibility for themselves.

The stage is finally reached at which the mother alone is not sufficient to provide for and protect her young. The father must be more than a mere progenitor. He becomes part of the parental team. A point is even reached at which older brothers and sisters lend a hand in caring for the new baby.

At the human level, therefore, the evolution of the family reached the point at which the task of protecting and providing for the young demanded the teamwork of both parents. It was out of this need that marriage evolved. And as human civilization developed, the period of maturing needed to socialize and educate a child has extended to about twenty years—between one-quarter and one-third of the human life span. Throughout that period, both parents may be needed to provide the developing child with all it requires for the maturing process. The bond between father and mother, during these long years of cooperation, could easily develop into a habitual association. Indeed, as the parents grew older, they could look to their grown children to care for them in their later years, thus reversing the parenting process.

The sustained cooperative relationship of a man and a woman therefore developed out of needs that were vital to human survival, and it is easy to see how, as human society became organized, this developed into the institution of marriage. It is also easy to see how the nuclear family—two parents and their children—became the basic building block for other kinds of organized social groupings.

Of course it was not as simple as that. The course of evolution is never a straight line. There were digressions and deviations in all directions, and many experiments that didn't work for every one that did. In the course of human history, it is probable that every variant pattern that could have been tried actually *was* tried. The wide variety of forms marriage has taken is well illustrated in Edward Westermarck's definition: "Marriage is a relation of one or more men to one or more women which is recognized by custom or law and involves certain rights and duties both in the case of the parties entering the union and in the case of the children born of it" (Westermarck, 1925, vol. 1, p. 26).

Some of the various models that emerged have fared better than others. Group marriage, for example, has probably never existed as a settled, continuing pat-

tern. Polygamy, on the other hand, has been widespread, and is still extensively practiced in Africa, and less extensively in Asia. However, it has succeeded much better in the form of polygyny (one husband to several wives)
than in the form of polyandry (one wife to several husbands).

The particular marriage form adopted in any human community has tended
to be the one that best suited the group's needs at the time. In the early nomadic period when our ancestors were hunters and foragers and food was scarce,
small family units probably would have managed best, because they are highly
mobile and small enough in numbers to keep alive during a lean period. Later,
when agriculture had developed and tamed domestic animals were available,
family groups living on the land would not be short of food as long as they
had plenty of hands to work, so larger groupings were more desirable.

In the period of recorded history, we have seen marriage progressively insti-
tutionalized as civilization developed. With minor variations, all the great human cultures have followed broadly the same course, which is defined by the
word *patriarchal*. Since our own cultural roots in the Hebrew, Greek, and
Roman civilizations all adopted this pattern, we had better take a brief look at
it.

Marriage in Western Culture

The patriarchal family, as its name implies, was father dominated. The man
was considered superior to the woman as fighter, leader, and ruler; he therefore
assumed the power to make decisions. There was also another important factor,
which has not been given the recognition it deserves. In the ancient world, the
process of reproduction was not well understood. Since the microscope had not
yet been invented, the sperm and ovum could not be identified. Therefore,
reasoning from what could be observed, people in the old cultures came to the
conclusion that the seminal fluid of the man was in fact the incipient child and
the womb of the woman served simply as an incubator for its development.
The child was therefore the product of the man's seed, planted in the woman's
body as the seed of corn is planted in the earth. This concept is found in early
Hebrew and Greek writings, and continues to be held among primitive African
tribes. What it means is that, in the vital process of transmitting life, the woman
contributed nothing of her essential self, but simply provided a mechanical aid.
This naturally placed her at an inferior level to the man.

There was another advantage in keeping the wife in a submissive role, and
we shall see the importance of this more clearly later. As long as the power
was vested entirely in the husband, marriage was a one-vote system. This obviated the risk of conflict arising out of a clash of wills, and contributed decisively to maintaining the stability of the family.

The Hebrew culture could be taken as a classic illustration of patriarchal
marriage. Indeed, the entire nation was frequently referred to as the "children

of Israel,'' all having come from the loins of the original patriarch. This illustrates vividly Plato's observation that "the nation is the family writ large." The tribal chiefs, and later the kings, were all viewed as father figures, while law and custom alike affirmed the dominance of the husband and the submissiveness of the wife. Divorce, for example, was the right of the Hebrew husband but not of his wife, although her family could intervene for her protection in any situation where she was threatened with injustice.

Greek culture likewise was patriarchal; but it was in Rome that our Western law originated, and Roman law is of great importance to our inquiry. The old Roman *patria potestas* gave the husband supreme power, even the power of life and death, over his wife as well as his children. Although wives acquired some rights of their own in the later centuries, there was never any real question about where authority was vested in the family.

What we see clearly in Roman law is the manner in which marriage was viewed as the foundation stone of the system for preserving social order. The family had to be subservient to the authority of the state; and in turn family members had to be subservient to the authority of the family head. The whims of individual choice and preference could not be allowed to unsettle the rigidity of this monolithic system. We find similar arrangements in all the great cultures based on the ancient religions: Buddhism, Hinduism, and Mohammedanism, as well as Judaism and Christianity.

The Christian era took over this concept and gave it the support of the Church as well as of the Law. The rituals of most traditional marriage ceremonies began with a preamble about the three causes for which marriage was divinely ordained. Procreation naturally came first. The second was to keep sex under proper control, lest it become the source of discord by inciting jealousy, contention, and conspiracy in the body politic (history has provided plenty of evidence of the way in which wayward sexual desires could disrupt the life of the community and even plunge countries and nations into war). The third cause was the companionship that a man and woman could enjoy together, based upon rendering mutual service to one another. We may remember that in the Book of Genesis, God said that it was not good for Adam to be alone. This element in marriage, though it was recognized, was given scant attention by church or state until our own era, when it has emerged as the dominant issue.

The Catholic Church made marriage a sacrament, and in the process subjected it to rigid ecclesiastical controls. Despite its sacramental nature, it was viewed as a way of life spiritually inferior to that of celibacy—a scale of values given full affirmation at the Council of Trent (1545–63). This was largely an outcome of the Church's ascetic view of sexuality, which Augustine had regarded as sinful except when used expressly to beget children, and venial if enjoyed by the participants.

Ecclesiastical law made divorce impossible, and this was later reflected in state law. In England, until 1857, a divorce could be procured only by a special

Act of Parliament. Likewise, the subservience of the wife was assured in England by a legal enactment that upon marriage, all of a woman's property passed to her husband's control—a state of affairs that was not ended until the passing of the Married Women's Property Acts in the late nineteenth century.

The Contemporary Cultural Revolution

The rigid legal and religious controls over marriage had already begun to lose their power, especially in North America, at the beginning of this century. But the scope and vigor of the revolutionary changes that were to come could not have been imagined at that time.

The rebellion against the rigidities surrounding marriage marked the convergence of many forces, only a few of which can be mentioned here. The rapid rise of urban culture, following the earlier agricultural settlements, uprooted multitudes of people and broke the power of social and neighborhood controls. The vast development of travel from railroad to automobile to aviation produced high rates of mobility. The mass media opened up communication and brought diversity of opinions on all subjects right into family living rooms. Scientific humanism led a sustained attack on the rigid ethical standards of conservative religious groups. Some liberation movements fought for almost unlimited individual freedom. Affluence opened doors of opportunity, while hedonism offered for sale a wide selection of hitherto forbidden fruit. These and many other influences created a completely new social climate, which encouraged experimentation and pluralism while it undermined the traditional system of controls.

This cultural revolution has come quickly—too quickly for any kind of orderly adaptation to take place. It has created for marriage and the family a state of bewildering confusion, with traditional and avant-garde philosophies coexisting almost side by side. But there can now be little doubt about the ultimate issue. Rallying conservative groups have tried to make a last stand here and there and are still doing so; but the momentum of the new value system is sweeping them aside, and with the youth culture almost totally indoctrinated the outcome appears certain.

What outcome? I mean simply that the traditional family system, with its built-in rigidities, is no longer enforceable. If it has a case, it can still plead for recognition in the marketplace; but it no longer has the power to compel obedience. The family has in fact been stripped of most of its traditional functions. We no longer build our own homes or make our own clothes or furniture. We no longer grow our own food, administer folk medicine, organize home recreation. Our children now get their religious education from the church, their secular education from the public school, and most of their values from the mass media. Our homes are now largely unoccupied on weekdays—the parents (or parent) at work, the older children at school, the younger children at the day-care center. It is relatively rare for the family members to be all together at home in the evenings or at the weekends. It is relatively rare for the whole family to be together outside the home. Our leisure activities are largely fragmented.

Under these conditions, marriages are crumbling at an increasing rate. American divorce rates, already among the highest in the world, have been soaring higher still in the last few years. Esteem for marriage seems to be at an all-time low. Once viewed as a sacred institution, it is now kicked around like an old football. The prevailing cynical attitudes, vigorously propagated in the mass media, have convinced some people that we are witnessing its final demise. A Yankelovich poll of college students a few years ago found that 34 percent of them viewed marriage as "an obsolete institution"; and someone offered the opinion that this might be the last generation of young people who would marry on any significant scale.

The demise of marriage would clearly leave a vacuum. But don't worry, we were told, everything is arranged. Experimental new life styles, we have been confidently assured, are on the way and will replace our obsolete family system. When we examine these new social experiments, some of them do indeed offer improvements in community living. But when we focus on the substitutes for marriage, we find that some of them bear a striking resemblance to variants that we discarded earlier in the evolutionary process—such as polygamy (as before, with polygyny decidedly in the ascendant) and group marriage, which seems no more durable now than in the past. Another substitute form is the one-parent family, but this usually consists of a discarded or disenchanted ex-wife making the best of it with her children until she can do better the next time around, or an unmarried mother bravely struggling to raise her child or children without benefit of father. When we inquire about other variant forms, we are referred to marriages in which extramarital sex is accepted more extensively, and more openly, than it has been in the past; to couples living together very much as the legally married do, but without a certificate; and to cohabiting homosexuals who wish their union to be legally recognized.

These experiments have, no doubt, served some useful purposes; but they have been given an amount of publicity altogether out of proportion to their importance. I have examined them quite closely, but I find little evidence that they could, in the near future, offer fulfilling lives to any more than a fraction of our present population on an enduring basis. They are in fact far from durable—most of those who participate in them seem to be young and transient. And not a few of them turn out to be in fact marriages of a novel kind, or very typical marriages in all but name.

Apart from the comparative handful of people really involved in the true variant styles, the vast majority of the unmarried are genuine singles—ex-husbands or ex-wives in transition from one marriage to the next (between two-thirds and three-quarters of all divorced persons remarry), or couples who are to all intents and purposes in what I prefer to call "unregistered marriages." Even if you want to call the modern trend "serial monogamy," each union is a marriage as long as it lasts, and if it doesn't last the obvious reason is that it didn't come up to expectations. If it had proved satisfying, it would probably still be intact. So what is really happening is that people on a very large scale are still seeking what they believe marriage has to offer but are failing dismally to find it.

Surely what we need to do, therefore, is not to hunt around for alternatives to marriage, but to discover why so many people are failing to find satisfaction in married life; and then to consider whether we can do something about it. This is in fact what marriage enrichment, in its true meaning, is all about. We *are* exploring, and we *are* finding answers. But when we try to say so, we are met with cries of derision from some people who seem not to *want* marriages to be improved, but only to have the whole system abolished, with nothing of any substance to take its place. This seems at times to be a form of nihilism.

However, while all this doubting and arguing have been going on, something quite promising has been taking place. Quietly, almost unnoticed at first, a really effective alternative life style has emerged—one that can very fittingly fill the empty space left by the collapse of the traditional marriage system. We shall examine this interesting new phenomenon in the next chapter.

2

THE NEW
COMPANIONSHIP STYLE

ERNEST Burgess has justly been called the father of American family sociology. He was a small, modest, unassuming man, but a distinguished scholar.
He set out, with well-chosen professional colleagues, to make a thorough study
of marriage and the family in North American culture. His best-known book,
The Family—from Institution to Companionship (Burgess and Locke), provides, in eight hundred pages, a summary of his findings and recommenda-
tions, following years of investigation. It was first published in 1945—and
would that it had been better known and taken more seriously!

Burgess said, in effect, that *the family is undergoing a major transition. The
institutional form, as he called it, has served its purpose in maintaining social
order in closed, hierarchical cultures. But in our open democratic society the
primary emphasis on social order has been replaced by a new emphasis on the
quality of the relationships between the family members.*

In a broad sense this is so obvious that it might seem hardly worth writing a
book about it. But our present dilemma concerning marriage and the family
would have been much less acute if we had really listened to Burgess. We have
continued not to listen in the more than thirty-five years that have passed since,
and still are not paying heed to his vitally important message.

Burgess saw the marriage of the past as being legalistic, hierarchical, and
based on the performance of closely defined roles leading to cramping, confining relationships, with little room for growth or change. He saw the new companionship model as fluid, flexible, based on loving and creative interaction,
and open to growth. He considered the transition to be inevitable and irreversible, and he tried to spell out the means by which we might enable it to take
place as smoothly as possible. The implication was that the new pattern would

14

be quite difficult to learn, but when learned would result in rich and meaningful relationships between husband and wife, between parent and child.

I am deeply convinced that Burgess provided us with the key to understanding what is happening to marriage and the family today. He further elaborated his views in a second eight hundred-page volume, *Engagement and Marriage* (1953), coauthored with Paul Wallin.

I prefer to speak of the "traditional" rather than the "institutional" family as the form that is passing away. It was rooted in the traditions of the past, and served well enough in its time; but it is now anachronistic. The word *institution* has, I think, a somewhat different nuance. My dictionary defines it as "a relationship or behavior pattern of importance in the life of a community or society." In that sense, I think we shall always need institutions, but with the onward march of progress we should be able from time to time to discard the traditional ones and replace them with new and more relevant forms.

The word *companionship,* on the other hand, very neatly describes the new marriage style that has emerged to replace the traditional one. We need to avoid, however, any possible confusion of this with the "companionate marriage," advocated in a 1927 book by Judge Ben Lindsey as a sanctioned form of trial marriage for young people.

Another term that would serve would be the "partnership marriage," which was frequently used by the distinguished European marriage specialist Theodor Bovet. But I think "companionship" includes all that "partnership" does, and perhaps a more warmly loving dimension as well.

Comparing the Old and the New

In order to provide a broad basis for comparing the two marriage models, I have compiled a list (see Table 1) of some of the differences between them. It is by no means exhaustive, but the ten items it contains should be enough for our present purpose.

In Chapter 6, I will describe some of these differences between the old and the new marriage patterns in greater detail. The transition now taking place is of course a gradual process, likely to span about a century; and the pace at which it is proceeding may vary greatly between one community and another.

However, the difference between the old marriage pattern and the new is very clear. The first conforms to a rigid system, which provides ready-made answers to most questions that are likely to arise. The couple don't have to struggle with differences; and they don't have to be much involved in each other's inner thoughts and feelings. The second pattern, by contrast, involves husband and wife in a continuing series of interpersonal interactions and is virtually unworkable unless they can establish the kind of flexible relationship that only companionship makes possible.

The emergence of the companionship marriage was inevitable, and it repre-

TABLE I

MARRIAGE, OLD AND NEW

A Comparison of the Traditional and the Companionship Models

Traditional	Companionship
One-vote system—husband makes all major decisions	Two-vote system—decisions jointly made by husband and wife
Fixed roles—husband's and wife's roles clearly differentiated by gender	Fluid roles—roles based on personal choice and competence, with little emphasis on gender difference
Husband provider—wife homemaker	Flexible division of provider and homemaker functions
Husband initiates sex—wife complies	Sex initiated by either husband or wife
Basic concept—marriage a hierarchy	Basic concept—marriage an equal partnership
Issues settled with reference to legalistic principles and rules	Issues settled with reference to personal and interpersonal needs
Wife close to children—husband disciplinarian and authority figure	Husband and wife both close to children, both represent authority
Husband assumes role of religious head of family	Religious functions of family shared by husband and wife
Further education important for husband, not for wife	Further education equally important for both
Husband's vocation decides family residence	Family residence takes account of both husband's and wife's vocations

sents a transition process arising out of a revolt against the rigidities of traditional marriage, in an increasingly open democratic culture. The struggle is epitomized in two highly significant words: *Love* and *Equality*.

The Love Marriage Is New

We need to recognize the fact that marriage in human history was not based on love—at least not on romantic love. Until China went Communist in 1949, more than half of all the world's marriages were "arranged" by parents or other persons in authority. They were not based on natural attraction or affection between the boy and the girl, but rather on considerations of convenience and social advantage to the two families concerned. True, the dream of romantic love was always there—in the poetry, the songs, and the legends—but young people had an awkward way of falling in love across the established frontiers of tribe, class, and religion, and the only way to avoid these inconveniences was to take the matter firmly in hand and treat marriage as a strictly utilitarian operation. Its purposes were to produce offspring to continue the family line, to provide for the management of the family property and the maintenance of the family traditions.

Romantic love, therefore, was considered not only as something not connected with marriage, but even as introducing undesirable complications. The romantic tradition was rich in premarital and extramarital fantasies; but marriage itself was seen as generally dull and unexciting, associated more with duty than with pleasure.

Gradually, however, and especially as young people gained greater freedom of choice, marriage for love ousted the older emphasis on convenience and security. By the first half of this century the love marriage was established as the norm. The American girl in particular was encouraged to dream of the Prince Charming who one day would enter her life, sweep her up in his arms, and carry her off to a life of endless bliss. The boys perhaps were rather less starry-eyed, being more interested in sex than in love; but they were quite ready to go along with the game.

The women's magazines of the time dutifully sustained the romantic legends. They were replete with articles about the unending joy that awaited the young wife who knew how to keep herself attractive and who had learned the subtle arts and skills that would make her "lovable."

In today's youth culture, the romantic dream has been rudely shattered and replaced by a stern realism, sex in the here and now, and a cynical attitude toward marriage. At any rate, that's the surface reaction. Yet beneath the surface, the dream of love still lingers, and will surely revive, though in a more sober and realistic form. The present rejection of marriage is only a phase, an understandable and forgivable reaction to the grossly oversold and sickly romanticism inflicted upon the previous generation. We shall return to this important question.

Changing Roles for Wives

The other key word is *equality*. The women's liberation movement has assiduously searched the historical records for evidence of discrimination against the female of the species and has reaped a rich harvest among the archives of traditional marriage. I have no wish to argue the point. There is no doubt that in traditional marriage women were conspicuously put down, slighted, depersonalized, and humiliated. So universal was this, in fact, that women simply accepted the situation and made the best of it; and at least it gave them security and protection in a world often viciously tough and hazardous to live in. The hot indignation felt by the liberated woman of today as she reads about the confined life of her great-great-grandmother is, however, largely wasted, because the lady in question would have been greatly surprised if anyone had commiserated with her about the injustice of her lot.

Anyway, the banner of equality in marriage has now been unfurled and run up to the masthead. A generation ago, the "fifty-fifty marriage" was proclaimed as the ideal, and a strenuous campaign has been going on ever since to enforce it, a campaign so vigorous that a counterattack has been mounted with surprising energy by Marabel Morgan, author of *The Total Woman,* and her disciples and imitators. In our age of personal freedom, I predict that this will be short-lived.

I completely agree with the principle that the personhood of woman must be given the opportunity for full development. This is a reform that is long overdue. In the far distant future, as historians look back, it may be seen as the most significant event of the twentieth century.

I am obliged to point out, however, that putting this into operation literally delivers the coup de grâce to traditional marriage, so we must realistically balance our gains and losses. Let it be done, by all means, because justice demands it. But the blundering, insensitive way in which we are presently doing it is rather like dismantling an obsolete building in a busy city street at high noon by exploding a bomb under it. A lot of innocent people are getting hurt by the falling wreckage.

We need to remember that, if in past ages the personhood of woman was sacrificed on the altar in order to insure the stability of family life, the goal was a pretty important one. It is much easier to rewrite history than to reenact it. To suggest that the woman's subject status in the traditional home was a vicious manifestation of deliberate brutality on the part of the males of the population represents a highly prejudiced and totally unrealistic appraisal of the facts. For every human culture, the top priority must be sheer survival. And it is arguable that the early human communities that finally created our Western society might not have survived without stable families; in which case we would not be here, comfortable and secure in our twentieth-century affluence, to point accusing fingers at them. Even if our superior wisdom after the event can come up with a workable formula that might have made it all different, our ancestors probably lacked the wit to invent it at the time.

Let me put the issue very plainly: a marriage that is a one-vote system is largely conflict-free. All major decisions are made by one person and accepted by the other. Some pain and humiliation are inevitably involved for the submissive partner, especially when the dominant partner acts exploitatively or punitively. But at least it results in a general state of order and stability. So if stability is your goal, the price might be worth paying.

Switch to a two-vote system, however, and you have a situation vastly more difficult to manage. Two conflicting wills mean the possibility of endless disagreement and strife, and if the two persons concerned have plenty of basic differences in their needs and wishes, a state of chronic acerbity is introduced into the relationship. In other words, demand equality in marriage and you take the risk of all hell breaking loose. Unless the couple have highly developed skills in the very complex art of negotiating disagreements, their relationship may soon be in serious trouble.

This then is the practical significance of the transition Burgess saw taking place in marriage. The demand for love and equality turned a relationship that was relatively easy to handle into a very difficult task requiring much more skill than the average couple possessed. It was like getting off a cart horse and mounting a race horse.

An Era of Confusion

All this was not at all clearly understood by the starry-eyed couples who were involved in the transition. They eagerly bought the love marriage and the fifty-fifty marriage, expecting to be ushered into a relationship of instant happiness and effortless harmony. The rude discovery that this was not so shocked them deeply. But because of the heavy veil of privacy that surrounds the marriage relationship, they did not cry aloud. They plodded doggedly on, hoping that somehow the dream might still come true, but inwardly becoming progressively disillusioned. Each couple in turn struggled with a secret guilt that they, alone among their friends and neighbors, were failing to do something that other people did with comparative ease. With courage and fortitude they kept up the pretense in public, hiding their deep disillusionment with cheerful smiles. For some of them the effort to keep smiling became intolerable, and they secretly sought out marriage counseling, shamed into the painful admission that they were "having problems."

We can now understand quite clearly what was going on. But we didn't at the time. And unfortunately, because the real issue was seldom faced, when the great sham broke open and was publicly revealed in the form of a flood of divorces, the wrong conclusions were drawn. When emergence of the companionship model ended in an epidemic of marriage failures, the inference was that marriage itself had now been unmasked, and that it was a cruel deception. One writer even described it as a trap set by society, into which young people were enticed by promises of love and happiness, and then the trap snapped shut and they found themselves confined in a den of misery.

To make the issue more confusing, hardly anyone understood that the marriage model had changed and that this important fact had to be taken into account. The conclusion was that the blame lay entirely with the traditional marriage—usually identified in terms of monogamy and the nuclear family—and its shortcomings were loudly denounced and its early demise jubilantly proclaimed. The fact that it was already all but dead, and that it was the new form replacing it that was failing (for the simple reason that the new form required quite different skills, which the couples simply did not possess) was completely obscured in the general chorus of recrimination and the hot pursuit of "alternatives to marriage" that soon followed.

It is both startling and shocking that such an egregiously misleading misinterpretation of a major social event should have been so widely and naively accepted by almost an entire generation of the very people whose lives were so intimately and immediately involved in what was happening. Even the people who resisted the attack on marriage and came to its defense were for the most part unaware of the fact that the traditional marriage was not only past the point of being defended, but not worth defending because the new companionship form is so much better suited to the new world in which we are now living, if only we will take the trouble to understand it and learn how to make it work.

This piece of recent history is so vital to the whole theme of this book that I wish at this point to summarize what the event was, and how different are the two interpretations that can be offered.

The Event. A quiet cultural transition took place in which the rigid traditional marriage was replaced by the new companionship form, based primarily on the concepts of love and equality. The unfortunate, though quite logical, result was a massive flood of marital failures.

Interpretations. 1. Traditional marriage (the transition to the new form went unnoticed) is now revealed as a hollow sham and doesn't bring the fulfillment it promises. Therefore we must abandon it and turn to new alternative forms (these were neither clearly defined nor their shortcomings admitted).

2. Traditional marriage is anachronistic in our open society, and the emerging companionship form replacing it requires entirely new skills, which most couples do not at present possess. We must, therefore teach these skills if we are to prevent marriages from breaking down to a disturbing degree.

What Can Now Be Done?

In 1955, ten years after Ernest Burgess had first published his findings, Nelson Foote, another family sociologist, wrote a book (coauthored by Leonard Cottrell) in which he coined the term "interpersonal competence." What he tried to do was to define in specific terms some of the new skills we need to make companionship marriage work. Burgess had spoken of new services that would be needed, but had not very clearly identified the kind of retraining that couples would require. Foote made a good start toward filling this gap; but much more progress has been made quite recently. We owe to Foote, however, both the concept and a vivid descriptive term he coined to describe it.

What *is* "interpersonal competence"? Before we can answer this question, we must take a look at the ways in which people are in fact trained to relate to each other in human society.

Most of the older cultures, as we have seen, were hierarchical. Traditional Japan furnishes a recent and classic illustration. If you learn to speak Japanese, you can use three ways of addressing another person: deferential, as you speak up to a superior; patronizing, as you speak down to an inferior; relaxed and friendly, as you speak across to an equal. You and the other people around you accept the social status into which you were born, and you don't try to change it. But above all, you are always polite. The first day I spent in Tokyo I ended up with a backache because of the bowing I was so unaccustomed to!

These are all defensive measures well designed to keep you out of trouble. And the way to keep out of trouble, above all else, is to learn not to communicate your true inner feelings.

American society has never adopted the rigid hierarchical structures of the older cultures, but has opened the door wide for people to "get ahead." However, this has made for a highly competitive situation, with very much the same need to conceal your real feelings, though for a quite different reason. To climb the social ladder you must present yourself as a self-confident, successful person—stressing your achievements and carefully hiding your weaknesses.

In either kind of society, we soon learn to guard carefully our inner thoughts, feelings, and wishes. We learn to wear a mask in order to hide our real selves, to project an image we think will make a good impression, to be pleasing to those whose favor we seek, even if this means being completely dishonest and hypocritical. We simply take all this for granted, blissfully unaware of the fact that we are telling little white lies all day long. We smile indulgently at the straightforward honesty of young children, and we comfort their parents with the assurance that they will soon learn to behave properly.

Our patterns of social behavior are probably necessary—at least until we can do some drastic restructuring. I am simply pointing out that this is the way we are trained to interact with others.

However, many people pay a heavy price for this practice of unreality. It is the cause of most mental illness. It places great stress upon our society. And it deprives us of the simple, artless happiness of just being ourselves, and the fulfillment of becoming ourselves in any true sense.

What we need, and need desperately, is a protected inner world in which we can take off our masks, relax, and learn to develop our hidden potential as loving, caring persons, This however is denied us. Our very training to live in society robs us of the power and skill we need to satisfy our deep craving for intimacy.

We are, in fact, so habituated to "transactional" relationships, geared to a limited exchange of services or favors, that we are unable to function in any other way. The result is that when we marry, in quest of intimacy, love, and tenderness, we are almost completely unable to function at the levels necessary to achieve our goals. Ian Suttie, a British psychiatrist, spoke in 1935 of the "taboo on tenderness" that permeates our Western society.

In the traditional marriage, this deficiency didn't matter. The goal of stable marriage was in the past achieved not only by enforcing a one-vote system, but also by establishing stereotyped roles for husband and wife, which had the effect of clearly defining their separate spheres of influence so that they would not clash or compete. Young people were thoroughly trained for these pre-scribed roles. In a few intimate areas like sex, they had to go into it blind and follow their instincts; but since there were no established norms except to achieve pregnancy, most couples managed to reach this simple goal. Beyond that, noth-ing else was required.

The French word *rôle* means the script you memorize before you go on the stage. Once the couple got over the strangeness of actual experience, they soon picked up each other's clues and worked out the appropriate set of stereotypes.

The companionship marriage, however, calls for something entirely differ-ent. It is not playacting, but a genuine encounter between two persons who are committed to being their true selves and to being equal partners, and within that context finding a way to meet each other's needs with understanding and compassion. This is a very complex and demanding task, and the possibilities of failure are frightening. Yet the rewards, for those who succeed, are tremen-dous.

Today people are going into marriage in search of these rewards but with almost none of the necessary equipment to achieve them. It is as if we sent them out on a journey in wilderness country, described the destination clearly, but gave them no directions and provided them with no map or compass.

My favorite illustration of this is what happened in the field of aeronautics when we made the switch from piston-engine to jet-engine planes. The new planes were superior in every way—they flew higher and faster and were much more comfortable. However, when the transition took place, all the pilots had to be retrained. If we had simply put them in the jet planes and told them to do their best to get the machines off the ground, the results would have been disastrous, and jet planes would have been crashing all over the place.

This is what has been happening to marriage. A fundamental change of de-sign has taken place. The new design is much better suited to our needs in contemporary society. But, disregarding the warnings of Ernest Burgess and others, we have failed almost completely, not only to provide the retraining necessary, but even to make it clear that a change of design has in fact taken place.

What is needed now is to retrace our steps and begin to do what we should have been doing before. We must learn what interpersonal competence really is as it applies to the companionship marriage, and how we can provide couples with the necessary skills to succeed in the new kind of relationship.

This is the task before us. The future happiness of millions, and even per-haps the survival of democratic society, depends on its successful accomplish-ment.

In 1978, I attempted to define the companionship marriage as follows: "Companionship marriage is a socially registered commitment between a man and a woman, in which they seek to know themselves and each other as far as they are capable of being known, and, through mutual affection and affirmation, help each other to grow and change in order to become the loving and creative persons they are capable of becoming."

Let me add some notes by way of commentary:

1. Although the social registration of marriage can be given undue importance, it represents a responsible intention to establish a new unit of human society, and this commitment provides strength to the relationship in making difficult adjustments.

2. Knowing each other as persons requires an effective functioning communication system; but it also requires the courage and fortitude to accept the pain that mutual self-disclosure may bring about and that may be necessary for growth and change.

3. There are limits to the extent to which we can ever know ourselves and each other, and these limits must be realistically accepted. An area of unfathomable mystery must remain in the closest of human relationships.

4. Growth can take place only in fertile soil. In marriage, that soil is provided by the continuous practice of affection and affirmation and, because of our human frailty, by the exercise when necessary of forgiveness and reconciliation.

5. Given a fertile soil, growth in relationship represents the progressive development of the potential that is within us, combined with constant adaptation to the processes of change that are continually occurring in each other and in our social environment. Growth and change must go on throughout the whole of life. A companionship marriage can never cease to grow.

6. The product of a companionship marriage must be two loving and creative persons. Any other goal must be considered secondary.

3

INTERPERSONAL COMPETENCE: THE KEY CONCEPT

MARRIAGE today can be likened to that mythical bird the phoenix. Dying, it was consumed by fire, until there was nothing left but a heap of ashes. Then, miraculously, from the ashes there arose a new phoenix, vigorous and very much alive.

Far from being dead and done for, marriage has in reality been liberated and resurrected. As we have seen, what has died is the rigid, legalistic, traditional pattern; and its death is not tragic—it has served well enough the kind of human society out of which it emerged. Now a new kind of society needs a new kind of marriage, and that is exactly what is emerging from the ashes. The marriage scene of today presents us, therefore, with an astonishing confusion—some marriages dying, while others are springing into new life, and all side by side.

What People Want from Marriage

Before we can discuss what kinds of resources are now needed by married couples, we must be quite clear on what it is people want out of marriage today.

When I say that marriage has been liberated, I mean that it is no longer required to submit to the social order as in the past. We do not need to marry primarily to produce children; in a world already overpopulated, and in an age when the death of a child is fortunately a rare event, the ancient injunction to be fruitful and multiply is not always good advice. Nor need a man any longer marry in order to secure a housekeeper. The local restaurant can cook his meals and the laundry can take care of his clothes; or he can do both himself.

A woman need no longer marry for economic security. If she is at all qual-

24

ified she can earn a good living, do a minimum of housework, and enjoy full freedom and independence.

It isn't even necessary any more to marry for sex, which seems to be freely available, in great variety, in most communities.

So people today are not driven into marriage by their relatives, by necessity, or out of a sense of duty. Unmarried people today are no longer considered odd or deficient or deprived.

What all this means is that for the first time in human history, people are free to marry for love, and for love alone. This is a dream that has tantalized people all through the ages, and it seems almost unbelievable that at long last it has really come true.

Now, indeed, the traditional reasons for marriage, as they appear in the wedding service, stand in reverse order—companionship first, then sex, then procreation.

'All this has happened with the emergence of the companionship marriage. What, then, is it that people are really looking for? We have already seen that most people today want love and equality in marriage; and we have also referred to intimacy. There may be others, but these are the main objectives, so we had better look at them more closely:

Equality. I would put equality first, not because it is more important than love, but because I think it is a precondition for the kind of love that is today held in the highest esteem. Love can of course exist in a hierarchical system. You can love a child in a protective way, in a pitying way, even in a possessive way. A child can love its parents in a dutiful way and in a dependently grateful way.

But I believe love between two people reaches its greatest height when they stand on a level of equality, neither dominating the other nor submitting to the other, each viewing the other with respect as an equal, each according to the other full personhood.

However, when we create these conditions, we also, inevitably, create the conditions for interpersonal conflict!

When differences arise, as they inevitably do, how do two equal persons resolve them? Equality in marriage, again and again, creates deadlock and can set up a power struggle that threatens the whole relationship. This is where the couple in a companionship marriage need special skills that were not required in a traditional marriage. Lacking these skills, the advantages of equality are soon overwhelmed by the disadvantages.

Equality, therefore, cannot be managed unless with it the couple acquire quite complicated skills that are needed for the resolution of interpersonal conflict. This must be a very vital part of training in interpersonal competence.

Love. Most married people today want love above all else. It is a very complex subject, about which many books have been written. It includes esteem for the partner, affection, warmth, and tenderness. One of our most vital human needs, perhaps the most vital of all, is the need to love and be loved. In marriage, love cannot be feigned, as it can be in more superficial relationships. A verbal declaration of love has no validity if the nonverbal messages cancel it out.

Love in marriage must also be sustained if it is to be meaningful. Shallow love that comes and goes in favorable and unfavorable conditions is not enough. The times when we most need to be loved are the times when we feel ourselves to be, and probably are, somewhat unlovable. Love must be deep and strong to be sustained in such conditions.

In marriage, love is not dependable if it is based on partial knowledge. The only basis for a secure sense of identity and self-worth is the knowledge that you are fully known and at the same time deeply loved. This calls for a high degree of self-disclosure, and many married people shrink from this, fearing that if they were in fact fully known they would not be loved, but rejected.

Love also needs to be nourished. Few of us can go on loving someone who doesn't give love in return. In the close life married couples lead, frustration and irritation can often arise, generating anger, which quenches love. Unless couples have the skills to deal with these situations creatively and clear them up, love can soon wither. Love also needs to be constantly renewed through mutual affirmation and, if need be, through mutual forgiveness.

Without understanding of the intricacies of loving, the best-intentioned couples can blunder and extinguish the flame that once brought warmth and light into their lives. So often does this happen that many people believe the slow cooling of love in marriage is an inevitable process. On the contrary, in a well-nourished marriage, love should increase, rather than decrease, as the years pass. But this cannot happen to couples unless they know how to guard and nourish tenderness and affection.

Intimacy. This word is also difficult to define. Even without knowing clearly what they mean, many couples declare their need for intimacy. What they mean is essentially closeness, and the feeling of security and support that comes from closeness. Today the word is often given a sexual connotation, and that is certainly an important element of it. But there is much more to it than that, as Thomas Oden (1974, p. 33) implied when he said, "Sexual intimacy without interpersonal intimacy is like a diploma without an education."

Intimacy has been briefly defined as "shared privacy." It involves a high level of trust, and this has to be built up slowly over time. Any occasion that destroys trust sets the process back a long way. Intimacy means making oneself vulnerable and defenseless; and any attempt on the part of the other to exploit this in demanding or controlling ways can be devastating. Although intimacy meets our dependency needs (and we all have times when we need to lean on a friendly shoulder), too much dependence can become enervating to one partner and imprisoning to the other; or worse still, it can tempt the stronger partner to gain power by taking control.

Through sustained intimacy a sense of unity develops in the marriage partners, and this is strengthening. But unity must never be considered union. In a poetic sense we use the concept of "two becoming one" in marriage; but outside the sphere of poetry it is a dangerous idea. The union of two persons would literally mean the annihilation of one and probably of both.

Even in a deeply loving marriage, there can be no forceful penetration of one person into the inner life of the other. That would be a violation of all that love means. There is a deep truth in the often-quoted words of Kahlil Gibran, the Lebanese poet, "Let there be spaces in your togetherness."

Thus, in all our seeking together for love and intimacy, each person must remain free to be, and to continue to become, his or her own self. Any violation of the other's selfhood spells the death of love. It is here that the principle of equality provides a valuable safeguard.

In this brief discussion we have looked at three of the goals that are most often desired in the companionship marriage. It can all be summed up in the term "relationship-in-depth." This is something that has to be actively cultivated; it never happens by chance or comes naturally. And it requires skills that few are ever taught.

Even this brief discussion surely reveals that all this had little or no place in the traditional marriage. In my boyhood in Scotland I was able to observe closely many marriages among relatives and family friends. They were all stable, and the couples maintained at least an outward appearance of mutual respect and occasionally even of affection. But I can remember only one couple in whom I really saw genuine equality, love, and intimacy, and the warmth of that particular marriage still stands out in my memory, in contrast to the tepid quality of the others.

Three Essentials for Successful Companionship Marriage

How, then, can we train people for companionship marriage? Much of the rest of the book will be devoted to answering this important question. Let me summarize here what I have come to believe is possible and then fill in the details later.

Interpersonal competence means skill in relating to others. In marriage, I believe that the critical question is whether or not the couple possess what I call a "primary coping system." If they do, with the addition of a little relevant information when the need arises, a little wise guidance in an occasional perplexing situation, and the availability of skilled counseling in a real crisis, the couple can handle their marriage in such a way that it will grow and flourish. Without this primary coping system, however, they are not much better off than a rudderless ship on the high seas. And it will require little more than a miracle for them to achieve otherwise reasonable goals.

A "primary coping system" consists of three essentials:

A Commitment to Growth. We have seen that the traditional marriage was used primarily to preserve social order, and that its stability was the highest priority. It was recognized, however, that some kind of "compatibility" between husband and wife was desirable, and in arranged marriages this was often given careful consideration when the choice was made. Beyond that, however, any idea that significant growth would take place was not viewed with favor. It was recognized that people will inevitably change somewhat as they move through the life cycle, and that these changes affect their close relationships. But just as two-vote systems and shared spheres of influence were viewed as threatening to marital stability, so were growth and change. The word went out, therefore, that the wedding was expected to be followed by a process of "settling down." Too much concern about growth might have unsettling consequences, so it was better not to encourage it.

By contrast, the companionship marriage depends for its effectiveness on the growth process, in order to bring about changes that are essential if the couple are to adapt flexibly to each other in a shared life. However much they have in common when they marry, no couple can possibly expect to fit neatly and precisely the contours of each other's personal behavior patterns. Only by working patiently and persistently on the task of smoothing out the rough areas of their relationship can they reach the delicate articulation and flexible mutuality that make for a harmonious marriage. Like two dancers who perfectly match each other's body movements, the well-married couple learn to integrate their lives in creative harmony.

And all this, of course, must not hinder or block the separate individual growth of each of the partners. In a shallow marriage, insecure people will cling compulsively to their partners and in the process deny them personal freedom. In a truly loving relationship, by contrast, there is always enough trust to enable each partner to encourage and foster the personal growth of the other.

Unless the couple have made a clear commitment to each other that they intend to work for ongoing growth in their relationship, the strong likelihood is that they will do nothing about it, or that they will make a few half-hearted efforts and then give up.

The commitment to growth therefore provides the motivation that is essential for sustained effort, and it must be the first action taken by any couple who are really serious. Until the couple have looked into each other's eyes and solemnly made their commitment to each other to promote mutual growth, it cannot be said that they have really started on the task of achieving a companionship marriage.

An Effectively Functioning Communication System. A decision to work for mutual growth will not get very far unless the couple clearly understand where they are in their relationship and what their goals are. Oddly enough, many

couples seem never to have reached clear agreement on these two vital questions. Even when they try to do so, they tend to run into communication difficulties.

A major study undertaken and published by the Family Service Association
of America in 1973, by Dorothy Fahs Beck and Mary Ann Jones, included an
extensive investigation of couples with marital conflicts who sought help from
the association's agencies. The major areas of difficulty, and their frequency of
occurrence, are shown on the following diagram (reproduced with permission).
The areas of conflict that are generally recognized, such as infidelity, relatives,
money, and sex, appear on an ascending scale from 25.6 to 45.7 percent.
Then, far above any of these and in splendid isolation, we find ''communication'' at the 86.6 percent level.

Among these nearly nine out of ten couples whose marital conflicts included
communication difficulties, frequent complaints were: ''We can't talk to each

DIAGRAM 1
Areas of Marital Conflict or Difficulty

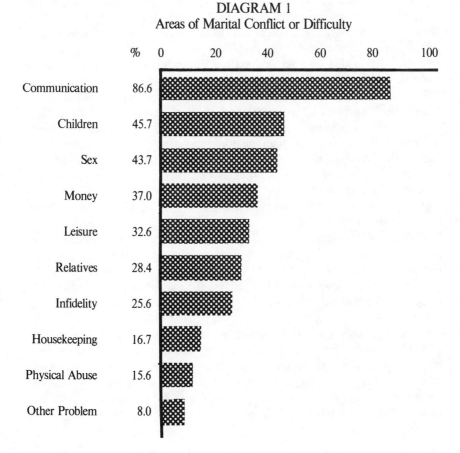

	%	0	20	40	60	80	100
Communication	86.6						
Children	45.7						
Sex	43.7						
Money	37.0						
Leisure	32.6						
Relatives	28.4						
Infidelity	25.6						
Housekeeping	16.7						
Physical Abuse	15.6						
Other Problem	8.0						

other''; ''I can't reach him''; ''She doesn't understand me''; ''When we try to talk, it ends in an argument.'' There is a significant comment in the accompanying explanation: ''Without communication, how can one know what the problem is, much less resolve it?''

So a very basic part of a coping system for successful marriage must be really effective communication. Fortunately, we now have well-developed couple-communication programs that can be very helpful to those who participate in them (more about this later).

The Ability to Make Creative Use of Conflict. It is sometimes suggested that effective communication is all a couple need to develop a successful marriage. I cannot agree. Important as it is, good communication does little more than show the couple clearly where they are and accurately identify the adjustment tasks they have to carry out. This of course represents a great deal; but the work still remains to be done.

I would go even further, and suggest that to do no more than help couples to open up communication between them might of itself be a harmful process. To begin to communicate in areas of the relationship that have previously been closed off might only reactivate painful conflicts that have been avoided by a tacit mutual agreement not to discuss them. If they are now reopened, and the couples are provided with no new skills for their resolution, the relationship could be further damaged instead of improved.

The major barrier to be overcome in the adjustment process, therefore, is interpersonal conflict. So long as the goal of marriage was defined as stability, the strategy was to avoid conflict, which only caused unpleasantness. Indeed, as we have already seen, the traditional marriage was ingeniously structured to exclude the possibility of conflict—first by making it a one-vote system; second, by carefully separating the ''spheres of influence'' of husband and wife through the allocation of separate roles to each.

Now that we have discarded both of these protective mechanisms, modern marriages inevitably produce a great deal of conflict. But since the traditional habit of avoiding conflict is still widely accepted, the average couple are caught in a trap. As we shall see later, the closer couples try to move to each other, the more conflict they tend to develop; and when this becomes too painful for them to tolerate, they have no alternative but to abandon their quest for intimacy and take refuge in distance. This is happening again and again in American marriages today.

In fact, we now know that conflict resolution is the vital key to effective growth in love and intimacy. But it is a tricky business, involving the processing of anger and a high degree of skill in negotiation. My counseling experience in dealing with average American couples is that they have virtually no developed skills in this complex field. And this is not because they have been offered these skills and have refused to learn them. They simply don't know that there are any skills to be learned. On the subject of conflict in marriage, most couples are in a state of either total ignorance or utter confusion.

Yet, thanks to recent psychological studies, the art of conflict resolution is becoming quite well understood, and I am convinced that the average couple can now be given the necessary tools. Most of the marriages breaking down all around us need not, in my opinion, break down. The couples concerned have tried hard. They are not failures; rather, they are the unhappy victims of *our* failure to make the necessary training available to them.

I recently accepted an invitation to spend an evening with a group of nearly forty "parents without partners," most of whom had been divorced. I began by telling them that I viewed them as victims rather than failures, and that I would explain to them why I believed this.

For an hour I presented to them, as clearly and simply as I could, with the help of diagrams, what we now know about marital interaction, and how we can train couples in interpersonal competence. When I had finished, I gave each of them a sheet of paper and asked them to write down how they reacted to what they had heard.

Later, I read their statements. Many of them said that if they had understood earlier what they had just learned, their marriage might not have failed. Of course, much of this may have been wishful thinking. But what was quite clear from my discussion with them afterward was that none of them had had any previous understanding or clear comprehension of what I had explained to them. As one of them expressed it, "I now see that I went into marriage completely blind, with no understanding of what could have been vital information. Why did this have to happen to me?" A number of them said, "It's too late now for me to learn, but I sure hope my children can be given this knowledge before *they* marry."

The kind of training we can now offer to married couples has developed from the clinical experience of marriage counselors, and from research in the behavioral sciences. Consequently, we have vital knowledge we did not have before—knowledge that could, for many couples, bring happiness where there is now misery. In recent years, mainly through the marriage enrichment movement, these new approaches have begun to be tested out and have been found effective. There is no reason why programs using these new procedures could not be made available on a very wide scale.

Later in this book I will explain in detail just how this knowledge can be applied and the kinds of programs that are now being developed, or could be developed, to put it to use. But before getting into that, we must look more closely at the concept of marital growth, which is vital to the argument I am presenting.

4

COUPLE GROWTH AND POTENTIAL

IN the old nursery rhyme "Mary, Mary, quite contrary" the question was asked, "How does your garden grow?" The reply she gave was rather confusing, which is probably why she is described as "contrary"!

But today just try asking any average citizen who happens to be married, "How does your *marriage* grow?" If your experience is anything like mine, the response will be one of complete bewilderment. Most of the people I have questioned have eventually struggled to give some kind of intelligible reply. But they have had to confess that the first thing that happened to them was that their minds went completely blank. The concept of marriage *growing* was startling; they had just never thought of it in that way before.

Why is this? Probably because our culture has consistently portrayed marriage as *static*. Legally it is described as a "state" or "estate" into which you enter by way of a formal ceremony—rather like an alien becoming an American citizen and taking the oath of allegiance to the flag. He walks out saying to himself, "Now I'm an American." Similarly, the bride and the bridegroom leave the church saying, "Now we are married."

What next? Our culture offers three answers. The romantic view is: "Why, you live happily ever after, of course!" The supposedly realistic answer is: "Well, you furnish a home, start a family and then settle down." A more recent and very cynical answer has been: "You find out that you've been deceived, and you're caught in a trap."

There is a fourth answer, but I would not expect to hear it from any except a few very enlightened people: "You get to work on the job of growing together." Yet, if you are looking for a successful companionship marriage, that is the only answer that is anywhere near correct.

One dramatic way of putting it is to say that a wedding is not a marriage.

32

To most people, there is no clear difference between the two words. But in fact, the two are as different as the egg and the chicken. An egg *might* grow into a chicken but it might not. Likewise, a wedding could, under favorable circumstances, lead in time to a marriage. But it might not. Each year in the United States, over a million couples who have gone through a perfectly proper legal wedding acknowledge that they have failed to achieve a marriage they can live with, and they give up.

What went wrong? In the case of both the egg and the wedding, the necessary growth process didn't take place.

How Marriage Can Grow

Growth can have several meanings. The simplest definition is that it is simply an increase in size, number, or intensity. But in this case, what grows doesn't change, but only gets bigger. Another meaning is that growth is development toward completeness and maturity. It is in this sense that we are using the term here.

Let's begin by considering the growth of a baby. Three processes are at work:

Maturing. Like the seed becoming a flower, or the acorn becoming an oak, the hidden blueprint unfolds as the baby changes into a child, a youth, an adult. Physically and mentally, the capacities for development stored in the genes are translated into reality as the original design is completed. What was inherently a possibility becomes an actuality.

Assimilating. Growth cannot, of course, take place in a vacuum. The seed and the acorn have to draw sustenance from the soil, or they would perish. Likewise the child's growth is profoundly affected by the favorable or unfavorable nature of the environment. If children don't get enough food, their bodily development will suffer. If they are not provided with parental love, their emotional development may be stunted. If they have no opportunity to get an education, they will fail to learn what they should know in order to become intelligent adults.

Adapting. Growth seldom has a chance to take place in a perfect environment. A plant or tree may in the process of growing have to get around obstacles. To a far greater extent, children growing up will meet adversity in one form or another—poverty, uncongenial playmates, missed opportunities, hostile competition, unfulfilled hopes. If they have the ingenuity to deal wisely with disadvantages of this kind, their growth may not be hindered. Indeed, they may even use adversity to increase their strength, endurance, and wisdom. However, they may fail to cope, give up, and stop developing. It is possible to use the word *growth* in a negative sense. You can grow better—and you can grow worse.

Closely linked to growth is the word *potential*. There are upper limits to the possibility of growth. No human being will be likely to grow ten feet tall although you might at a peak moment feel that way. Only a few select people will ever run the mile in under four minutes, or become concert pianists or distinguished poets. Each of us seems to have an upper limit to how intelligent we may become. On the other hand, most people *could* make much more of themselves than they actually do. Albert Einstein once suggested that most of us go through life without ever using more than about 10 percent of our intellectual potential.

In our growing as individuals, we have to accept inevitable limitations. Life cannot provide the time and opportunity we would need to develop all our potential in all the areas where we could grow. So we have to make choices as to where we will live, what subject we will study, what vocation we will follow, how we will spend our time, what church we will join, what forms of recreation we will cultivate, who will be our friends, whom we will marry. Each choice sets limits to our future and narrows our options. It is like going through a particular door and giving up the chance of going through other doors that had previously been open to us.

All this is quite familiar to us and makes sense, at least as long as we apply it to ourselves as individuals. But it seldom occurs to us to apply it to our relationships, and particularly to our marriages. Yet that also makes sense. Complications certainly arise when we are dealing with two people interacting with each other. Yet, all the principles we have established hold true. Let us put this to the test, first in the three growth processes:

Maturing. A relationship develops over time, just as a person does. Each member of the couple brings certain capacities for relating, resulting from earlier experiences with others. People who marry very young may be quite poorly developed and interact on a very low level, and this can create serious difficulties. Such marriages are notoriously prone to failure. Yet, all except severely disturbed personalities have some potential for giving and receiving love, for feeling sympathy for another, for communicating thoughts and feelings, for sharing joys and sorrows, for making reasonable concessions in order to meet another's needs or to give pleasure, for tolerating a certain amount of frustration, for controlling destructive impulses, for deferring gratification—the list could go on and on. Of course, the growth process in which these potential capacities are developed is complicated by the parallel need for each partner to grow, individually, in tandem with the other. Obviously, this will not always be easy, and crises will develop. What I am saying, however, is that the maturing of a relationship is entirely possible, given some understanding of how to promote it and a joint determination to see it through.

Assimilating. Getting married involves each partner in deliberately choosing a limited environment, governed by the need to consider the wishes of the other partner. Of course, most of us have been through this kind of experience already in selecting our circle of friends, but in marriage the choice normally involves more concentration and more lasting commitment. Each enters to some extent the world of the other and must seek to draw sustenance from it, as well as from a wider range of sources. It is to some extent an exchange of breadth for depth, and the exchange is a good one if the couple can achieve intimacy and respond to the challenge to grow that this makes possible. Without intimacy, however, it may come to look like a bad bargain, because all that is experienced is a limiting of options. Young people today, having had the opportunity to see only shallow and superficial marriages, often decide against marriage because they perceive it as a loss of breadth, but are unaware of the compensating gain in depth. Experienced at only superficial levels, another person may soon appear to be dull and uninteresting. At deeper levels, that same person may surprise us with unexpected qualities that have not appeared on the surface. Every perceptive counselor becomes aware of this hidden richness in ordinary people.

There is another aspect of growing by assimilation. Because both marriage partners share much of the same external environment—common friends and neighbors, interests and hobbies, significant experiences of joy and sorrow, overcoming obstacles together, accumulating memories, and many other aspects of the shared life—they tend to grow alike in some of their habits, tasks, preferences, and values, all of which builds a foundation of compatibility and unity into their relationship. The static view of marriage sees compatibility as a prerequisite for success. In the dynamic marriage increasing compatibility is experienced *as a product of the growing relationship.*

Adapting. Adapting also has two aspects in marriage. Adjusting to each other's differences is a task of primary importance in the early years of the young couple, and adapting to each other's continuing personal growth is a process that never comes to an end. Traditional marriages reduced these processes to the irreducible minimum by discouraging intimacy. But in a marriage that seeks intimacy as its goal, this task of continuing adaptation cannot possibly be avoided. It is in fact one of the most creative aspects of couple growth and of individual growth. Without it, marriages are likely to become dull and stale.

In addition, however, the couple can learn to adapt jointly to the ever-changing opportunities and demands of their social and cultural environment, to exciting new experiences and to demanding crises. Successful joint coping with an endless variety of new life situations develops in the couple an accumulating sense of confidence in each other, which deepens and strengthens their love.

The Power to Change

These processes of personal and relational growth are fairly complex, and it is unfortunate that they are seldom explored because our mistaken concept of marriage as static firmly closes our minds. There is, however, more to be said. An important question is: Exactly *how* does growth take place in marriage?

Part of the answer is that *experience* generally promotes growth. By repeating unfamiliar actions we make them familiar and habitual, and we can then perform them with increasing skill and confidence. This takes place, of course, in all marriages. Even if our general view is that marriage is static, in fact it is not so. The most rigidly structured relationship can undergo some growth even if this is never recognized or acknowledged. But a rigid and inflexible relationship provides a very poor medium for creative growth and is more likely to produce firmly established habit patterns. A marriage with no opportunity for growth may also die of suffocation.

The other factor that promotes growth is *change*. It is here that our understanding of human life has made enormous and exciting progress, especially in recent years. And it is here that new hope for better and happier marriages has been born.

Today it is hard for people living in the Western world to realize that in most of human history change was not welcomed but opposed. In Asia, for example, all the great religions are based on a philosophy of acceptance. "Fate has placed me where I am. This is my destiny. I must bow to it with resignation. I must simply take life as it comes."

Even in our own recent history, although Americans have developed an indomitable confidence in their ability to manipulate their material environment, they have not been as ready to believe in their power to change themselves. Many of our familiar sayings illustrate our fatalism: "That's the way it is"; "Don't tempt providence"; "Take it easy"; "You can't teach an old dog new tricks"; "You've made your bed, so you must lie on it."

The behavioral sciences have been investigating this tendency to avoid change and have come up with some interesting conclusions. I spent the summer of 1960 in the Soviet Union, and discovered that Soviet psychologists totally rejected Freud and put their faith instead in the Pavlovian theory of behavioral change. On my return here I found little interest in such ideas, although I had been impressed with some of the things the Russians were achieving.

Now, twenty years later, behavior modification is a flourishing branch of American psychology; all kinds of organizations and movements are busily promoting change as the best way to solve human problems. Wide acceptance of systems theory has opened the way for new forms of family therapy, which recognize how changing individual patterns can affect the relationships of all family members. In particular, studies of aging have come up with unexpected new concepts of the power older people have to change their ways. One highly esteemed specialist in the field, after years of studying the aging process, said to me, "I now believe that older people retain the power to change their behavior up to the day of their death."

I am not saying that behavioral change can be made quickly or without effort. What I am saying is that it *can* be made. We should be clear, however, in understanding that fundamental change in your personality pattern is virtually impossible; it has been determined by your genes and by your conditioning in very early life. But behavior is the way you *use* your personality to relate to other people. Your capacity to adapt your behavior is considerable, provided that the *motivation* to change is there and provided that the *rewards* are sufficient to sustain that motivation.

Fortunately, there is no need to press these general statements to their ultimate logical applications. The kinds of changes needed to promote growth in marriage are really not very difficult to achieve. What is wrong with us is that we resist the *idea* of change because we are skeptical about it, or because we get bogged down into a state of paralysis or inaction. What we are really saying is not "I *can't* change," but "I *won't* change."

This has been dramatically described by psychologist Sidney Jourard:

> I have been struck by the incredible lack of artistry and creativity in marriage partners. Either person may be immersed in making money or in decorating a house, but when it comes to altering the design for their relationship, it is as if both imaginations had burnt out. For years, spouses go to sleep night after night, with their relationship pattern one way, a way that perhaps satisfies neither—too close, too distant, boring or suffocating—and on awaking the next morning they reinvent their relationship *in the same way*. There is nothing sacred to the wife about the last way she decorated her house; as soon as it begins to pall, she shuffles things around until the new decor pleases her. But the way she and her husband interact will persist for years unchallenged and unchanged, long after it has ceased to engender delight, zest or growth (1970).

A moment's reflection will show quite clearly that these people are just stuck in ruts. They have accepted a static concept of marriage, and by doing so they have paralyzed their power to use capacities for growth and improvement to good purpose in other areas of their lives.

Changing your behavior in marriage requires an investment of energy and effort. It may involve some discomfort and even pain. You will also need to have faith that the change will lead to improvement in the relationship, which will bring rewards to you and to your partner; and the rewards must in fact be forthcoming if you are to keep up the changed behavior.

If you don't believe in marital growth, of course all of this is quite irrelevant, because your mind will be closed to the possibility that something much better is in fact available to you if only you will stir yourself to action. You will be in the state of paralysis that Sidney Jourard has so vividly described.

What is needed to stir married couples out of their lethargy and seeming indifference? I believe we must find ways to kindle new *hope* in them that their marriages can really be much more satisfying and rewarding. And that brings us to the subject of marriage potential.

Measuring Marriage Potential

Once we have recognized the fact that marriages can change, grow, and get progressively better, we are confronted with the question: "What are the upper limits? *How much better* could my marriage really be?"

If the idea of marital growth is new and strange to the average couple, the concept of marriage potential is positively mind-boggling! Yet, when we examine it, it becomes perfectly reasonable and entirely logical. We have already seen that in the growth of plants and of persons there is a terminal level, which can be roughly determined, and which represents full maturity. Exactly the same is true of relationships.

I was first confronted by the concept of marriage potential almost accidentally. In the course of reading Lederer and Jackson's book *The Mirages of Marriage* (1968), I found a rough attempt to classify marriages on a scale representing their quality. An estimate is then given by the writers that marriages in a top bracket, described as the "harmonious and collaborative union," would not exceed more than 5 to 10 percent of all marriages. A further comment, however, points out that "marriage is a continuous process, involving constant growth and metamorphosis . . . the marital state may move from one category into another" (pp. 128–29).

From my own close and extensive observation of marriages, which extends over more than forty years, I would be inclined to agree that only about 5 to 10 percent of them are functioning at a really high level of mutual satisfaction. This may sound somewhat alarming and depressing; it means that more than 90 percent of the marriages around us are not in very good shape. But it does help to explain the widespread dissatisfaction with marriage today, which of course is a function of our higher expectations. And, most important of all, it indicates that many more of our marriages *could* reach a far higher level of satisfaction, if only the couples could be motivated and helped to realize their potential.

The next question that naturally arises is: "How can ordinary couples be made to see this so that they may claim what is available to them?" I am very familiar with the couple who, invited to participate in a marriage-enrichment event, react defensively and reply, "Oh, but we don't need that sort of thing. You see, our marriage is all right." I have often been tempted to reply, "That's fine. But, wouldn't you like to find out just *how* 'all right' your marriage really is?"

I finally found a way to do just that. My wife and I concocted what we call the Marriage Potential Inventory. It is a very simple instrument, which any couple can use. They are asked each to write down a list of ten areas of marital adjustment. Almost any ten would do, but this list happens to represent the ten areas most often brought up by couples with whom Vera and I have worked:

1. common goals and values
2. commitment to growth
3. communication skills
4. creative use of conflict
5. appreciation and affection
6. agreement on gender roles
7. cooperation and teamwork
8. sexual fulfillment
9. money management
10. (a) parent effectiveness
    (b) decision making (as an alternative,
        if the couple are not presently parenting)

Acting quite separately and without collaboration, the husband and wife are asked to assign a score from zero to ten for each area. The figure is arrived at as follows: in each area consider what your marriage *could* be like if you had developed your full potential. This means you would have worked on this aspect of your relationship sincerely and diligently together; learned all you could about it; sought all the help you could command; made all the progress of which you are capable. This would represent your full marital potential in this area, according to your best judgment. Now, look at your marriage as it presently is and consider how much progress you have already made toward claiming your potential. Be honest about it but also be fair to yourselves. Then, give the marriage a score that would represent where you consider you are right now.

When you have done this for all ten areas, add up all your scores. The result will be the percentage of the perceived potential that you have already claimed. The difference between that figure and one hundred will be the percentage of your potential that you have not yet appropriated.

After thoughtfully completing the test, the couple then spend at least a full hour alone together, sharing their scores with each other. On the basis of the discussion that follows, we encourage them to make a growth plan for their marriage, to put it in writing, and both to sign it. Neither the test score nor the growth plan need be reported to anyone. We purposely don't give them typed or printed copies of the test because that would suggest that it might have to be "handed in" for someone to assess. The test is entirely subjective and would serve no useful purpose as a basis of comparison with other couples, or as a means of establishing norms. It is simply a device to encourage couples to look realistically at their marriage as it now is—not in order to find out what is wrong but in order to become aware of their unclaimed riches. By doing this test they discover, usually for the first time, just where their marriage is, in relation to where it could be. They discover how far they are in agreement about the progress they are making. They also find out what their expectations are; low scores usually mean high expectations and high scores mean low expectations. We find that levels of expectation sometimes differ markedly between husbands and wives. In one extreme case, the wife's percentage of achieved potential was 55 percent and the husband's was only 25 percent. This was, however, a couple in therapy and the test provided the clue to their almost fundamentally different evaluations of the marriage.

This simple instrument, which I warmly invite any couple to try out for themselves, has proved quite helpful in opening the minds of husbands and wives to the reality and the possibility of marital growth. As one couple expressed it, "we really thought we had a good marriage, and said so to all our friends. We still think that this is generally true, but we now realize that we were complacently settled on a plateau, and that we have a lot of growing still to do. This discovery is very exciting to us, and we are now ready to get to work. It's as if we discovered we had a whole lot of money in the bank that we didn't know about!"

5

SOME QUESTIONS
AND ANSWERS

IN the previous chapters, I put forward a theory concerning what is happening to marriage in our contemporary culture. I suggested that the traditional marriage as an institutional system is now dead or dying; that Ernest Burgess was correct when he described the new companionship form that is now replacing it; that the new model is more rewarding to the partners, but also more difficult to achieve; that this difficulty can be overcome through training in what Nelson Foote called "interpersonal competence"; that the training consists in providing couples with a "primary coping system"; and that couples thus equipped should be better able to achieve relational growth together and to appropriate their marital potential.

I will spell out many of these concepts in greater detail later, and I will describe how they can be implemented through the provision of appropriate services. Before moving on, however, I want to consider some of the questions that are likely to arise in the mind of the reader, and to try to answer them.

Why should this transition be taking place at this particular point in human history?

The answer is complex and not easy to summarize briefly. We have already seen that marriage has been, throughout human history, a very flexible institution. The form it takes in a particular time and place tends to reflect the current needs of the culture concerned. Although human history has passed through a vast and complex series of changes, we may nevertheless identify three major cultural patterns.

Over a period of as many as three or four million years, our earliest ancestors were nomadic food-gatherers and hunters, struggling to survive in a hostile environment. Then, about ten thousand years ago, the development of agriculture and ownership of land led to a more secure and prosperous way of life

41

that made possible the emergence of what we call civilization. Finally, for a mere two hundred and fifty years, since the Industrial Revolution, we have seen the establishment of a technological culture, which has put enormous power into our hands and produced the affluent society.

The family, it is generally agreed, has from the beginning been the basic human institution, and its form has been determined by the kind of culture it is called upon to sustain and to serve. We know little about the family system in the early nomadic period, although archeologists generally tend to see it in terms of relatively small, simple, and flexible kinship groupings. In the agricultural period, families have been larger in size, hierarchical in structure, and mainly patriarchal—all of which tends to be favorable to a stable corporate life based on the ownership, use, and protection of land and property.

The rapid social changes resulting from our developing technology have proved very disturbing to the rigid institutions that characterized the earlier era and have led to a strong emphasis on individual freedom and autonomy, which has eroded the traditional stereotype and brought about widespread family fragmentation. In such a cultural climate, marriages can no longer be held together, as they were in the past, by *external coercion*—social pressures imposed mainly by religion, law, and the resulting public opinion. Increasingly in contemporary society, marriages will have to be held together instead by *internal cohesion*. In other words, the emphasis must now be upon the *quality of the relationship*. Traditional marriages were based on social duty ("for better or for worse"). The marriages of today are increasingly based on personal fulfillment; if they are not rewarding to the partners, they will not be sustained. The transition from the traditional marriage to the companionship marriage clearly reflects this shift in social values.

Do we need to retain marriage at all? In our new open society, can't we dispense with it altogether?

A number of people have taken this view, but their arguments are not very convincing. What they are contending generally is not that marriage itself should be abandoned, but that the traditional form should be replaced by "alternative life styles." When we examine these alternatives, as we have already seen, they generally turn out to be no more than variant forms of marriage, most of which have already been tried out in earlier stages of civilization.

The word *marriage* can have a variety of different connotations, but in Western culture, its meaning has been narrowed to represent only the traditional model in its most rigid form. The implication, that every arrangement for men and women to live together that is other than traditional marriage is nonmarriage, and should not be described as marriage, is of course quite inaccurate. This confusion in our terminology has resulted in giving marriage a bad name, and implying that it is a form of bondage that imposes all kinds of exploitation upon those who enter it.

Perhaps we should define the companionship marriage more clearly. Is it necessarily monogamous? Must it insist on sexual fidelity? Should it require lifelong commitment? Does it demand adherence to certain predetermined gender roles? Must it be registered legally? Is it expected to produce children?

Burgess gave little attention to these questions, because they were not being vigorously debated in his time. Today they are all controversial, because they raise the subject of personal freedom. Let us consider this broad issue.

The quest for freedom is closely linked to our understanding of democracy. Historically, the democratic ideal represented a rebellion against the tyranny of despots who denied what we now call "human rights" to those over whom they ruled, and who imposed social obligations on people who had been given no share whatever in deciding whether they were wise and just.

The progressive emancipation movements that in recent years have championed the cause of individual freedom have brought some welcome changes. But now they are in danger of swinging the pendulum to the opposite extreme—to the point at which, instead of one all-powerful tyrant, we have to suffer from the irresponsible actions of a multitude of petty tyrants who insist on almost complete personal freedom and recognize few if any social obligations. Democracy is not simply the opposite of tyranny; it is the point of balance, the middle position of the pendulum, between two different forms of tyranny. It represents a society in which individual freedom and social responsibility are equally respected, but neither is given complete dominion over the other.

My personal view is that marriage still involves certain social responsibilities that must be accepted if public order is to be preserved. Marriage is not a purely private matter, because it is closely related to such major social concerns as protection from exploitation, the transfer of property, and the welfare of children. However, there is no doubt that in the past rules and regulations that paid too little attention to married people's legitimate needs and wishes were imposed upon them, and in our open society of today some readjustments have become necessary.

How far these readjustments should go in the direction of personal freedom is a central issue, one that is now being worked out in our society. We have yet to define just how far, in the marriage relationship, the quest for personal freedom ("the pursuit of happiness") can be recognized, consistent with the responsible discharge of necessary social obligations. I believe that a functioning companionship marriage produces the kind of people who are highly likely to achieve that balance; and I am therefore prepared to trust such people to answer the broader ethical questions for themselves. I am aware that this involves risks; but that is equally true of every step we take in the direction of human freedom.

How far along is the transition from traditional to companionship marriage?

This is impossible to answer with any precision, so I can only offer my opinion.

The classic traditional marriage, as we have known it in the past, is now almost extinct. In remote rural areas, and in extreme religious groups, a few marriages that adhere strictly to the criteria listed in Table 1 can still be found. There have also been recent attempts to reaffirm the traditional values in books such as Larry Christenson's *The Christian Family* (1970) and Marabel Morgan's *The Total Woman* (1973).

The rationale for these reactionary movements is easy to understand. Our disturbingly high rates of marriage and family breakdown are interpreted by some religious groups as manifestations of moral corruption, and it is reasoned that the only way to avoid disaster is to go back to a literal reconstruction of the past, to the "good old days" when virtue abounded. But in fact distance lends enchantment to the view, because the old days were not as good as we think they were, and our nostalgia might quickly be dissipated if we actually could return for a season to the past as it really was.

Enquiries have convinced me that few of those influenced by these doctrines do in fact adopt them in their entirety. To do so in our contemporary culture is an increasingly difficult task.

Large numbers of older couples, however, have made only a limited accommodation to the new trends; and often they have done so almost without being aware of it. By contrast, today's young couples have supported broadly the companionship concept, at least in theory, but they too can be observed in many respects as clinging still to traditional roles. Few of them truly practice, either in marriage or in the freer forms of association, the egalitarian principles that both the women's and men's liberation movements advocate.

The great majority of couples today are somewhere along the continuum. A distinction has to be made, however, between the two main characteristics of the companionship marriage—equality and love. Equality in its narrow quantitative sense is not a goal widely sought by marriage partners. What is favored is rather *equity*—fair shares of both the advantages and disadvantages of living together. When it comes to love and intimacy, however, this is widely desired, though often fear of the implications suppresses awareness of the desire.

The trend toward the companionship model is better demonstrated negatively than positively. It is the millions who move out of marriage, only in most instances to move in again later, who are saying loudly and clearly what they want. I believe most of the unacceptable marriages of today would have been acceptable a generation ago. What has happened is that *expectations* of marriage have become much more demanding, and the shift has in my opinion been decisively in the direction of the companionship model as the desired ideal.

What are the obstacles that hinder the widespread achievement of companionship marriage?

The major obstacle, as we have already seen, is that the necessary training in interpersonal competence has not been available. Ernest Burgess made some attempts to define appropriate new services to couples, especially in his later volume (Burgess and Wallin, *Engagement and Marriage,* 1953). Nelson Foote attempted to carry the process further in experimental studies at the Family Study Center of the University of Chicago; he reported them in his book *Identity and Interpersonal Competence* (Foote and Cottrell, 1955). But we simply did not have the basic knowledge at that time to do the job. It was not until we got into the 1970s that the behavioral sciences began to grapple seriously with the dynamics of interpersonal interaction, and particularly of dyadic interaction. The tools and skills we are now using successfully in marriage enrichment are largely the result of quite recent research.

However, now that we can deliver the goods, we are confronted by a host of obstacles, both on the part of married couples themselves, and on the part of the culture generally. These obstacles are quite formidable; and although time is on our side, it will nevertheless take years of effort to overcome them.

First, let us consider *obstacles in married couples themselves.* Because the nature of the transition taking place in marriage has not been clearly understood or widely interpreted, current concepts about marriage are often grossly inaccurate and misleading. Here are some examples:

1. The view is widely held that *no special knowledge or skill is required to make a marriage work,* and that to need help of any kind in such an elementary task is a sign of incompetence or even stupidity. This of course represents the survival of the static concept of marriage.

2. Arising directly out of this is the view that *most people have "good" marriages; and that such marriages are free from "problems,"* which imply the need for adjustments that "normal" people don't have to make. If, therefore, you seek marriage counseling, that may suggest that you have a "bad" marriage, and of course, this reveals you to be a weak and inferior person. Consequently, any suggestion that your marriage could be "improved" or "enriched" can be highly threatening, because it could put you in this despised category.

3. The *idea that marriage involves a need to change is viewed as ridiculous,* because everybody knows that people *can't* change their behavior, any more than a leopard can change its spots. If two people don't naturally get along smoothly in marriage, it means that they are incompatible; and quite apart from the fact that nothing can be done about this, it also reflects upon their intelligence and judgment because they ought to have known better than to marry unsuitable partners.

4. Another widely held misconception is that *conflict in marriage is abnormal and destructive, and therefore to be avoided.* Similarly, anger felt toward the marriage partner is often regarded as sinful, or at least something not experienced by "nice" people. These quite inaccurate ideas prevent millions of couples from working through their natural and inevitable differences and disagreements, and deny them the achievement of intimacy.

Attitudes of this kind compel most married people to put on an act in order to conceal the real facts about their mediocre relationship from others, and even from themselves. This leads to the widespread cultivation of *privatism* about marriage, sometimes justified on the grounds that the interior life of the couple is too "sacred" to discuss with others. I would define privatism as an excessive and needless preoccupation with privacy, in situations where it serves no useful purpose and only deprives those concerned of help and support they need from each other.

These obstacles to facing the realities of marriage create a climate of confusion, which is reflected in the public avoidance of the subject, reflecting the intermarital taboo (see Chapter 14). It is highly unusual for a natural, comfortable discussion of the marriage relationship to take place in any ordinary social group. When the subject does arise, it is either talked about very intellectually and with an air of clinical detachment, or it is treated as a joke in order to cover up and divert the self-conscious feelings it evokes.

This widespread policy of evasion is projected into the Establishment, where marriage is strictly relegated to the "private sector." Government agencies leave marriage strictly alone, even when, on a national scale, it is in serious trouble and needs help. Foundations asked to make grants for the study of marriage have almost invariably turned down the applications, as the record will testify. The mass media either treat marriage as a joke, or join in the negative propaganda that has pervaded our culture in recent years. (I shall say more about this later.)

To sum up, our entire society is pervaded by an atmosphere of awkward self-consciousness about marriage, which makes it very difficult to face the reality that it is today in serious trouble, even when we are beginning at last to come up with some workable answers. This creates an absurd situation in which, when we try to offer married couples the key to the deep and rich happiness that in their hearts they desperately want and need, they often respond as if we were trying to hurt them.

This strange situation will almost certainly change. Meanwhile, we may console ourselves by remembering that the Church once condemned investing money at interest as a deadly sin, and that when scientific birth control first became available it was attacked in almost every quarter as an iniquitous idea.

Can all marriages be expected to make the transition to the companionship model?

Probably not. The question isn't a vital one at this time, because the number of couples who have shown any desire to be trained in interpersonal competence constitutes only a small minority. A rough estimate suggests that something like a million and a half couples may have been involved in some kind of marriage-enrichment program. However, this represents roughly only 3 percent of American marriages; and of course it doesn't follow that all these couples, as a result of whatever they have learned, have followed up by continuing to work for ongoing growth in their relationships.

In the cultural climate of today, with all the barriers I have just been describing, it requires determination and perseverance to set the companionship marriage as a realistic objective and then press on toward the goal. At the present time, most of the couples who get seriously into marriage enrichment are of the pioneering type, people who are strongly autonomous and have the courage and resolution to go after what they want.

Yet it must be added that couples of almost every type, when really confronted with the promise the companionship marriage holds out, in circumstances where they were reasonably free to respond, have done so gladly and gratefully. There is no doubt in my mind that, in a more favorable climate, large numbers of couples would welcome the chance to enrich their marriages. For that reason, I believe we can speak of the marriage-enrichment movement as "the wave of the future." The concept is so eminently sensible, so logically sound, that whatever opposition exists cannot long be sustained—especially when increasing numbers of couples are ready to testify, out of their own experience, that it really works.

There are of course married people who might never be likely to meet the requirements for making the transition. Some are deeply prejudiced and therefore unable to accept the logic of what is being offered. Some are not ready to undertake the behavioral changes that would be involved; they simply lack the motivation. Some suffer from personality disorders that make them incapable of embarking on a deep relationship of any kind. Some are "loners," unable to tolerate the idea of entering into close association with others. Some, committed to the extreme philosophy of arrogant individualism, believe that the way to fulfillment in life lies in the rejection of all commitment to relationship.

Yet I believe there is abundant evidence that, as the Bible story of the Creation asserts, it is not good for a man (or woman) to be alone; that we are so made that the fullest realization of our identity comes, not through unyielding isolation from others, but through close and continuing relationships in which we become fully known and at the same time deeply loved. When Havelock Ellis said, "To live is to love and to love is to live," he never spoke a truer word. Of course marriage is not the only relationship in which love and fulfillment can be found. But for those who choose marriage, it seems tragic that they should have to settle for anything less than relationship-in-depth.

What about the companionship family?

This is of course a natural corollary of the companionship marriage. It has always puzzled me that anyone viewing a family could consider the husband-wife relationship and the parent-child relationship in totally separate compartments, as though a truly loving couple could be anything other than loving parents. Again and again I have received reports from married couples about the change that took place in their children's attitudes when as husband and wife they had broken through to a relationship of genuine intimacy.

I recall one couple who were quite astonished at the change in their ten-year-old son. "We had been having a lot of trouble with Johnny," they explained, "but since we came home from the marriage-enrichment retreat and told him what had happened to us, he has been quite different." There is no mystery here. A child's emotional security is deeply invested, not only in the way his parents behave toward him, but also in the way they behave toward each other. When he senses stress and conflict in the marriage, he internalizes his anxieties, and a clash takes place between the loyalties he feels to each of his parents. This can produce conflict within him, and can be acted out in the form of bad behavior. Remove this source of stress and show him that his parents are warm and tender in their love for each other, and his anxiety and insecurity melt away.

Cultivation of the companionship marriage should therefore lead naturally to the companionship family. The opposite process is much more difficult, and indeed highly unlikely. For that reason, greatly as I welcome programs for improving parent effectiveness, I feel that these should ideally follow marriage enrichment. Attempts on the part of one parent (usually the mother) to change patterns of interaction with the children, when the other parent is not participating, are hard to sustain. The quality of the marriage is the key to the quality of the family. I am aware that there are situations where it seems impossible to involve the other marriage partner or where there is only one parent present; and in these situations parent-effectiveness training can greatly improve the atmosphere of the home. What I am emphasizing is that in an intact family the primary objective should be to get the marriage functioning creatively. This done, improvement in parent-child relationships often follows naturally, or is much more easily brought about.

In the area of parenting, a transition is in process in our culture that is as significant as the transition from the traditional marriage to the companionship model. The traditional parent was normally a dominating, authoritative figure, and children in the past were expected to respond with respectful obedience, usually simulated in order to avoid punishment. When this system became impossible in our new open society, there was an unfortunate swing to an attitude on the part of parents of detached indulgence. This became known as "permissiveness"—a regrettable distortion of the true meaning of the term.

In fact, "permissiveness" exactly describes what the companionship form of the parent-child relationship ought to be. It can be loving; but it cannot be equal because of the vast difference between the child's limited experience of life and that of the parent. So the parent enters into a cooperative relationship with the child, granting him progressively increasing freedom as a reward for his furnishing proof that he can handle it responsibly, but limiting his freedom, for his own protection, when he shows that he is not yet ready to cope with it.

As the child grows older, the parent gradually relinquishes authority and withdraws control—a helpful process that could appropriately be described as "permissiveness," if the word had not been given a misleading and degraded connotation.

The companionship family becomes in due course the basic social unit of the companionship community. This, surely, is the democratic ideal. We have seen that marriage and the family must reflect the culture, because their task is the socialization of the individual to live in the culture and to strive for the fulfillment of its goals.

The older human cultures were authoritarian and hierarchical. This was the only way they knew of holding communities—tribes or nations—together in the enforced unity that was essential for survival. So all human relationships tended to be based on authority and obedience, dominance and submission—from the despotic chief or king down to the youngest female child. The only kinds of relationships that could be trusted in those days were *vertical* relationships. *Horizontal* relationships were just too dangerous. Make people equal to each other, and they become divided by differences, disagreements, and conflicts. The only way our forefathers knew of to deal with interpersonal conflict was to avoid it as far as possible; and the older cultures were elaborately structured to achieve that end.

Now we have embarked on an exciting but dangerous venture. We are committed to the concepts of individual freedom and the equality of all men and women. This involves adoption of the principle of progressively substituting horizontal relationships for vertical relationships. The hazards are great, and they can be overcome only if we can learn to resolve interpersonal conflict by using processes that achieve the growth of trust and cooperation.

This must be achieved first in the family, if it is ever to become workable in the wider community. In order to achieve the companionship family we must first make the companionship marriage work. That is the vital key to the building of a true democratic society. For this reason the promotion of effective marriage enrichment on a large scale becomes a task of the first magnitude.

In the rest of the book we shall consider how, in practice, this task could be accomplished.

6

THE GREAT TRANSITION

IMAGINE a human community, long settled in a narrow valley overshadowed by towering mountains. Life for those people has not been easy; but they have managed to survive, and they feel secure in their simple dwellings.

Now, word has come from an exploring party that they have discovered much better land on the other side of the mountain. They speak of fertile plains, abundant pastures, dense forests, and broad rivers. A new and better life beckons.

The migration begins. The bolder spirits go first. Then others follow. Some hesitate, then decide, pack, and set off. Now there are scattered parties on the move, taking various routes. Some go straight over the mountains, others take the longer but less arduous way round. A few grow weary of the journey and establish settlements along the route. Some even turn back.

This provides a fair picture of our cultural transition from the traditional to the companionship marriage. Families everywhere are on the move. Some have already reached the new country; some lag far behind; some are en route, struggling with unanticipated difficulties, exploring new trails and finding they lead nowhere.

In this chapter we shall try to understand this complex transition: what it is doing to us, what we are leaving behind, what lies before us, and finally, how we can make the journey as safely and smoothly as possible.

We can best accomplish this by looking at the whole process in its three stages: the traditional marriage that lies behind us; the changes and adjustments in the transition period through which we are living; and the companionship marriage that represents our goal. We shall look first at the process as it is experienced by the young, as they consider what marriage has to offer them; then at the adjustments that face the couple already embarked on their life together. At each stage and in each area we shall offer comparisons between the old and the new.

50

Looking Toward Marriage

Under this heading we need to examine four stages.

Learning about Marriage. Children everywhere begin to learn by observation and experience. In traditional families, boys and girls could see clearly what a marriage meant. They observed their parents, other relatives, and neighbors and thus learned the separate and distinct roles performed by husband and wife. The boy grew up clearly understanding what it meant to be a man, a husband, and a father; the girl, what it meant to be a woman, a wife, and a mother. They internalized their awareness of these roles and practiced them in their play. Consequently, when they reached the appropriate age, they were fairly clear about what was expected of them. The prescribed behavior allowed for a few individual variations; but the broad pattern was rigid and clear. Little in the way of formal teaching was given, and it was not really necessary.

Transitional children have by contrast grown up in a milieu of chaotic confusion. They have observed a bewildering variety of patterns and standards in the significant adults around them and in the wider society portrayed in the mass media. They therefore approach marriage with no clear sense of what is expected of them.

The children of functioning companionship marriages are exposed in their own homes to a fairly consistent pattern of flexible interpersonal interaction in which they have shared, and they should have learned the skills necessary for achieving open, honest, and mutually supportive relationships. They have probably also been free to increase their understanding through full discussion with their parents and siblings. They should be well prepared for possible later marriage, and they should know how to make it succeed. At this time, however, the number of such children is probably quite small. Our hope is that in the future it will greatly increase.

Mate Selection. In the really traditional families, marriages were invariably arranged, either by the parents or by the professional go-between. The choosing was often done with great care, and many of these unions turned out happily according to the modest expectations then entertained. In less rigid cultures (including our own), the young people were given some limited freedom of choice, but were always subject to the parental veto.

During the transition, a progressive shift has taken place as youth gained more and more freedom. The parental veto lost power, until it was little more than unavoidable parental acquiescence. In recent years, young people who were in college or at work, far distant from their homes, have often made their own choices, then presented the future mate to their parents as a fait accompli—even, in some instances, after the wedding! For most people there is now total freedom of choice. There is, however, no evidence that the choices made by youth are any better than those that responsible parents might make for them, or at least with them.

This same freedom belongs to the children of companionship marriages. Knowing clearly what a creative marriage is like, they should presumably be well equipped to choose a suitable partner; and the closer, freer quality of their relationship in the family might be expected to make them more ready to give consideration to parental opinion.

Courtship. This term had very precise meaning in the past, although it is seldom used today. In the old "arranged" marriage, it really *followed* the wedding, as a process of getting acquainted and mutually accepting each other—a first stage in marriage clearly recognized by the older cultures. In the Orient, the wedding is sometimes symbolized by a pile of dry sticks arranged for the lighting of a fire. Then, as the newly married couple fall in love, the sticks are ignited and kindled, create warmth and light, and get the relationship off to a good start! In traditional cultures that allowed some choice of mate, courtship was part of the boy's attempt to win the girl. After securing her parents' permission, he would make a proposal of marriage to her; and, if accepted, he would then meet with her regularly, with or without an attending chaperone, to enable the couple to get to know each other better. During the courtship period the intention to marry might be canceled if serious doubts arose. This was harder to do, though still possible, after the formal engagement, which replaced the ancient betrothal.

For young people in the transition period, most of these formalities have been abandoned. The almost complete freedom of boys and girls to be alone together today has rendered such formalities unnecessary. The American dating system, which had no precise equivalent in any other culture, allowed teenaged boys and girls to experience personal encounters with large numbers of potential marriage partners, which was believed to aid wise mate selection. However, dating has become so informal in today's youth culture that most of the traditional rules no longer operate. The wide extent of sexual freedom has now been further extended to allow the custom of cohabitation, which might be viewed as a kind of trial marriage, although some family specialists prefer to regard it as the new form of courtship—a thorough testing of all the aspects of the relationship before a final commitment is made. Unhappily, this development in the transitional period has resulted in extensive alienation between some of the young people concerned and their disapproving parents.

Since the children of companionship marriages generally live in the same cultural climate as young people, they have wide options regarding courtship. In general, their more open relationship to their parents enables their choices to be better understood and accepted and makes painful alienation less likely.

The Wedding. This was always a highly significant event in the older cultures; a Hindu wedding, attended by hosts of relatives, can still cover five days of ritual and feasting and can leave the bride's father bankrupt. The tradition of the elegant wedding has also characterized our own culture, marking an occasion of great social significance in the lives of two individuals and of their families. The solemnity of the rite was greatly heightened by the fact that it was virtually an irreversible commitment.

Like other traditional customs, the significance of the wedding has been diminished in the transitional period. The ease with which divorce can now be obtained, and the frequency of its occurrence, diminish the wedding as a rite of passage. And the fact that the couples have often already had sexual intercourse or lived together makes it no longer, for many, a process of initiation. It has become in some respects little more than a somewhat special social event, an opportunity to meet old friends and make new friends while celebrating the registration of a legal union. The ceremony itself has for some been made less formal by being held in unusual locations, and by the couple's exercising their ingenuity in writing their own versions of the religious ritual.

Again, there is no special emphasis that characterizes couples who favor the companionship marriage. Most of them would, however, recognize the inconsistency of making elaborate and costly preparations for the wedding, which lasts but a few hours, while offering little preparation of the couple for married living, which is expected to last a lifetime.

The Adjustments of Marriage

The changes we have already looked at prove to be quite extensive. The traditional concept of the wedding as the great divide between all that the couple had experienced before and all that they would experience thereafter has become so attenuated that it must now be abandoned. The ceremony in itself has profound religious, social, and legal significance. But the myths of the past, which saw it as a magical rite that opened to the couple an entirely new and different life, a gateway to enduring happiness and bliss hitherto unknown—these fantasies have had to be discarded.

What we must now recognize clearly is that a wedding is not a marriage. It is no more than a public declaration by two people that they *want to achieve a marriage.* They may or may not succeed; for, as we have already seen, the nature of marriage has now been so greatly changed that its achievement is a much tougher task than it has ever been before.

The plain fact is that all the couple have on their wedding day is a heap of raw materials. Out of these, somehow, they hope to fashion a relationship that will bring them both deep and lasting personal fulfillment. Will they achieve this or not? The answer does not lie in anything the wedding ceremony can of itself do for them. The answer lies in the readiness to work hard, and to persevere, which they bring with them and lay upon the altar. Even more, the answer lies in whatever skills they have attained, or are willing to attain, for the task of achieving what Clark Vincent has described as the most complex relationship into which any two people will ever enter. Their chances of success depend very little on the charm of the bridegroom or the beauty of the bride; very little on the fervent good wishes of their relatives and friends; very little even on the dreams they dream as they stand together to make their vows. The issue for them is largely decided in advance, by these questions: "Do you, or do you not, possess interpersonal competence? If not, are you, or are you not, willing to be trained for the task that lies before you? If so, are the opportunities to secure such training available, or are they not?"

These are decisive questions. For these two people are already confronted, and will continue to be confronted, by the need to make a whole series of complex adjustments.

In Table 1, we looked briefly at some of those adjustment areas—what they meant for couples in the traditional marriage and for those entering the new companionship marriage. Now we need to look more closely at some critical comparisons between the two.

Decision Making. In the traditional marriage, the spheres of interests of husband and wife were clearly defined. The wife was concerned with the running of the home and the care of the children. The husband worked outside the home and acted as disciplinarian when the children misbehaved. These divisions of responsibility were clearly understood, and each partner was free to make decisions in his or her sphere, without any necessity to consult the other. A Japanese grandfather of our acquaintance in Tokyo assured us that he had brought his wife as a bride to their present home, but had never at any time since entered the kitchen. "I would no more intrude there," he said, "than allow my wife to visit my place of business."

Beyond these strictly defined areas, all other major decisions were traditionally made by the husband. These rules were usually strictly honored.

In the transition period, these spheres have more and more become merged. As husband and wife moved progressively toward the concept of being equals, they both became involved in *all* areas of their family life. What had been a clearly defined division into separate one-vote systems became a vast, overall two-vote system, consuming time and energy, and often stirring up disagreement and bitterness.

Gender Roles. The different and separate functions of husband and wife, as illustrated by the Japanese couple, were clearly and sharply defined. It was a matter not only of decision making, but of proper function. I can remember the time when it would have been unthinkable for a woman to cut her hair short or drive a car, or for a man to enter a woman's store or be seen (publicly at least) holding his baby in his arms. Large numbers of everyday functions and operations were predetermined so that husbands and wives had to give very little time to discussing who did what and when. There was a clearly defined blueprint that settled it all effortlessly for them.

The wheel has now turned full cycle. It is the proud boast of some liberated couples today that there is *nothing* (apart from breast-feeding the baby or using the toilet in a standing position) that cannot be done by either partner. Equal shares is a fine principle; but we must not overlook the complexity that is added to the couple's life when all tasks have to be allocated between them by mutual agreement.

Sex. The traditional husband initiated sex, and it was clearly understood by the wife that this was a "marriage right" for him, and that it was her duty to be available at all reasonable times. Since the news of the female orgasm had not then broken upon a breathless world, this made it very easy for the husband's sexual needs to be met. And what of the wife's sexual needs? They just didn't exist.

Now we know all about female orgasms, and a lot about the technique of intercourse. This of course offers us heightened pleasure, but in the process sexual interaction has become very much more complicated. Traditional couples would have been astonished to learn, as Masters and Johnson have confidently assured us, that 50 percent of all married couples get into difficulties about their sex life at one time or another. Short of impotence, it would have been hard for those old-time couples to think of what *could* go wrong!

Vocation. The husband in the old culture brought home the bacon, and the residence and life style of the couple were settled in terms of the needs of his job. Married women simply did not, except in the rarest instances, work outside the home. When I married, my wife was a well-qualified teacher; but it would have been exceptional for her, as a married woman, to pursue her vocation. Homemaking and child rearing were honorable vocations and required full-time attention.

Today, with more than half of all wives gainfully employed, the complications of setting up a home are greatly compounded. I stand in awe at the manner in which many couples manage to cook the meals, get the children to school and back again, go off themselves in quite different directions for an eight-hour day, and generally keep the ship on an even keel. The endless adjustments and readjustments involved, especially when complications arise, stagger the imagination.

Relatives. Traditional families were usually close-knit and lived near each other. This involved certain disadvantages, but it also provided staunch support and succor in times of crisis. Young couples generally avoided conflict and maintained an attitude of respect for their own and each other's parents, whatever their underlying sentiments might have been.

Today, young nuclear families are often isolated, with close relatives far away, so that contact can be maintained only by costly telephone calls or long days of driving. There is also more open airing of grievances, and sometimes deep alienation between the generations, which strains loyalties and produces painful conflicts between husband and wife.

Money Management. Prudent management of financial resources was the rule in traditional families. "Buy now, pay later" was considered bad advice; and the multibillion-dollar advertising industry had not beamed its subtle propaganda to Americans to persuade them to live beyond their means. Nor was there any possibility of serious division of opinion between spouses as to how the income should be spent. The husband earned it, so the power was in his hands. I can remember counseling with many working-class wives who had no idea how much money their husbands earned; they only knew how much they gave them for housekeeping.

Now, at least half of all wives earn separate incomes, and some of them bring home more money than their husbands do. And spending habits suggest that large numbers of couples are unable to live within their means; the total burden of debt resting on American families is awesome. This means constant struggles to adjust and readjust, as is evidenced by the high ranking of "money troubles" on lists of causes of family stress.

Use of Time. Couples I work with are always complaining that they don't get enough time together to maintain effective communication and to make the many decisions that reflect the complexity of their lives. I am not surprised. I have already referred to the pressures of the two-job marriage. But other couples have their pressures, too. Many husbands hold down more than one job. Often both husbands and wives are heavily involved in community and church programs, in hobbies and spare-time pursuits, in social activities, in sports and other recreations. All these may be undertaken for commendable reasons; yet the sum total represents a consumption of time that leaves them out of touch with their inner selves, with each other, and with their children.

By way of contrast, consider the traditional family, without benefit of automobile, radio, television, or even telephone. The thought of such deprivation might seem intolerable to today's married couple; yet is there any real advantage in going to the other extreme? Couples who come to marriage-enrichment weekends often comment that it has been years since they had unhurried leisure time to open their hearts and minds to each other.

Values. In traditional marriage, homogamy (partners with similar backgrounds) was very much the rule. For a good marriage, bring together a couple who grew up in the same community, who went to the same school or similar schools, whose parents belonged to the same religious denomination and voted for the same political party. Again and again sociological studies have confirmed that these marriages show the greatest stability.

Nowadays, our geographical mobility mixes us all up so that such marriages rarely happen. In the mate-selection years, young people are often away from home, making friends who have very different values from those they learned as children; this results in marriages that are embarked upon with clashing religious and ethical standards.

Differences are not necessarily bad in themselves. Too much sameness in marriage partners can produce a dull, unexciting relationship. Adjusting to people who see life in other perspectives can mean a challenge to find common ground, and this can activate growth. But the adaptations called for are quite demanding and can be painful. Tensions mount, and the motivation to bridge the gulf ebbs away. Without great patience and negotiating skills, the task of mutual accommodation can become insuperable.

Conclusion

Adjustments, adjustments, adjustments. The list could go on and on, almost indefinitely. Lewis Terman, who conducted one of the earliest and most extensive studies of American marriages back in the 1930s, compiled a list of complaints his couples made about each other's behavior. The list of husbands' complaints about their wives runs to fifty-seven items, the wives' complaints about their husbands to fifty-three. And that was more than forty years ago, before marriage got really complicated!

Is it not obvious that marriage is failing today on a huge scale, not because it is unworkable, but because its complexity has been greatly increased, and we have failed to make this clear to those who enter it, and failed to provide them with the resources necessary for the task? Many of the changes that are part of the great transition are in fact conducive to better and more satisfying relationships; but they call for altogether higher levels of interpersonal competence than most of us possess, and we have done very little to grasp this fact and act upon it. I have already suggested that most of those unhappy men and women around us whose marriages are breaking up are not failures, but rather victims—victims of a culture that allows them to embark on perilous seas not only without chart or compass, but with only the most rudimentary skill in navigation.

What is the answer? Surely it is to equip them with what I call "primary coping systems." This is not a new idea. In *Identity and Interpersonal Competence,* Nelson Foote and Leonard Cottrell said, "Interpersonal competence is neither a trait nor a state. Competence denotes capabilities to meet and deal with a changing world, to formulate ends and implement them" (p. 49). It is not a new idea; it is an old idea that we never put into practice.

There has perhaps been some excuse for not doing so until now, because our knowledge of the necessary skills, and how to enable couples to learn them, has been quite limited. But this is no longer true. We now have the resources to provide couples with very effective coping systems. In the second part of this book, I will describe what these resources are and how they can be put to use.

PART TWO

Marital Interaction in Process

The following chapters explain the dynamics of marital interaction in the companionship marriage, in terms of a primary coping system that can enable the couple to embark on a process of growth and change, to develop effective communication, and to deal effectively with disagreement, conflict, and anger. With this coping system, the chances of achieving a successful companionship marriage should be good. Without it, the chances of success will be very limited.

7

HOW WE LEARN TO BUILD RELATIONSHIPS

M Y purpose in this second part of the book is to explain in some detail what "interpersonal competence" means, at least as far as marriage is concerned. The task of marriage enrichment is to equip couples with better insights, skills, and tools than they normally possess, in order that they may appropriate, in much fuller measure than they normally do, the rewards a fully functioning companionship marriage has to offer.

We shall examine in some detail the "coping system," which provides the key to success in marriage. Essentially, this adds up to the capacity to develop warm and creative relationships. It is not enough, however, to know what it is that we are seeking to teach; because, as we shall see, learning for living is a very different process than learning for knowing. We must therefore begin, in this chapter, by trying to understand just how people learn the complex art of establishing good relationships.

Marriage was traditionally viewed as an institution. It is, however, first and foremost a relationship. It is two people coming together with the intention of staying together. And it is an *intimate* relationship. Its biological base is sexual union—the meeting and joining of two living bodies to create new living bodies. At the reproduction level, nature leaves nothing to chance. It takes an urgent and powerful set of forces to overcome the natural protective defenses with which we shield our bodies from invasion; but the elaborate courtship rituals of many birds and animals reveal how male and female make themselves vulnerable in order to achieve physical intimacy.

Much more complex are the processes by which humans move from separateness into relationships. Beginning as strangers, with all defenses at the ready, two people go through a series of maneuvers in a preliminary probing of each other, gradually risking enough vulnerability and mutual trust to carry out whatever transaction is their immediate objective. If the transaction is limited in time, and in the degree of mutual involvement, they will then disengage and go their separate ways. If their purpose has wider and deeper implications, the processes are more complex. The intention to marry, which implies the greatest attainable intimacy and the expectation of a continuing cooperative association for the whole of life, surely involves the most complex process of all.

To understand marital interaction, therefore, we must begin by asking how we learn to relate to the other significant persons in our lives. The word *learn* is of central importance. Simple creatures, for whom life is brief and relatively uncomplicated, are endowed from the start with a set of built-in mechanisms, which we usually call "instincts." These serve their purpose well, and little further learning is required.

We humans, in contrast, need to learn almost all our behaviors. And we start in a condition of almost complete helplessness, totally dependent on our parents, from whom we learn our early coping skills—first by responding to their encouraging or restraining actions, and later by imitating what we see them do. This process of watching others and trying to copy them continues in the form of children's play, a large part of which consists of acting out experimentally the behaviors of the people who are the "significant others" in their lives. As we have already noted, this is the way in which boys and girls internalize the roles that will later become their behavior patterns when they grow up, marry, and become parents.

Relationships are, in fact, the main business of human life. It is doubtful whether an individual, in the strict sense of the term, can actually exist. We are what we are as a result of a vast multitude of interactions we have experienced with the many people whose lives have touched ours, although to some extent the particular ways in which we react are determined by our own unique personalities.

All this is common knowledge so far as children are concerned; but many of us tend to believe that later in life this process is replaced by a different arrangement, in which we decide how to behave as a result of intellectual judgments based on information received. There is no doubt that this is sometimes true. In recent years, however, I have come to believe that it doesn't happen to nearly the extent we imagine; the childhood pattern of learning to live by observing others and copying them remains the most powerful factor in deciding our behavior patterns.

Learning for Living

Since this question of how we learn to behave in relationships is vital to the marriage-enrichment process, we must now pursue it further.

As we saw in an earlier chapter, married couples often get locked into an unsatisfactory behavior pattern, which they seem unable to change. The passage I quoted from Sidney Jourard made this vividly clear. As we often express it, we "get set in our ways," and we seem unable to break out and change for the better. It has often been suggested that this is an inevitable process that is part of maturing, and that it tightens its grip on us further as we begin to grow old. What this implies is that, once we have established a set of patterns for relating to others, and especially for close relationships within the family, these patterns, for good or ill, must be accepted as established and incapable of significant change. This is a widely held notion.

If this were indeed true, of course, the case for marriage enrichment would collapse. The only way to improve most marriages is by enabling the partners to change their behavior toward each other. The whole marriage-enrichment movement rests on the conviction that this can really happen.

However, it can happen only if the necessary conditions are met. The extensive psychological studies recently undertaken in the field of behavior modification have established clearly what these conditions are. The first is that you must be *motivated* to initiate change; and the motivation comes from a strong conviction that the change is possible. The second condition is that, once you have acted to initiate the desired change, you must be sufficiently *rewarded* to go on repeating the new behavior pattern until it has been firmly established.

It takes careful planning to provide these conditions; and our traditional ways of attempting to change behavior have been almost entirely on the wrong track. We have made a major error in confusing the process of "learning for knowing" with the very different process of "learning for living."

The root of our trouble lies in the false belief that we can change people's behavior by giving them *information*. This is not, however, a complete fallacy; if it were, we would not have clung to it so stubbornly. Two things *are* true: that new information frequently *does* provide the basis for behavior change; and that nonhabitual behaviors are indeed often promoted on the basis of information received. These established facts have, however, led us to the false conclusion that information given can and should of itself change our established habit patterns. This very seldom happens.

Ever since the Greek philosophers of the fourth century B.C., our Western culture has been dominated by the idea that human behavior is dictated by *rational* considerations. The medieval theologians reinforced this concept, and modern academic education, with its heavy emphasis on assimilating facts, has given it further impetus. Indeed, the root meaning of the word *education*—to draw out what is already there—has been reversed, and the schoolteacher today sees his or her task as being to pump into the minds of the students, from outside, what is *not* already there!

I am not opposed to academic education. Learning for knowing has as its aim the accumulation of facts, which are filed systematically as a body of knowledge, so as to be available for future use in that amazing computer system the human brain. It is obviously necessary for a specialist in any field to have a large mass of relevant facts readily available.

What I *do* deplore is the facile assumption that we can apply this same process of pumping in facts to the business of learning for living. And this is just what we have been trying to do, on a colossal scale. The classroom is in fact a most unsuitable setting for the process of behavioral change, because it traditionally stands for authoritarian leadership and a highly competitive atmosphere among the learners—conditions that are about as unfavorable for learning to live as they are supposedly favorable for learning to know.

In fact, information must go through four successive processes before it has any real chance to influence behavior. Only the first of these is provided for in the academic setting. The other three require quite different conditions in order to operate.

This can best be explained by Diagram 2. At the upper level we see information descending like a shower of rain on two troughs, which represent the minds of a husband and wife. The information collects like water in the troughs; but notice that it is only retained at one end. At the other end the trough is nearly open, and most of the accumulating material just pours away. We are assailed daily by massive amounts of information, and nearly all of it makes a very superficial impact on our minds and is soon completely forgotten. Some, however, does remain and is processed as knowledge, which may be put to later use. Knowledge is simply information systematically filed for ready reference.

Notice also that there is a small pipe in the base of the trough, which allows a few drops to fall into another less-extensive trough immediately beneath the first. This represents a very small amount of the information we receive, retained and processed as *knowledge,* some of which seeps down to a deeper level within us and becomes *insight.* This can be defined as knowledge that is especially relevant to our personal life situation, so that it is perceived by our inner awareness as offering us some advantage, such as a possible improvement in our marriage relationship. At this point, however, no step has been taken to make use of the new knowledge. All that happens is that we entertain *a fantasy about what might happen if we acted on it.* Insight and fantasy are closely related, and fantasy represents the private imagining of an experience we do not normally undergo in reality.

Some early exponents of psychotherapy held the view that to enable the patient to gain insight into his condition was almost equivalent to a cure. This is not so. There are plenty of people in the world who go about loaded with insight, but never do anything to translate it into action. So this trough, like the other, has an open end, out of which most of the insight pours away and is never acted upon.

It also, however, has a thin pipe through which a few precious drops penetrate to another still smaller trough beneath. This takes us to the third level, which is *experimental action.* Now we are really making some progress.

This time, the husband sees something he can do that might make his marriage happier, and he summons up the courage to try it out. However, it doesn't follow that the results will correspond to what happened in his fantasy. He may

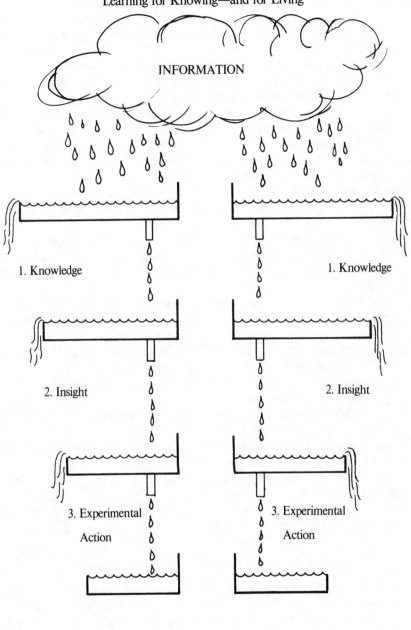

DIAGRAM 2
Learning for Knowing—and for Living

INFORMATION

1. Knowledge

2. Insight

3. Experimental
Action

4. Behavior Change

HUSBAND

1. Knowledge

2. Insight

3. Experimental
Action

4. Behavior Change

WIFE

choose the wrong time, or go about it in the wrong way, or meet with a negative or disinterested response from his wife. In any of these events he will
probably be discouraged and will not try again. He may however score a partial
success the first time, but be prevented from following it up, or later get a
discouraging response. He may be diverted in some other direction and not get
around to repeating the experiment. So once more, there is leakage from the
trough, but not as much as at the higher levels.

Again there is that little pipe, and another quite small trough underneath.
But now there is no more leakage, because we now have at last reached the
level of *behavioral change*. This time, the experimental action is repeated and
repeated and repeated until it brings about a new habit pattern, which replaces
the old one. Now, at last, something has really been achieved!

But we have come a long way from the mere receiving of information. All
four stages must be completed before we can claim that relational enrichment
takes place.

Notice, too, a further complication. Because this is a married couple, *both*
partners must go successfully through all four stages, and both must do so
together. At any point in the process it takes two to promote progress; but one
alone can stop it.

Notice something else: for an *individual* to arrive at the point of decision to
change behavior is easier than for a couple; but when the change is decided on
by two together, the chances are much better than it will be sustained, because
they will encourage, support, and stimulate each other to keep up the new behavior pattern if both have a stake in seeing it through.

In order to make the process quite clear, let us summarize the four stages
we have examined in detail:

Stage 1. Selected information is processed as knowledge and registered in
the memory for possible later use.

Stage 2. A relevant piece of knowledge is processed as *insight,* and its application to our life situation is dwelt upon in fantasy.

Stage 3. The new behavior suggested by insight is tried out in real life as
experimental action.

Stage 4. The experimental action proves successful and is repeated frequently until it achieves *behavioral change*.

Inadequacy of Our Present Educational Programs

Such then is the process that takes place when a relationship comes alive
and begins to grow. It is a complex process, and seldom does the mere giving
of information provide the necessary momentum to carry it through to its logical conclusion. For that reason, with great reluctance, I have to give my considered opinion that most of the educational procedures we are presently using
in the attempt to improve relationships are of very low effectiveness. Consider
a few examples:

1. A classroom teacher offers a course on marriage and the family. The information provided is processed as knowledge and becomes stored in the minds of the students. Possibly some of the knowledge generates insight, so that some students imagine themselves as prospective future spouses and parents. However, unless they are already married, there is little possibility of direct experimental action, except in the distant future, by which time most of what they learned will probably have been forgotten. If some of them *are* married, unless their spouses are also taking the course, the chances of both developing the same insight together are probably poor; and if the insight is not shared, the motivation for experimental action will be one-sided and will probably fail. The chances of behavioral change, now or later, are probably quite remote.

2. A pastor preaches a sermon on marriage. What he says includes helpful information, which his hearers process as knowledge. He also holds up before them an idealized picture of a deeply satisfying marriage, which has an emotional impact and generates fantasies. A few of the married members of the congregation begin to see new possibilities for their relationships and entertain th idea of trying out a new approach. After the service, one or two may even discuss this with their spouses as they drive home. However, as the atmosphere of the service is lost, and the demands of the daily routines press upon them, the chances are good that no further action will be taken.

3. A wife reads a self-help book on marriage. She learns some new facts, and her suppressed longings for a better relationship with her husband are reactivated. She has strong and alluring fantasies about the possibilities of an improved relationship. She tells her husband about the book, but he responds without enthusiasm, and she is discouraged. Perhaps she asks him to read the book, but he is busy and doesn't get around to it. Maybe he does read it in the end, but is not motivated to take any action. Finally the matter is dropped and life goes on as before. The evidence is that it takes an unusual combination of favorable circumstances to bring an isolated married couple to the point of working through a self-help book together and really acting on it. There is a possibility, but a rather remote one.

4. A group of married couples agree to meet together weekly to talk about their relationships. They may work through a book on marriage, reading a portion each week and then discussing it. They will all probably gain some new knowledge and they may well develop some new insight. Since they are involved together as couples, they have a good chance of processing some of their knowledge into shared insight about how to improve their relationships. And this should create quite favorable conditions for their embarking together on experimental action. If the group encourages the sharing of experiences as well as the discussion of ideas, some of the couples may extend their experimental action into behavioral change, and support each other in the process.

As we look at these four hypothetical situations, we see that, in terms of the conditions that favor learning for living, the first three offer very little chance that much will be achieved. Yet these three—the classroom course, the preacher's sermon, the reading of the self-help book—represent to an overwhelming extent the methods now being widely used in what is often called "education for marriage and family living." Only the fourth method—a group of couples meeting to learn and share together—begins to create effective conditions for the real improvement of relationships; and outside the marriage-enrichment movement, how many such growth groups for couples are getting together?

Accepting a realistic appraisal of the ways in which people develop effective relationships is for most of us a painful process. I myself have given innumerable lectures, taught many courses, written a number of books and a much greater number of articles, all in the sincere belief that I was helping married couples and family members to grow. I would not be so foolish as to think that all these activities have been worthless. Indeed, I have some concrete evidence of their effectiveness. But by comparison, the evidence I have of the effectiveness of the enrichment approach leaves me in no doubt about how learning for living should now be undertaken. When we knew no better, we had no alternative but to use the methods with which we were familiar. When we discover better ways, we have no real alternative but to employ them.

Increasing involvement in the emergence and development of marriage enrichment over the past twenty years has been for me a highly significant learning experience. Later in this book I shall describe the methods and procedures we are now using. I do not claim that they are by any means the best possible approaches. Indeed, they still remain largely experimental. Nevertheless, their effectiveness has been established by independent research, and I am convinced that they can and will become more effective as our understanding and experience grow.

Our goal, therefore, is to establish a setting in which the processes illustrated in Diagram 2 can take place as smoothly and effectively as possible. We certainly have to begin by communicating the new knowledge we possess, and which I am trying to summarize in this book. Until married couples understand some of our new concepts, they remain under the power of the myths and misconceptions that still dominate the thinking of the vast majority of people. To open up their minds to new ways of looking at marriage is certainly the first step. It is no more than the beginning of our task—but it *is* that.

Creating Environments for Change

We now have to create an environment in which couples are given every possible opportunity to move together through the remaining three stages that lead to behavioral change. The taboos and avoidances our culture places in the way of this add up to formidable obstacles, and I know of no existing social setting in which these have been circumvented. The only way is to set up special environments where what we want to happen can actually happen. This is the way in which other special services to people are made available: we provide churches for worship, hospitals for treating the sick, schools for educating children, theaters for acting plays, stadiums for sporting events, restaurants for eating meals, shopping centers for making purchases. Each setting is designed to facilitate what people want to do in it.

Fortunately, the prescription for couples who wish to learn better relationships is now clearly established. The three basic needs are seclusion, stimulus, and support.

Seclusion takes the couples out of their normal home environment and away from the paralyzing pressures of the daily routine. The weekend is a perfect time, and the residential retreat is generally considered the ideal. The Marriage Encounter has sometimes described what it offers as a "child-free, television-free, phone-free weekend"—an opportunity for the couple to be together with other couples in a relaxed atmosphere in which all share the avowed purpose of quietly reflecting on where they are in their marriages right now, and the new directions in which they would like to grow in the future. My colleague Paul Hopkins once remarked that a group of couples who spent a weekend in this way, without any leadership or any program, would probably have a profitable experience.

However, the right kind of *stimulus* is also highly desirable. There is as yet no unanimity about what kind of program is the most effective; but we are learning all the time and improving our methods. Some teaching—just the basics, to give uninformed couples orientation—is invariably included, though highly didactic presentations are not favored. Leadership of the group by one or more carefully selected and trained married couples is the accepted procedure, although we would prefer to substitute for the term "leaders," which has an authoritarian flavor, the concept of "participating facilitators."

What is going on here is a process that recapitulates the stages described in Diagram 2. First, the leader couple provide *information,* usually in the form of a brief talk on a particular area of marriage. The talk is often illustrated by using one or more diagrams, in order to encourage rapid comprehension. Often the leader couple offer illustrations of the concept out of their own marital experience; they may openly dialogue with each other about it, thus providing a demonstration in action of the concept they are trying to communicate. We call this "modeling."

Next, an *exercise* may be given to all the couples. They may be asked to write down how they could apply what they have just learned to their own relationship. First they do this separately, then they turn to each other and privately share what they have written. Sometimes they are given the opportunity, if they wish to take it, to share whatever insight they have gained with the other couples in the group. They are never *required* to do this, but they may volunteer.

This approach serves to emphasize the dynamic, as opposed to the didactic, learning process, and to exemplify the concept of "experiential education." The idea is that you learn a new way of interacting, and then immediately have an opportunity as a couple to try it out in practice and see how you like the feel of it. This moves the couples swiftly and naturally into experimental action, as opposed to the stereotyped procedure where they simply sit on chairs and absorb information.

Of great value, too, are organized periods of time when the couples can be alone together, after being carefully instructed about how the time should be used, and often after writing down separately their personal reactions to questions they are asked on the quality of their relationship.

The element of *support* is developed by creating an atmosphere of mutual trust in the group of couples, a process sometimes described as "community building." Every effort is made to free them from the defenses and pretenses that are part of the usual social stereotypes. Sitting in a circle instead of in formal rows or sitting on the floor if they prefer it; wearing casual clothes; joining in friendly, playful activities; using first names all around—these are some of the ways in which a warm, relaxed atmosphere is quickly generated. And the sense of common purpose that soon develops creates a remarkable spirit of loving and caring, which many couples affirm they have never before experienced even with their closest friends.

I never cease to wonder at the warmth, the trust, and the creativity that a group of couples can achieve during an enrichment weekend. It takes a little time, of course, and some couples move faster than others. Experience has taught us that, to be on the safe side, a minimum of fifteen to eighteen hours together is needed to get the group functioning at high potential. But once the setting has been established, the learning process really gets going. What is surprising, too, is that a couple can move right through the four stages quite swiftly—at least to the point of *commitment* to behavioral change. Of course, the process of actual change is only *initiated* in the weekend experience, and the real test comes in the followup; but when we consider the slow and very limited progress achieved by our conventional procedures, the contrast is positively startling. It is nothing short of amazing how far a given couple, ready and responsive, can move in the course of one weekend. One husband said, "I am not the same man who came here on Friday evening."

This, then, is what marriage enrichment aims to do: to create a unique environment in which a married couple can, under the most favorable conditions possible, learn experientially, and commit themselves to continue, the kind of creative love and companionship that is their hearts' desire.

I am not suggesting, of course, that this is a "miracle cure." It is only a beginning; and we have to continue to provide for the couples, in our "support systems," the conditions for ongoing growth. In the chapters that immediately follow, I shall try to define in more detail what this ongoing growth process involves.

8

DEVELOPING COUPLE
COMMUNICATION

THERE is overwhelming evidence that married couples who don't communicate effectively with each other are prevented from achieving close interpersonal relationships. Clearly, therefore, training couples in the necessary skills could greatly increase their chances.

How much do we really know about communication in marriage, and what can we do to give couples training in this important area of interpersonal competence?

As I sought answers to these questions, my first discovery, an astonishing one, was that the subject of communication between married couples was given very little attention until the 1970s. It would seem obvious that a marriage could be barely sustained, let alone improved and enriched, unless husband and wife could be in real touch with each other's thoughts, feelings, wishes, and intentions—so that careful study of the couple-communication process would be basic to the understanding of marital functioning.

Until quite recently, however, this was apparently not clearly perceived. I discovered this by going back to some of the basic books on marriage published before 1970. I selected twenty-six of these, dating from 1930 to 1970, on the basis of the reputations of their authors, all of whom were acknowledged authorities in the field. All but two of the volumes were college texts, which I assumed would include any major findings of studies on couple communication. The other two volumes (one published in 1947, the other in 1964) were scholarly symposia with contributions from a number of leading experts.

Having assembled these volumes without any reference to their specific content, I then looked up the word *communication* in the index of each. In nineteen of the volumes the word did not occur at all; nor could I discover any real reference to the subject under any other entry.

Seven of the volumes *did* have the word *communication* listed. In two of these, however, the references were not to interpersonal communication, but to what we now call the mass media. Two more *did* discuss interpersonal communication, though very briefly. In Clifford Kirkpatrick's *The Family as Process and Institution* (second edition, 1963), there was one page on the subject out of a total of seven hundred pages. In *Marriage and the Family* (1956), by Carle Zimmerman and Lucius Cervantes, a half of a page (also out of seven hundred) referred to *sexual* communication in marriage.

I may have missed something, but it is obvious that in twenty-three of these major works on marriage the topic of couple communication is given short shrift.

In the three remaining volumes I *did* find significant material. Harold Christensen's *Handbook of Marriage and the Family* (1964), a scholarly symposium of a thousand pages, included two and a half pages specifically on marital communication, written by Jessie Bernard; and James Peterson's *Education for Marriage* (1964) dealt with the subject at four different points for a total of seven and a half pages out of five hundred.

The third writer who got into couple communication was Henry Bowman, in his very popular text *Marriage for Moderns*. Since this book has gone through many editions, all carefully revised, I took soundings over a twenty-year period. In 1954 the word *communication* did not occur in the index. In 1960 half a page was devoted to the subject. In 1965 there was an extended discussion covering nine and a half pages. In 1975, however, the material on couple communication had been condensed to three and a half pages—perhaps because a number of other current topics were now calling for extended treatment.

I cannot close this brief historical survey without noting that the early pioneer who wrote most extensively in this field was not an American, but a Swede. In 1951 Georg Karlsson, at the University of Uppsala, published *Adaptability and Communication in Marriage,* a study of a group of couples in which he gave special attention to their communication systems. On a visit to Europe in 1962 I sought him out personally for discussion of some of his concepts.

Karlsson developed a ''communication index'' to measure how well his couples were communicating with and understanding each other. Using this, he concludes that good communication was related to high levels of marital satisfaction. Harvey Locke, a colleague of Ernest Burgess, reported the same conclusion in his book *Predicting Adjustment in Marriage: A Comparison of a Divorced and a Happily Married Group* (1951).

A sampling of these scattered pre–1972 discussions shows that they include the following points:

1. Much of the communication between marriage partners is nonverbal and lacks precision. Couples must therefore make the effort to clarify these vague messages through verbal explanations. This is especially important in the area of sex adjustment.

2. There is need for couples to share their role expectations in order to avoid negative responses to each other's behavior. They should also learn to announce their intentions clearly so as to make their future actions predictable. One way is to try reversing roles so that each can get the feel of the other's behavior. This helps to create empathy.

3. Learning to listen attentively, and to prove that the message has been heard by giving feedback, will avoid needless misunderstandings.

4. Expressing feelings is helpful—especially affection and tenderness. Affirming each other builds mutual respect and increases toleration of differences.

5. Talking about conflict areas can help to remove misunderstandings: it is better to "open up" than to "bottle up." But communicating dissatisfaction and negative feelings is risky and should be approached with caution.

These are all basically sound concepts; but one gets the feeling that the writers were groping for more light. There is no evidence that any of them, writing at that time, had a clearly formulated theoretical framework to which their scattered pieces of helpful advice could be related. They were moving in the right directions, but they had not yet arrived.

However, work *was* being done in the field of couple communication. As early as the 1950s a group of psychologists and psychiatrists, some of whom later became the founders of the family therapy movement, began to suspect that schizophrenia might have something to do with the patient's family environment. This launched them on studies of family interaction; but they were not in touch with the findings of the sociologists; so they developed their own conceptual framework. This soon led them to investigate the patterns of communication among family members, including couple interaction. This group included Eric Berne, whose investigations provided the groundwork for transactional analysis; Jay Haley, for many years the editor of the journal *Family Process;* Don Jackson and Paul Watzlawick, who with Janet Beavin published in 1967 *The Pragmatics of Human Communication,* which contains the first serious theoretical statement on couple communication. In 1968 Don Jackson, with William Lederer, wrote *The Mirages of Marriage,* which for the first time presented some of the new insights to the general reader.

By the time this material began to make any significant impact, however, we were already into the 1970s. Obviously, before that time couple communication was only dimly understood, even by most of the marriage specialists.

The 1970s Bring New Knowledge

It would not be inaccurate to state that we have achieved, in the last few years, a major breakthrough in this field. The pieces have been put together. A good deal is now being written on the subject of couple communication; but the real forward thrust has come from two research teams: Sherod Miller and his colleagues at the University of Minnesota, with constant encouragement and support from Reuben Hill; and Bernard Guerney and his colleagues at Pennsylvania State University. Significant material on specific aspects of the subject has also come from other investigators, such as Sidney Jourard's studies on self-disclosure and William Hill's "interaction matrix."

In the remainder of this chapter I will try to chart the new insights we now have, and how they are being used to help married couples. One of the very gratifying aspects of the major studies is that in both instances the teams concerned have not just carried out research. They have also designed highly effective training programs that are being made available to married couples. Sherod Miller's program was formerly called the Minnesota Couples' Communication Program, but is now known simply as Couple Communication (CC), a service of Interpersonal Communication Programs, Inc. (1925 Nicollet Avenue, Minneapolis, Minnesota 55403). It is fully described in the very readable book *Straight Talk,* by Sherod Miller and his associates. Bernard Guerney's program is known as Couple Relationship Enhancement (CRE) and is described in his book *Relationship Enhancement: Skill Training Programs for Therapy, Prevention, and Enrichment* (1977).

The essential elements in an effective communication system for married couples can be classified in various ways. For our present purpose, I shall arrange them under six headings:

Developing Self-awareness. Effective couple communication in marriage goes a long way beyond the primary level of passing on information. For two people to live a shared life, it is necessary that they share themselves; that each should know, in considerable depth, who the other is.

It is quite possible for two people to live together under the same roof, as husband and wife, for many years; to sit together at meals three times a day; to sleep in the same bed every night, and to join their bodies together in sexual intercourse. It is possible for a husband and wife to do this for a lifetime, and yet not really know each other as persons. This was in fact true of many traditional marriages, and it is true of many marriages today. Every marriage counselor has had the strange experience of hearing a husband describe his absent wife, or a wife her absent husband; and then, on meeting the other partner personally, failing to recognize this person as the one described. The degree of inaccuracy and distortion that can occur in the concept each partner has of the other is sometimes hard to understand.

Probably the main reason why marriage partners cannot communicate themselves to each other is that they really don't know themselves. So training for couple communication has to begin there. The CC program begins with what it calls the "awareness wheel." A Marriage Encounter weekend begins with an opportunity for self-examination.

Behind this emphasis there lies a very important fact; namely, that you cannot enter into a meaningful companionship relationship until you have established your own personhood. The traditional marriage did not require this condition. Indeed, it tended to make the wife an appendage of her husband. She was a *dependent* wife. She might find security in this role, and many wives were content to do so. But companionship must be based on a respectful recognition by each of the personal identity of the other.

Another way of expressing this is that you cannot truly love another person until you have come to love yourself as a person. If this sounds like arrogant egotism, remember that the Bible enjoins you to love your neighbor *as you love yourself*. The person whose self-esteem is critically low is simply incapable of giving love to another; he or she can only be grateful to lean abjectly on another. This could offer the other some kind of relationship. It could that of a protegé or a servant, but not a companion.

Some have criticized marriage as a confining relationship that denies to people the freedom to be and to become themselves. That *could* happen, and it *has* happened in the past. But it couldn't happen in a companionship marriage, because such a relationship tends to improve progressively as the partners increase their individual self-esteem and establish their individual identities.

So, communication training for couples begins by showing them how to become increasingly aware of themselves. The awareness wheel of CC has five spokes: sensing, or awareness of what your five physical senses are experiencing; thinking, or knowing how your mind is interpreting what is going on in your life; feeling, or identifying the emotional states you get into; wanting, or recognizing your needs as a person; and doing, or observing what action you are performing.

Full awareness eludes us all. But it is quite definitely possible to increase your awareness. This can be done in several ways: by forming the habit of focusing your attention in turn on each spoke of the wheel, so as to get a composite picture of your total awareness at a given time; by writing down a list of your thoughts, feelings, and wishes for the purpose of clarifying a disturbed emotional condition, or just as a way of checking up on yourself (most marriage-enrichment programs include exercises of this kind); or, best of all, by forming the habit of setting up a mutual reporting dialogue with your spouse, preferably on a daily basis. Through regular practice of such procedures, you can in time greatly expand your self-awareness and give special attention to thoughts, feelings, and actions that you have not previously recognized, and that you may want either to own or to change. Expanding your self-awareness is very definitely a growth process.

Practicing Self-disclosure. Since the publication of Sidney Jourard's *The Transparent Self* in 1964, the psychology of self-disclosure has been extensively investigated. An excellent summary of the findings of these studies is given in *Sharing Intimacy: What We Reveal and Why* (1975), by Valerian Derlega and Alan Chaikin.

What follows are some relevant facts about self-disclosure as we now understand it.

Almost all real friendships are based on mutual self-disclosure. If in a group of people I take you aside and tell you something about myself that I have not told any of the others, you feel honored by my trust, and you may reciprocate by sharing something in your life that you wouldn't care to tell any other member of the group. These exchanges create a special relationship between us, and as our sense of trust in each other grows stronger, we may both disclose more and more of ourselves. The result is that we become increasingly comfortable in each other's presence, because we can relax and be our real selves, without defenses or pretenses.

This happens in a special way in marriage. When two people are in love, they seek to prove their love by being open to each other. Physically, this is symbolized by sexual intimacy. But it is also true of uncovering our personal lives. Remember the fairy tales in which the prince sat down with the fair maiden he had rescued from the dragon, and "he told her all his heart"?

People who can't open up to others generally can't make friends. They become more and more lonely and isolated. They may develop paranoid tendencies and suspect that others around them are rejecting them and even plotting against them. Likewise, neurotics don't respond reciprocally to the self-disclosure of others.

Too much disclosure too soon may produce a backfiring effect and bring a negative response. Making disclosures requires the right setting and the right time. In a few situations, unwise disclosures can be damaging—for example, betraying the confidences of others, or telling your partner you don't like him or her. Honesty in marriage is a good principle; but the ethic of honesty must always give way to the higher ethic of love.

The supportive atmosphere of a marriage-enrichment weekend provides an excellent setting for couples to open up to each other, and this is generally a healing and renewing process. It is almost the basic operation in the Marriage Encounter, which is designed to bring husband and wife out of the strained detachment and unreality into which many conventional marriages settle and to get the couple started on a new life together, characterized by new openness and new trust. Many couples with dull, dreary marriages long for something to happen that will take down the walls of deception they have built between them.

Completing Your Communication Cycles. Almost the first lesson in communication theory introduces you to the three-step communication cycle. In Step 1, I send a verbal message to you. In Step 2, you repeat what you heard me say, so that I may know you heard me; this is what we call "feedback." In Step 3, I either confirm your feedback, indicating that you heard the message correctly, or, if you got it wrong, I correct your feedback and give you the true version.

The following diagram illustrates this clearly:

DIAGRAM 3
The Communication Cycle

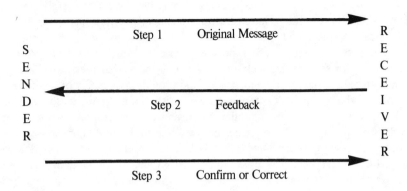

This simple procedure effectively excludes the possibility of a misunderstanding arising between us. It is confidently used by airline pilots, whose lives may depend on it.

The Couple Communication course calls this "shared meaning." Consider how many unhappy situations, how many bitter quarrels, arise in marriage because of misunderstandings. Here is a simple device, readily available to all married couples, which could space them from any possibility of a misunderstanding ever again arising between them.

Couples should learn this three-step process. They can do so during a meal, while driving, or at leisure moments. Some couples feel self-conscious at first about doing this. They say it makes them feel silly. But when they consider what a valuable tool it is, and how useful it could be in a crisis, they can easily overcome their awkwardness, especially if the sequence is first demonstrated to them, and they have the chance to try it out with a group of other couples.

Learning to Listen and Respond with Empathy. The word *empathy* means more than sympathy. The distinction between these two words derives from their semantic roots. When you sympathize with another person, you get alongside him and in some measure share his feelings *by association.* But to empathize is to get right inside him and share his feelings *by identification.* It means, in popular parlance, "standing in his shoes."

Although complete identification with another is impossible, to go as far as possible in this direction is obviously to develop deep understanding. We all feel comforted and supported when someone says, with obvious sincerity, "I know how you feel."

Clearly this capacity to identify with another could contribute very considerably to the husband-wife relationship, where two people are committed to sharing their lives at a deep level.

The key to learning empathic response is the cultivation of your capacity for what has been called "creative listening." It is this aspect of couple communication that the Couple Relationship Enhancement program has made its central focus. Couples, under the guidance of a trained instructor, go through a series of sessions, with appropriate homework, in which they learn to listen perceptively to each other, picking up not only the verbal messages, but also the emotional overtones and undertones, and providing evidence of this through feedback, which is called "empathic response." Some would reason that this is the very heart of couple communication, and that couples who achieve high levels of empathy need little further training in effective communication.

Using the Appropriate Communication Styles. If Couple Communication had done nothing else than pick up William Hill's four communication styles and popularize them, it would already have saved many marriages from ending in disaster.

When people communicate, they always do so in one or more of four styles. All married couples should be aware of the style they are using at any given time and learn to use the right one at the right time. What follows is a somewhat simplified description.

Style 1 is the most common one. We use it when we are simply passing on information or engaging in casual conversation. It is generally not accompanied by strong emotions, which might disturb the relationship.

Style 2 is the "putting down" way of addressing your spouse. You are blaming, attacking, nagging, manipulating. My wife and I call it "the style with the sting in its tail." If the receiver feels the sting, then it *is* Style 2, even if the sender is unaware of it.

This style is usually damaging to the relationship, though unfortunately most of us use it frequently until we become aware of what we are doing. It is not a good way to deal with stresses in a relationship, so couples who want to improve their marriages often make a contract not to use it, and to be willing to be challenged if they slip up. The challenge, however, should not itself be in Style 2! The best approach is a simple question: "I wonder if that was Style 2. What do you think?"

Style 3 is an exploring, wondering, speculative way of looking at a situation—a rational, investigative inquiry to see if we can understand what's going on between us. A couple might be getting into a quarrel when one says, "Let's be reasonable about this and see if we can settle it in a calm, rational manner."

In this sense it is a "working style." But attempting to move from a heated Style 2 exchange to Style 3 may not be successful, because what you are doing is saying in effect, "Let's put away our nasty feelings and settle this intellectually." That won't work, because it's the feelings that are causing the trouble, and you can't solve the problem by ignoring them. So it is much better to approach Style 3 through Style 4, the other working style.

Style 4 is a process of self-disclosure in which you communicate where you are and what you are feeling, without blaming your partner or justifying yourself. You simply say, "My feelings are giving me trouble, and I need your help to straighten them out."

This constitutes an invitation to work. It may or may not be accepted, but it's more likely to be if the couple have made a contract beforehand to use Style 4 in any emotionally charged situation, and to respond positively to an approach in Style 4 from the partner. When this happens, the couple can then move to Style 3; and this time they are taking the feelings with them, so they are much more likely to be able to work out a solution. Anyway, this is their only hope; there *is* no Style 5!

After a little practice, couples learn to be aware of what style they are using. This has enabled some couples literally to change the whole pattern of their relationship from one of continuous mutual antagonism to a happier state of mental cooperation.

Maintaining Mutual Self-esteem. The five procedures we have been examining are in a sense devices to get a couple's marital communication functioning at a productive level. Once they have both developed self-awareness, opened up to each other, learned in a situation of uncertainty to complete their communication cycles, and become skilled in using the right styles, they should have made considerable progress. All that remains is to keep it up!

The best way I know of doing this is by frequent affirmation of each other. What this amounts to is never missing an opportunity to express appreciation, encouragement, and affection. This may sound childishly simple, but the plain fact is that very few married couples take it seriously.

Ian Suttie, a British psychiatrist, wrote *The Origins of Love and Hate* in 1952. In it he drew attention to what he called the "taboo on tenderness" that exists in our Western culture. We are all aware of the inhibitions that exist in most northern European countries, as compared with southern European countries, about expressing feelings. We may not understand so clearly that, especially among men, these inhibitions operate more strongly to restrain positive emotions than negative emotions. This is well illustrated by the story of the husband who was interviewed by a reporter on his fiftieth wedding anniversary. Asked whether after all these years together he still loved his wife, he replied, "Indeed I do. In fact, sometimes it's all I can do not to tell her so!"

In modern families there is more freedom to express emotions than there was in the past; but this applies more to negative than to positive emotions. Yet several studies have indicated that one of the major characteristics of "well" families is that their members habitually affirm each other and warmly express love and affection. This was reported in the recent book *No Single Thread*

(1975) by Jerry Lewis and his associates; similar conclusions were reached in earlier family studies by Herbert Otto and Nicholas Stennett, and in a careful investigation by James Hine of eighteen very successful marriages.

Conclusion

We have come a long way, both in theory and in practice, in our understanding of couple communication. We shall no doubt continue to increase our knowledge and to improve the procedures we use to put it to work in the training of married couples. Already we have assembled a set of concepts about couple communication that in theory make sense; and by way of confirming the theory, they really work in practice. They are also being extended, beyond the marriage, to parent-child relationships, and indeed to all kinds of interpersonal interactions.

All these tested practical skills are now available to married couples for the increase of their happiness. However, not only do we meet couples who have had no opportunity to learn them, but most couples don't even know that they exist!

Can you imagine what would happen if someone invented a new gadget that could substantially improve efficiency in our homes, or in our cars? Surely it would be patented quickly and widely manufactured, advertised, and sold, and in a short time we would all have one. But when we discover resources that have the power to increase the capacity of husbands and wives to understand and support and cooperate with each other, almost nothing is done to make these resources available—because those who care do not have the power to act, and those who have the power to act do not seem to care!

9

UNDERSTANDING MARITAL
CONFLICT

FOLLOWING my discovery that our understanding of couple communication is a relatively recent development, I decided to apply the same test to our knowledge about the management of conflict in marriage.

I went back to the same twenty-six basic books. First, I looked up the word *conflict* in the index of each. It occurred in just about half of the volumes. Most of them, however, had something to say on the subject, often under such headings as "adaptation," "adjustment," "disagreement," "quarrels."

Some of the strictly sociological volumes did not deal with conflict at all. Among those that did, the older publications tended to focus on the *areas* of marriage in which conflict commonly occurs. Ray Baber, for example, in 1939, spoke of "classifying the causes of conflict."

Ernest Burgess, in his 1945 volume, defined conflict as "a fight of any sort, ranging from a slight difference of opinion to uncompromising warfare." In his 1953 volume, he devoted a chapter each to "adjustment" and "adaptability," and conflict is discussed in both, with illustrative case material.

The fullest discussion of the subject I could find in an early volume was by Joseph Folsom in 1934. He defined marital conflict simply as "a collision of wishes." The later writers (up to 1970) tended to give more attention to the *nature* of marital conflict than how to deal with it. As early as 1954, Henry Bowman said, "Some conflict in marriage is normal and to be expected." Jessie Bernard, in 1964, spoke of "the inevitability of conflict in marriage"; and James Peterson, in that same year, went further and said that "conflict is inevitable and continuous."

Peterson was one of the first writers to suggest that marital conflict could, if wisely used, actually be beneficial. He described it as "a means to the promotion of final family cohesion," and he elaborated his point in these words:

"Conflicts may be the stepping stones to a marriage of maximum cohesiveness combined with a maximum development of personality for both partners."

We can, therefore, trace an evolution of thought in attitudes toward marital conflict. This trend reaches its final consolidation today in the view now widely held by psychologists that a conflict in a close relationship can be viewed as a "growth point," or at least as a "choice point" at which the two people concerned may decide either to use the conflict as a means of further relational growth or to turn away from it and miss an opportunity to grow.

I see marital conflict as a central issue in the process of marriage enrichment. The development of my ideas has come in part from reading what has been written on the subject by others, but also relies heavily on my own experience of marriage, and on discussions with thousands of couples both in marriage counseling and in marriage-enrichment groups.

I have found that married couples react to conflict in a variety of ways. Among them are the following four.

1. *Avoid it.* A common policy is to maintain a superficial state of peace, sidestep every potential quarrel, and sweep all disagreements under the rug. The inevitable result is a very superficial relationship.

2. *Tolerate It.* Many couples simply shrug their shoulders and accept the fact that periodic quarrels are an inevitable part of marriage; that nothing can be done to alter this fact; and that the only course to follow is to bear with the unpleasantness, make up later, and enjoy a period of relative tranquility until the next quarrel breaks out. The result is a relationship with alternating phases of harmony and disharmony, what we often speak of as the "ups and downs of married life."

3. *Fight Fair.* This is the doctrine, widely promulgated by George Bach, that fighting in marriage is okay, but that it should be done in accordance with prescribed rules learned by taking a course in "fight training." I have met couples who said they found this helpful, and others who had been unable to make it work. To me, fighting in a love relationship seems totally inappropriate.

4. *Process It.* This attitude is increasingly being adopted by couples who accept Peterson's philosophy that conflict is a growth point and can be used to enrich the marriage. As I said earlier, this is the view I believe is appropriate to the marriage-enrichment movement.

What Is Conflict?

Folsom's definition of conflict as "a clash of wishes," though simple, goes to the heart of the matter. It is impossible to imagine any two people, however much they love each other, who would always want to do the same thing in the same way at the same time.

In other words, conflict is rooted in *difference*.

However, differences only cause trouble when the people concerned are *related* to each other. John Smith, who lives on the other side of town, may believe in a life style totally alien from the one I favor. If we never meet, that matters very little. If, however, we find ourselves together at a social event and exchange opinions, I may remark to my wife later, "What an unpleasant fellow that man Smith is!" He may make the same remark about me to *his* wife. And probably both of us will decide henceforth to keep out of each other's way.

Suppose, however, that I take a new job and find that Smith works in the same outfit. We can't entirely avoid each other now; but we probably keep as much distance as possible between us. Then one day there is a reshuffling of staff positions, and I become his colleague, so that we have to work together. Now the question of our differences becomes a major issue. Either we have to find some way of accommodating to each other; or one of us had better resign and find another job. If we don't, we shall be involved in continual differences of opinion, causing irritation and frustration on both sides.

It is clear, therefore, that difference plus involvement sets up disagreement, and disagreement disrupts a relationship. Two people who have to cooperate, but find themselves in disagreement, are in trouble. Unless they can either disengage from each other, or find a solution acceptable to both, there will be a head-on collision, a "clash of wishes."

What will happen then? Smith will be getting in my way, preventing me from doing what I want to do and what I feel I ought to do. I will, likewise, be doing all these same things to him. When this happens, my natural biological reaction is to build up a head of steam, so as to have an extra surge of energy available to break through the obstacle that is blocking my path. Smith, at the same time, is experiencing the same biological reaction. We are in conflict.

A conflict is a disagreement *heated up*. A disagreement is a difference accentuated by lack of space. So, there are two factors always present when conflict develops: our wishes are different, and our space is limited.

Now apply this to marriage. John and Mary, when they first met, were attracted to each other. John had met other girls, but Mary seemed special. To Mary, likewise, John seemed special. They were drawn to each other. Physically, they felt a strong urge to join their bodies. But in other areas also, there was the same longing to be close—to be joined in mind and in spirit. They wanted love, intimacy, unity, the sharing of life.

We needn't get far into the complexities of mate selection. But obviously one of the strong pulls that drew them together was *likeness*. They found they had many things in common; probably they went over some of these when they were deciding to marry and felt good about them.

Of course there were differences, too. But some of these were actually favorable. Robert Winch (1958) and others have found, in studies of mate selection, that *complementarity,* as well as similarity draws people toward each other. John saw that Mary had qualities he admired, and he hoped that in a shared life she would be supportive to him, that she might enhance his gifts, even that some of her good qualities might be transmitted to him. So, at least some of their differences could be counted as assets.

All differences, however, can't be assets. For John and Mary, there were touchy areas where they irritated each other, and even a few where they really clashed. Some of their tastes and preferences differed. Each liked to do some things in ways that seemed senseless, or even offensive, to the other. Some of their values, their standards, their life goals were not exactly the same.

All couples who marry take into their shared life a bundle of assets—and a bundle of liabilities! The assets provide sustaining strength to the relationship. The liabilities represent a hidden threat.

What exactly *is* that threat? It is a danger that, as they move into an intimate relationship, opposing forces will erupt which will defeat their desire by pushing them apart. Just when they need closeness, they will experience a compelling need for distance. Their desire to merge will be opposed by a contrary desire to disengage. The struggle between these contending forces within them will make them miserable just when they want to feel happy and harmonious.

We can see all this clearly in Diagram 4, which my wife and I developed some years ago and used in an earlier book (Mace and Mace, 1974).

We begin with John and Mary, at a distance from each other, but feeling the urge to get closer. They are aware of differences between them, but the strong pull of attraction masks the opposing forces, so that they don't seem to matter.

As they move closer, however, their differences are accentuated by their increased involvement, and as they become aware of disagreements developing, they begin to feel some tension. However, their urge toward intimacy is still strong, so they move closer still. As they do so, the tension between them gets stronger, and with the development of anger, in one or both, disagreement heats up into conflict.

Now the closeness is getting uncomfortable as anger takes over and quenches love. The urge to escape into the comforting safety of distance overpowers the urge toward intimacy, and they move away from each other, back to where they started.

After a time the hot anger dies down, and as they cool off, the desire for closeness gradually reasserts itself. Sooner or later, they begin to move again toward intimacy. Love revives, they are reconciled, and all is well until another conflict, or the original one again, is activated. Then the process repeats as it did before.

This recurring series of movements toward closeness, back toward distance, and forward again toward closeness, represents an experience most couples are very familiar with. Vera and I, who have often experienced this rhythm in our own relationship, call it the "love-anger cycle." It is a basic element in the

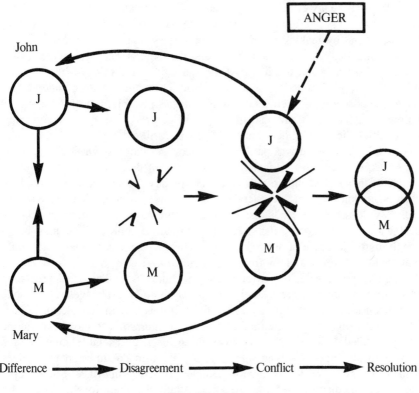

DIAGRAM 4
The Love-Anger Cycle

dynamics of marital interaction. Indeed, I would go so far as to suggest that it is *the* basic factor. Any couple who can deal constructively with interpersonal conflict in their relationship can move on to continuing growth and enrichment. Couples who *cannot* manage conflict successfully are doomed either to settle for a relatively unsatisfactory relationship characterized by "ups and downs," or to drift gradually into a state of marital separateness that mocks the dream of loving intimacy.

What can a couple do about conflict?

There are three possibilities, and the differences between them are sufficient to justify us in speaking of three different forms of marriage:

The Conflict-excluding Marriage. We have seen in an earlier chapter that in traditional marriages the primary value was *stability*. This being so, the disruptive power of conflict could not be allowed to threaten the security of the family unit. The only really effective way to achieve this was to structure the relationship so that the possibility of conflict was virtually excluded. As we have seen, this was done by making marriage a one-vote system, with all the power of decision making vested in one partner, and the requirement that the other partner be subservient and obedient. At the same time, the roles of husband and wife were closely defined so as to keep their spheres of influence widely separated, in order to limit their interactions as far as possible. Given these strictly enforced safeguards, traditional marriages in general were able to keep interpersonal conflict well under control. This was achieved, of course, at a price. The wife's personhood was partly suppressed, and intimacy was quite limited.

The Conflict-avoiding Marriage. This is an apt description of the average couple of today. The culture tells them very plainly that people who really love each other don't get into conflict, which of course is not at all true. When in fact they do develop serious disagreements, they have no appropriate skills to deal with the situation. After a few bitter quarrels, one or both may be so deeply hurt that peace at any price may seem the best deal to make. The only way to do this is to withdraw from each other. Physical withdrawal is of course not usually practicable; but psychological withdrawal is. The usual procedure is to close off areas of the relationship that prove to be explosive and to choke back intense feelings that might start a fight. In this way the couple make their life together tolerable by limiting their areas of interaction to those that can be safely handled. This of course means settling for a superficial relationship and giving up all hope of loving intimacy. People who do this find themselves denied the warm and tender love they hoped to find in marriage. Such people easily become disillusioned and are ready to turn elsewhere for the meaningful relationship they failed to find. Among these are the unhappy, frustrated husbands and wives who are divorcing on a large scale today.

The Conflict-resolving Marriage. This is simply another way of describing the enriched marriage. As I have already said, conflict is not something tragic in a human relationship. It is not to be feared and run away from. It is a normal and integral part of any close relationship. It is in fact raw material to be worked on and transmuted into an opportunity to grow. A conflict may even be welcomed, because it pinpoints an area where an adjustment has to be made—very much as an unusual noise in an automobile engine locates a fault, which, when corrected, makes the machine run more smoothly. Couples who learn the necessary skills to work on their conflicts therefore have the assurance that they are continually improving their relationships. Each conflict resolved marks another milestone in their progress toward relationship-in-depth.

Using Conflict Creatively

The art of conflict resolution is not simple. That is why comparatively few couples really understand it. This is not something you imbibe with your mother's milk. It is not something that life automatically teaches you. What you learn in the outside world is either to fight and win; or, if you *can't* win, how to exploit the resulting situation so as to placate your adversary and get the best deal possible.

Marriage, however, is not, or at least should not be, an adversary situation. It is a cooperative relationship, in which neither winning nor losing should be relevant. It is not a matter of my interest over against your interest—although many marriages do in fact degenerate to that level. In a loving marriage, it is *our* joint interest that is the goal. The trick, therefore, is to avoid getting into an adversary confrontation; and instead, to maneuver the conflict situation into a joint-growth opportunity.

Dealing with conflict in that context requires three distinct steps. I will introduce them briefly here; then I will deal with the second and third much more fully in the two following chapters. This material represents the very essence of how a companionship marriage can be made to work.

I. *The couple must clearly understand the true nature of conflict.* What is happening, as we have seen, is simply that one of the negative areas of difference between them is asserting itself and needs to be closely examined and dealt with. This is at least how a conflict *starts*. However, if it is not faced as it arises, the conflict can expand and pull in a whole set of other differences that have not been previously cleared up. It is as if you said to your partner, "I don't like what you're doing right now, and I'm angry about it. And, while I'm at it, let me add that there are several other things you do that I don't like either. These actions on your part make me feel hurt, slighted, and put down. And that reminds me, in the last few months there have been a number of occasions when I have felt hurt, slighted, and put down. For example . . . In fact, now that I come to think of it, this has been going on for years and years. I remember the time soon after we were married when you . . . And don't think I'm the only person you treat like this. I know for a fact that you have done the same thing to . . ."

This kind of piling up of unhealed injuries from the past can be terribly destructive and quite unproductive. There is only one way to avoid it, and that is to *take the conflicts one at a time and work each one through*. Of course this involves a lot of time and effort; but in the end it actually *saves* a lot of time and effort. There just isn't any effective way to keep a relationship warm and sweet except by working at every conflict as soon as it appears. Couples who are really serious about marriage enrichment make it a daily task to keep their relationship in good working order, and they find this well worth while.

But if conflicts reflect disturbing differences between the people concerned, *can* these really be removed? Is it fair for me to keep changing my behavior in order to humor my partner? Can't she just accept me as I am and be done with it?

These are questions that look only at one side of the equation. In dealing with an irritating difference, it isn't a matter of wrangling over who will give an inch here or an inch there. That kind of adversary attitude will achieve little or nothing. Rather, it is a matter of looking at the situation *together,* with all the facts and all the feelings out in the open, and planning *together* how to handle it in the best interests of *both.* But how can this be done between two people who are both insisting on having their way and confronting each other in anger?

That question leads us naturally to the second step in the art of conflict resolution.

2. *The anger must be taken out of the conflict before it can be effectively resolved.* Go back to Diagram 4. A latent difference between a husband and wife is activated when they have to maneuver in limited space—they are literally in a tight situation! Some decision has to be made or some action taken. The difference between John and Mary creates a disagreement, and as they struggle with it, hot emotions are generated within them. Anger takes over. The function of the anger is a perfectly healthy and legitimate one—it is a surge of power to enable each individual to break through the impasse and get his or her own way. For an individual acting alone, this could be entirely appropriate; it happens in many life situations we get into, and *not* to insist on what you believe is right could be weakness and even irresponsibility.

However, this is not an individual situation, but a relationship in which the goal is to achieve harmonious cooperation in a shared life. So the anger is pushing both persons in the wrong direction. However, anger is a physiological redeployment of the body's resources. And the body cannot know how to act until the mind gives it the necessary instruction. What we have here is not an occasion for a fight, but for a cool, carefully examined, mutually acceptable solution arrived at together by two people who are in a love relationship. The anger creates a crisis because when I am angry I cannot be loving, and when I am loving I cannot be angry—the two emotional states exclude each other. What I need is the ability to see and understand and accept my partner's position; but my capacity to do this is inhibited by the hot emotions surging through me. I cannot, while the anger lasts, identify with the other person, or concede the validity of his or her point of view. I cannot even hear, accurately and fairly, what he or she is saying.

So the anger paralyzes and temporarily suspends the capacity to act cooperatively. Until we can both take the anger out of the conflict, and get to work on the disagreement that activated it, we are unable to negotiate a solution. The anger must first be processed. (How that is done will be the subject of the next chapter.)

3. *A mutually acceptable settlement of the underlying disagreement must be negotiated.* Since in this chapter we are dealing with conflict, we have been thinking of a situation where anger has been released. In these circumstances,

it is only when the anger has been processed that any negotiation can be undertaken.

However, disagreements don't always explode into conflict, and there is no need for them to do so. Indeed, one important goal for an enriched marriage is for the couple to settle disagreements *before* they generate hot emotions that can paralyze their negotiating powers.

Whether anger has been present or not, however, the task of negotiation remains. And it has been my observation that few couples have learned much about the use of negotiating skills, or about the options that are open to them in clearing up a disagreement. (We shall discuss this fully in Chapter 11.)

10

LOVE, ANGER, AND INTIMACY

THERE will inevitably be an autobiographical component in this chapter. In the long quest for enrichment in our own marriage, Vera and I found that dealing constructively with anger proved to be one of the most difficult tasks we undertook, and probably the greatest triumph we achieved. This made us particularly sensitive to the role of anger in the relationships of other couples we have worked with, and in sharing our experiences with them we have learned a great deal. The conclusions at which we have arrived differ somewhat from those widely held. They certainly hold true for us, both in theory and in practice; and we have shared them with a number of other couples who have also found them workable. (I have described them in more detail in my 1982 book *Love and Anger in Marriage.*)

Having already consulted the twenty-six selected books on marriage written in the 1930–70 period to find out where the writers stood on couple communication and marital conflict, I decided to repeat this inquiry yet another time.

Since I am now inclined to believe that the most critical issue in the success or failure of a marriage may be the way in which the couple deal with anger, I wanted to find out how earlier marriage specialists viewed this matter. I was inclined to suspect that many of them would regard the most critical issue in marriage as being the way the couple dealt with sex. So, by consulting the index of each book, I decided to make a comparison.

What I found was very much what I had expected. The index of every book, without exception, listed the word *sex.* Indeed, there were often many references, enough in some volumes to take up a whole page of the index. But when I began to look up the word *anger,* in book after book I found no reference. I even began to think I might never find the word at all. However, it did finally appear in two volumes.

Remarkably, one of them was Joseph Folsom's *The Family and Democratic*

Society, first published in *1934!* Joe Folsom was a close friend of mine, and I regarded him as a highly creative thinker. I found that he treated the subject of anger in marriage quite forthrightly. In fact, he said specifically, "In the simplest and most direct terms, the main cause of the decline of love is *anger*" (p. 401). This is exactly what I have come to believe in recent years—and Joe Folsom knew it in 1934! The other book was Alexander Magoun's *Love and Marriage* (1948), which I have always especially liked. It contains a full discussion of anger in marriage; and although I could not now agree with all he said, it includes much homespun wisdom. For example, after describing a husband-wife quarrel: "Even if they should come to see at the same time that quarreling is destructive to both of them, there still remains the problem of finding the root cause instead of merely retiring to lick their wounds. It is of no use to try to do away with the harmful results of their quarreling without changing anything in the underlying causative situation" (p. 255).

These words of wisdom, however, come from only two of the twenty-six distinguished books about marriage. The rest gave the question of anger no particular attention, suggesting that they either didn't think it was important, or possibly didn't even think about it at all. Add this to what we have already discovered about the neglect of couple communication, and even somewhat of marital conflict, and it is not easy to deny that in the last decade we have made a quantum leap in our comprehension of the dynamics of marital interaction. Further, I do not hesitate to affirm that this flood of new knowledge, when we can get around to putting it to work in the lives of ordinary couples, may well make marriage enrichment immensely important in the future.

What Anger Does to Marriage

By way of beginning our discussion, let me make three statements about anger in marriage:

1. *The state of being married probably generates more anger in the average man or woman than does any other social situation in which he or she is habitually involved.* I feel sure that large numbers of married people would strongly disagree with this statement. After all, our culture has depicted marriage as a state of love, peace, and harmony, and it seems almost blasphemous to portray it in any other terms.

Yet I hold to my position. Indeed, my major concern is that in refusing to recognize this, many married couples are in fact revealing the extent to which they are suppressing and denying their real feelings. Some, of course, are only too well aware of the rage that sometimes consumes them. The startling revelation in recent years about battered wives, battered children, and even a few battered husbands lifts a veil that has in our respectable society discreetly concealed what is really going on in many families.

Despite all this battering, however, I am pretty sure that there is in our society a large number of wives, and a fair number of husbands too, who have formed the habit of suppressing their anger—choking it down, swallowing it, keeping it under firm control—until they have finally reached the point at which it is not only hidden from outside observers, but hidden also from their partners, and even from their own awareness.

Furthermore, this suppression of anger is often considered positively virtuous. For many husbands and wives, especially those with deep religious convictions, anger is regarded as wicked, sinful, something not experienced by "nice" people. Keeping it under firm control is therefore viewed as a manifestation of superior character. We shall discuss this and what it does to the people concerned in more detail later.

2. *Anger is the critical issue affecting the success or failure of the relationship in the great majority of couples who have set the companionship marriage as their goal.* This follows naturally from what I described in the last chapter. The quest for intimacy leads to a degree of closeness that at the same time initiates a sequence of events in which difference becomes disagreement, disagreement heats up into conflict, and the resulting anger then drives the couple apart and defeats their purpose.

Why this seeming contradiction? We need to understand clearly that a relationship of intimacy only becomes possible between two people when they are able to take down their defenses, open up their inner selves, and make themselves vulnerable to each other. This is actually what intimacy really means, as the definition "shared privacy" suggests. But *you can't take down your defenses in a relationship in which the possibility exists that your partner may suddenly explode in anger and attack you.* So long as there is any chance of anger breaking out, therefore, the atmosphere of complete trust that is necessary for the full blossoming of love and tenderness cannot be fully achieved.

We are of course speaking here of the companionship marriage. In the traditional marriage, anger caused little trouble so long as it did not lead to extreme violence. It was entirely appropriate for a husband to be angry. Indeed, if he stamped and bellowed he was simply exhibiting his masculine strength and showing that he was the master in his own home. The wife, on the other hand, was not expected to show anger, but to exhibit always the yielding sweetness and passive acquiescence that were lauded as the feminine virtues. By this ingenious arrangement, open conflict in marriage was neatly avoided. At least that was the expected cultural pattern. Of course it didn't always work, but on the whole marriages remained outwardly stable, which was all that mattered in those days.

There is, of course, no evidence that I have ever encountered that a woman, confronted with a corresponding stimulus, generates less anger than a man does. The quiescence of those traditional wives was entirely the result of social conditioning. So it is not at all surprising that when we switched from the traditional marriage to the companionship model, and gave husbands and wives equal opportunities to express their feelings, marital conflict broke out on a hitherto unprecedented scale.

3. *Most of our troubles in managing anger in marriage today arise from the fact that the average couple know of only two ways of dealing with anger: to vent it or to suppress it. No one has shown them how to process it; and until this is done, we shall make little progress.* In order to deal effectively with this vital issue, we shall have to consider what anger is, and what role it plays in human life. This is a vast subject, and we shall have to focus our attention on only a few relevant aspects of it.

Much of the literature about anger is based on widely accepted psychological and sociological theories about hostility and aggression. I prefer to begin with a *physiological* approach. As I have already suggested, anger is a complex series of body changes triggered by a sudden awareness of danger. It may be regarded as our survival kit, shared in some measure with all living creatures, and handed down to us during the long process of biological evolution.

All of us live, to some extent, in danger. At any moment an unforeseen catastrophe could overtake us. When this happens, the way we respond may decide whether or not we survive. In such a situation, we shall need two vital resources: first, an immediate surge of energy; and second, the necessary control of our actions to use that energy to good purpose.

The first need is met by the onset of anger. The process by which our bodies provide "instant energy" is a veritable miracle. As soon as a warning is received, with remarkable rapidity, a complex series of bodily changes takes place. The heartbeat speeds up, blood pressure rises, adrenalinlike substances pour out into the bloodstream, anticoagulants are withdrawn, muscles become tense. These and other changes ready us for either fight or flight—the two classical ways of responding to an attack.

How is the alarm signal given? Awareness of danger can be activated in a number of ways, all essentially through our five senses. It is hardly possible, however, that the first alarm could be dealt with effectively by our reasoning, conscious minds; there just wouldn't be time to analyze the nature of the stimulus and decide whether or not it called for an anger reaction. In any case, the simpler creatures from whom we inherited this alarm system didn't *have* analytical, reasoning minds! So it seems logical to conclude that, despite the teaching of some modern cults, *we do not make ourselves angry,* and are not responsible for being in such a state.

This is an important point. Many people feel ashamed and guilty about being angry, and try to deny their own feelings. I believe that anger is a natural, healthy emotional state, and should be accepted as such. Rightly used, anger could save our lives. Short of that, it can provide the motivation for personal and social action that could change all our lives for the better. Let us therefore affirm our anger and be thankful for it.

However, once the anger is there, it must be used correctly. If you are confronted by someone who has designs on your life, you must fight, and you had better use all your cunning and skill so that you have a good chance of winning. Or, if the best course seems to be to run for it, you had better run in the right direction, so that you don't land in a dead end or find your escape cut off by an accomplice of your attacker.

So you are not responsible for your anger being there—that is beyond the scope of your conscious mind; but you *are* responsible for what you *do* with the anger, as soon as you are consciously aware of it. In other words, you are capable of *controlling* your anger, so that you may use it effectively. You have in fact a choice of three ways in which you can deal with it (there is a fourth to which I shall refer later):

1. *Vent It*. Venting anger in the form of physical action is the most natural form of expression, because one of the physiological conditions that is caused by anger is muscular tension, and by *using* the muscles, as in fighting or running, the tension is somewhat relieved. What this means is that you begin to *expend* the energy supply your body has provided. However, when people sometimes speak of "getting rid" of their anger by venting it, this is not entirely accurate; drawing on the energy supply is actually a message to your body to keep the anger coming. We shall return to this point later.

2. *Suppress It*. Because we have the power to control the use we make of anger, we may choose not to make any use of it at all. There are situations in life where this is obviously the right course to take. If your boss bawls you out, and you experience a strong urge to respond by punching his nose, your superior wisdom tells you that this might lead to a chain of very inconvenient consequences, and you had better not do it.

3. *Freeze*. This capacity to take no action is also part of our biological inheritance. Many smaller creatures, in a situation of danger, respond neither by fight nor by flight—they freeze. They may "play dead" in the hope that no attack will be made. So we do have the capacity for control by the suppression of all action.

There are people who supposedly have "ungovernable" tempers. This may be true of a few people who are affected by a hormonal imbalance or a derangement of neuron circuits in the brain; but most people really use hostility because they have formed the habit, often since childhood, of throwing a temper tantrum in order to get attention or to develop power over other people.

It is not that they cannot control their anger, but that they choose, for what to them seem entirely desirable purposes, not to do so. We must never forget that a display of anger, especially in a parent, can be a very convenient (though not necessarily wise) way of asserting power and getting things done.

Let us return to suppressing anger. What happens when we do this? Does it "go away"? In time it does, because the body has no wish to remain in a state of internal crisis and welcomes a signal to return to a relaxed condition. However, if the stimulus that caused the anger is still there, it isn't easy to turn off the head of steam. What happens, if this kind of situation is frequently re-peated, is that the body establishes a state of continuing low-key tension—a kind of slow, simmering anger that never entirely subsides. We sometimes call this resentment, or residual hostility. It is an unhealthy state to be in and may result over time in psychosomatic illness.

This "bottling up" of anger is particularly harmful in the marriage relation-ship. Anger and love are mutually exclusive emotions. When you are con-sumed with anger, you can't be loving, especially toward the source of your anger. This is obviously true when a fight is on. However, when it is over, the two may make up and be warm and affectionate again. Some psychologists even suggest that this is a healthy process—that married people need distance, and that an occasional fight provides this, and makes their moving back toward intimacy all the sweeter. The weakness in this argument is that couples who need a period of separateness can surely communicate this fact to each other and arrange it, without the need for a fight!

Bottled-up resentment, however, can be a continuing condition between peo-ple, all the more difficult to deal with because it is often not openly acknowl-edged. It compels these people to keep at a distance from each other, because there is no "making-up" experience. It has been my observation as a marriage counselor, over many years, that couples who have habitually suppressed their anger become incapable of tenderness. The inner core of love between them withers away; and although they may go through the motions of being affec-tionate, it is not genuine. This is the tragic price they pay. Many counselors believe that even if venting anger is not appropriate in a loving relationship, bottling it up is even worse.

What then are couples to do? If venting anger is damaging to love and inti-macy, and suppressing anger is even more damaging, they seem to be con-fronted by a choice of two evils. Large numbers of husbands and wives live most of their lives in this unhappy predicament.

How to Process Anger

Fortunately, there is a way out, although it is known to few couples. These few seem to have stumbled on it by some lucky chance. This is simply not good enough. Even in the marriage-enrichment movement, I have encountered well-meaning couples who speak of learning the art of marital fighting, or of holding back their negative feelings toward each other.

In my own marriage, our discovery that anger could be *processed* came about almost by accident. We had found the other two approaches to be quite unsatisfactory and were looking for a better solution. It proved to be a long and discouraging search. The solution that finally emerged took the form of a three-step system, which we mutually agreed, by making appropriate contracts with each other, to put into practice.

We began by recognizing that, if anger is a healthy emotion and its incidence is beyond our control, we should freely give each other the right to be angry, without any negative judgments or penalties. We agreed, however, that when one of us *did* get angry with the other, this would be communicated *in words* as soon as possible. Since we had the gift of speech, there was no need to use nonverbal hostile gestures, as animals do. It should be as acceptable to say "I'm feeling angry" as to say "I'm feeling sad" or "I'm feeling hungry." All are bodily states that a caring partner should be able to understand.

However, we drew a clear line between acknowledging anger and venting anger. These can become confused when we speak of "expressing" anger, so we try to avoid using that ambiguous word. The clear distinction between acknowledging and venting was made necessary for us by our second step, which was a commitment that we would never again *attack* each other in a state of anger. We decided that such action was entirely inappropriate between two people who were seeking to establish a loving relationship.

The assurance that there would be no attack obviated the need for the other partner to go on the defensive and to develop retaliatory anger. This made possible a compassionate concern, rather than a sense of hostility toward the angry partner; and the desire to understand how and why the state of anger had arisen.

The third step developed naturally from this. Acknowledging anger, and promising not to vent it, doesn't remove the negative emotions that have been stored up. The anger is still there; and it will not be healthily cleared up until the stimulus that caused it has been faced, understood, and removed.

In dealing with this, we had to recognize the fact that a state of anger in one partner, evoked by the other, is a function of the total relationship, and that both have an equal responsibility to clear it up. This directly challenges the frequent assertion that my anger is mine alone, and that I must be responsible for dealing with it. We found that this simply did not work in an intimate relationship. Only when we saw our anger as a barrier between us, which must be removed by both of us acting together, did we find the answer. If you have made me angry, I cannot clear up the situation completely without your active sharing in the process. I readily admit that it would be impossible to clear up anger toward more distant people in this way, although we would be creating a wonderful world if this could actually be done. In an intimate relationship, however, I have come to believe that unless it *is* done, the relationship will inevitably be damaged, and if this continues to happen, the damage will be progressive. Indeed, my view is that the failure to deal realistically with every anger situation as it arises is the major cause of failure in modern marriages.

What do I mean by "dealing realistically with an anger situation"?

Another insight we gained about anger is that it is not a primary, but a secondary, emotion. As we have seen, in the evolutionary process it was triggered by an awareness of danger. The primary emotion that danger awakens is *fear*. It is also, however, and much more often in our complex human world, aroused by *frustration*. Anger is our response to a situation in which our sense of security is threatened, our self-esteem damaged, and our feelings hurt. In such a condition, the last thing we really want is to get into a fight. Our real need is to be understood, loved, and supported. As someone once said of teen-agers, the time they need love most is the time they seem most unlovable.

The approach therefore is: "I find myself getting angry with you. But you know I am pledged not to attack you, which would only make you angry, too, and alienate us. What I need is your help to get behind my anger to what is really causing it, so that we can do something about it together." The response to this is: "I don't like you being angry with me, but I don't blame you for it. And since I know you won't attack me, I needn't put up my defenses and get angry with you in turn. I appreciate your invitation to help you get through to the underlying cause of your anger, because I care about our relationship, and it should help both of us to find out what is really happening to us."

This must be followed up by a session in which the situation that produced the anger is examined carefully. And this must be done in an atmosphere of openness and honesty, with all relevant facts and feelings shared. If the anger is still too hot to handle, it may be necessary to wait. But postponement must not become shelving. Every angry situation must be worked through as soon as possible. If this is not done, as we have already seen, each new situation will gather up previously unsettled ones and build up to a level of tension in which anger is likely to recur and even to get out of control.

What in fact happens when anger situations in marriage are faced together in this way? Years of experience have shown us clearly that careful examination always reveals one of two situations. Either it turns out that my anger was based on misinterpretation of your words or deeds, in which case we must achieve improvement of our communication system so that I am less likely in the future to misinterpret your behavior; or on the other hand it turns out that you pushed me beyond the limits of my tolerance at that particular time, in which case the investigation will improve your understanding of my sensitivity to your words and deeds, and at the same time help me to widen the limits of my tolerance to sensitive issues that I need to learn to live with. In other words, the anger situation has been used to promote a growth experience for both of us.

I will readily admit that this is complex, and not likely to be stumbled upon accidentally by any but a few exceptionally fortunate couples. I am also aware that some couples are not even seeking a relationship of loving intimacy, and would therefore not be motivated to pay the price that has to be paid for it. I would not hesitate to concede, also, that the initial task of changing over to this approach from a fighting pattern or a suppressing pattern is a major under-taking, because you have to begin with a formidable backlog of unresolved conflict. However, I can only say that, when a marriage is finally freed from what anger can do to it, either by violent upheaval or by slow corrosion, it is like passing through a sound barrier into a new atmosphere of ongoing growth and creative love, which has to be experienced to be believed. I am, of course, speaking from experience. This is what I call "processing" anger. Let me in conclusion try to explain what I see as taking place while this goes on.

We have already recognized that, when the state of physiological tension we call anger develops, we have to decide how to handle it. When a real situation exists justifying fear or frustration, the natural response is to get into action, and by doing so you automatically signal to your body that the anger should be sustained so that the surge of extra energy will continue until the fight is over, or until you have escaped to a place of safety. Then, and only then, can you signal that your exhausted body may now relax and rest. When, however, there is genuine reason for anger, but the situation would make anger undesirable, a mixed signal goes to your body, calling for continuation of the anger but promising no action to deal with the cause. This is obviously an unhealthy state of affairs, and we have seen that it can do bodily and psychic harm. On occasion, however, there is no alternative but suppression, and it must be tolerated.

This brings us to the fourth way of dealing with anger, to which I have not yet referred.

Dissolve It. Imagine a situation in which you are annoyed by an event that seems threatening, but turns out to be a false alarm. For example, you hear your spouse saying something to someone else that seems critical of you. When you challenge this action, it turns out that you misunderstood what was said, and that in fact the reference to you was complimentary. The attack you imagined actually never happened. You respond by signaling to your body that there is no cause for anger. Then, quite quickly, body tension is relaxed, and you are soon back to normal. The anger has been dissolved.

This can happen in many ways. You may be indignant about an event you hear about in your community. Then you think it over and realize that you can do nothing whatever about it, because you have no contact with the persons concerned. You dismiss the matter from your mind and quickly cool down.

A couple with a loving relationship can use this process when there is genuine cause for anger, but circumstances make it impossible to clear up the issue right now. They know, however, that they *can* process it, and that they *will* do so as soon as a suitable opportunity arises. Meanwhile, the anger can be dissolved. A disagreement doesn't have to heat up into a conflict before it can be dealt with. And if some heat *has* developed, it need not be sustained.

No suppression of anger is involved in situations like these. Dissolving anger is quite different from suppressing it.

In observing marriages over the years, I have been interested in recognizing various combinations of types: venters married to venters are inveterate fighters; venters married to suppressers end up with a tyrant-slave relationship; suppressers married to suppressers achieve a peace-at-any-price relationship, which is drearily respectable but without warmth and tenderness. Processers, unfortunately, must exist in pairs, because this is an approach to anger that has to be cooperative. So a processer, unless married to another processer, must convert a venting or suppressing partner to become a processer too!

I hope I have done something in this chapter to substantiate my claim that dealing with anger is critical for the success of a companionship marriage. We have not, however, yet reached the end of the road. Taking the anger out of the conflict is a task of major importance, because apart from this there can be no really final solution. But even when the anger has been dealt with, the disagreement that caused the conflict still remains to be dealt with. How this is done will be the subject of our next chapter.

11

SETTLING DISAGREEMENTS BY NEGOTIATION

TWO countries with contiguous borders are involved in a bitter dispute over boundary lines. Marauders from one side have crossed the frontier in force and established themselves on land they claim as traditionally theirs. On the other side a military unit has taken up positions confronting the invaders. Both countries are in the process of calling up army reserves. Meanwhile, the United Nations has called an emergency meeting of the General Assembly in the hope that the dispute can be mediated before shots are fired and both countries are engulfed in war.

Representatives of labor and management are sitting grimly on opposite sides of a long table in a city hotel. The session has been going on for a long time, and the contestants are strained and weary. It is nearly midnight, but no solid hope for a settlement has yet appeared. Across the country, members of the labor union stand ready to organize a strike.

Delegates from many churches are assembled at a denominational synod. Speaker after speaker argues the pros or cons of an explosive policy issue that must be settled before the delegates can return home. Press representatives await the issue, ready to rush the news into print.

It is the annual general meeting of a sports club. A motion is on the floor to change the bylaws. The issue is a touchy one and is being hotly debated. A plan for adjournment has been voted down, and the issue must be settled within an hour.

The Robinson living room is packed with people. All neighbor families are represented. They have heard Martha Robinson explain the plan to buy a vacant lot and build a swimming pool, to be jointly paid for and jointly used by all the families on the street. Opinions for and against it are being expressed, and the atmosphere is getting tense.

Arthur and Nora Pittenger are seated in their living room with their three teenaged children. Arthur has explained the attractive job offer he has received from Australia. He would like to accept it. Nora dreads the upheaval that would be involved, and the move away from familiar people and places. They want to hear the children's opinion before reaching a final decision.

Peter and Beth are teenagers, very much in love. Peter wants Beth to move out from her parents so that they can set up house together, as many other young people are doing. Beth is afraid of alienating her family and some of her friends. Strongly opposed feelings are rising between them as they try to reach an agreement.

These are all credible human situations in which disagreements are being confronted. Some decision will have to be made in each case. They represent very different issues, both in nature and magnitude. Yet all of them are alike in that differences are causing disagreements. All will have to be settled by the same process.

That process is *negotiation*. It lies as the very heart of what we call democracy. It is very important for every companionship marriage, so we had better try to understand it.

A great deal has been written in books on marriage about the task of mutual accommodation of the partners to each other. Such terms as *adapting, adjusting, decision making,* and *problem solving* are often employed. As we have already seen, the tendency of earlier writers on marriage was to study the areas in which disagreements between spouses most commonly occur; long lists of these appear in the literature. Later writers have shifted the emphasis to studying the *methods* by which disagreements are resolved. This seems now to be the important question. It was anticipated by Burgess (1953) when he wrote, ''The area in which the adjustment arises may not be significant. The basic problem may be either in the relationship itself or in the decision-making process or both'' (p. 618).

In this chapter we will look at the decision-making process. My complaint about many writings on this subject is that they describe elaborate procedures, but omit to point out that none of them can be effectively used by angry husbands and wives. That is why I have felt the necessity to deal extensively with the management of anger, before coming to the problem-solving process. Having done this, we are ready to proceed.

How can marriage partners learn to use the negotiation process effectively?

Assuming that the traditional one-vote system is no longer acceptable to them, how do they reach a settlement on a two-vote basis?

According to my observations, few couples have learned much about the use of negotiating skills, or about the options that are open to them. So let us examine these options. There are three of them, and in order to help explain their meaning I am using Diagram 5, which I used in an earlier book (Mace and Mace, 1977).

The Three Available Options

Capitulation. This word conjures up the humiliating picture of a commander of a fortress finally surrendering after a long siege. But it also means simply "acquiescence," which can be a manifestation of love. It therefore has two very different meanings, and I want us to consider both. (Some writers prefer to use the word *conciliation*.)

Diagram 5 shows John and Mary at a distance from each other, which represents their disagreement. Their wish is to close that distance so that they may find themselves together, of one mind and happily reconciled.

Capitulation would mean that either John would close the distance by moving all the way over to where Mary is, or she would move over to where John is. Clearly this would settle the disagreement.

The critical question, though, is what could motivate either to make such a move? It could be done unwillingly, as a result of coercion; or willingly, as a result of caring. Between these two there is a world of difference.

We have seen that, in the traditional marriage, such issues were settled in advance, by making the husband the head of the house, and giving him, not the casting vote, but the *only* vote. The hope was that he would listen respectfully to his wife's opinions and wishes, and consider them carefully. But when the time came, he would simply announce his decision, his wife would accept his sovereign will, and that would settle the matter.

Coerced capitulation has no place in the companionship marriage; but caring capitulation has. Suppose that Mary wants John to go with her to an important church meeting on an evening when he had planned to go bowling with a group of his friends. He tells her frankly that he isn't much interested in the meeting, and that he is sure he would find it boring. But then, seeing the disappointment in her eyes, he says to himself, "This is my wife, and I love her. Obviously it would mean a lot to her if I went with her. So, why shouldn't I do it, as a gift of love?" When he tells her he has changed his mind, she is very grateful—not only because she will have him with her at the meeting, but even more because by his capitulation he has provided her with a token of his wish to make her happy. There is nothing of humiliation or surrender here. It is a pure gift of love, and it will contribute to the warmth and strength of the relationship. If Mary had been coercive and had nagged John into going to the meet-

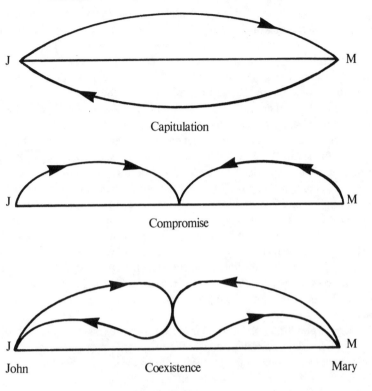

DIAGRAM 5
Settling Disagreements by Negotiation

From *How To Have A Happy Marriage* by David and Vera Mace, copyright © 1977 by Abingdon. Used by permission.

ing, he would have gone unwillingly, and it could have been a miserable evening. As it has now been arranged, it could be a very happy occasion. Love gifts of this kind mean a lot more than candy or flowers.

There is another aspect of caring capitulation that we must not overlook: John knows very well that what he has done could pay future dividends. "Next time I want Mary to do something special for me," he thinks to himself, "she may remember this, and *she* may be more willing to capitulate."

In fact, caring capitulation, as a way of resolving disagreements, should always be seen as a two-way process. Where one partner capitulates too often to the other, love gifts begin to be taken for granted and the relationship may soon look very like one of dominance on one hand and submission on the other. Over time, therefore, a just balance must be maintained. This means that the partners form the habit, in order to return favors formerly granted, of being on the lookout for little services and sacrifices they can plan for each other. This creates a very pleasant atmosphere, which contributes significantly to the happiness of the marriage; it is in sharp contrast to the kind of relationship in which the partners are constantly exploiting each other.

Not all disagreements can be resolved by caring capitulation. But couples should look at this option first and use it whenever they can.

Compromise. In Diagram 5 we see the compromise option in terms of both partners being willing to make concessions, though neither can go all the way. So they move toward each other, searching for an intermediate solution, a meeting point somewhere between them at which they can settle. Both will offer to make some sacrifice, but neither will do all the sacrificing.

This is of course nothing more or less than the ancient and honorable process of *bargaining.* Long before money was invented, business was transacted by barter, which means exchange of goods. Even when money came along, the prices of articles were settled by a lively process of negotiation. I once amused myself in Egypt by trying out every stratagem to see how far I could bring down the price of an inlaid wooden plate, which I still have in my possession. It was an interesting and amusing experience, both for me and for the Arab merchant. In the end I got the plate at a rock-bottom price, and we parted with mutual respect.

Actually, a good deal of bargaining goes on in most marriages. Not all of it is open and aboveboard. Often there is use of subtle manipulation in the form of mean strategies to punish the partner, such as the withholding of sex, money, or privileges. Eric Berne, in his book *Games People Play* (1964), exposed some of these strategies, and other writers have drawn attention to them also. In any marriage where open and honest communication is not the rule, a good deal of game playing is almost sure to go on. This is sad, because it undermines trust and puts the partners in an adversary position, in which they plan secretly to exploit each other.

A basic goal of marriage enrichment is to end these manipulative maneuvers and help couples to bring all the facts and feelings out in the open. The Marriage Encounter deliberately sets this as one of its primary objectives.

Bargaining openly is, of course, still bargaining. There must be back-and-forth negotiations in order to settle on a final meeting place. But when this is done with all cards on the table, the secret, devious elements that arouse suspicion and undermine trust are discarded. Under these conditions, a compromise arrived at is seen to be fair and is likely to be durable. Nothing could be more damaging to the relationship than to find out later, after an agreement had been arrived at, that essential information had been deliberately withheld, or that one partner had tricked the other in order to gain personal advantage.

Skill in communication plays a very important role in the bargaining process. A session planned to negotiate a disagreement should also allow adequate time for each to hear the other, and should use feedback to make sure that what is being offered is clearly understood. It may be helpful to put decisions arrived at in the form of written contracts and keep them for future reference. All contracts between marriage partners should, however, represent reasonably attainable goals, should begin on a short-term trial basis, and should be open for later renegotiation.

Coexistence. Although most disagreements in marriage can be settled by capitulation or compromise, the companionship marriage requires a third option: coexistence. It is shown on Diagram 5.

A companionship marriage is based on the principle of equity, which means that a roughly equal balance should exist between rights and responsibilities for both partners. This means, inevitably, that some differences may arise between them that are, for the present, irreconcilable; a state of disagreement has to be accepted and lived with, at least for a time. There is no alternative to this if each accords full respect to the personhood of the other.

In the traditional marriage, this could not be tolerated. In order to guarantee stability to the relationship, there had to be at least the external appearance of unity, in the form of apparent unanimity. Hence, it was necessary for the wife, as part of her marriage vows, to undertake to be *obedient* to her husband; which meant that he was able to overrule her wishes when the marriage was faced with an irreconcilable difference, so that no outward sign of disagreement remained.

Coexistence, therefore, means an open recognition that a disagreement cannot be resolved. The difficulty of living with such a situation must not be underestimated. Obviously, such a solution should not be arrived at until all possibilities of reconciliation have been thoroughly explored.

Diagram 5 illustrates this point. The picture is not of John and Mary stubbornly dug into defensive positions and unwilling to budge. On the contrary, each makes every effort to go out to meet the other, either by accepting a compromise or even exploring the possibility of capitulation. Only after a searching examination of all the facts and feelings on both sides should coexistence as a solution be considered. And it is not even accurate to describe it as a solution. The word *accommodation* would probably be more appropriate.

Living with an accepted disagreement, in mutual respect, does not imply a continuing state of conflict. We have seen that conflict is disagreement heated up by anger. A disagreement, however, doesn't inevitably explode into conflict. Indeed, one important goal in the enriched marriage is for the couple to learn to settle disagreements before they generate hot emotions that paralyze their negotiating power.

Even if John and Mary *have* been in conflict about the issue, but have been able to take the anger out of it, they should be able to live with it on the understanding that it cannot at present be resolved. Of course it will probably remain a sensitive issue, and care should be taken not to provoke strong feelings around it. But reasonably harmonious coexistence is entirely possible.

Notice that this is quite different from "burying" a serious disagreement and trying to live as though it didn't exist. Coexistence implies that the disagreement has been thoroughly explored, without anger, and is open to further exploration at any time. No avoidance is involved, only a recognition that no successful negotiation has yet been found possible. It might be described as an agreement to disagree.

You will observe that the language I use carries a tentative connotation. The solution of coexistence is for "now," and applies "at present." It is not a *permanent* settlement. The matter is, to use a colloquial term, "on the back burner."

What next? In loving marriages, over time, even long-standing disagreements tend to get settled. I don't mean that a process of attrition wears down the opposition on one side. On the contrary, I mean that living a shared life that is rich and fulfilling tends to bring about an ever-deeper meeting of minds and a clearer understanding of the partners' motivations.

This, of course, takes time. In the early years of marriage, it is unreasonable to expect that all controversial issues can be cleared up quickly. It is very easy, in an undeveloped relationship, to confuse virtues with associated vices.

For example, strong conviction can be interpreted as stubbornness, shyness as evasiveness, genuine zeal as fanaticism. I have long believed that all people—even so-called "crazy" people—have sound reasons for everything they do; but those reasons don't always appear clearly to the observer. Many a husband has castigated his wife for conduct that is only another facet of a quality for which he married her, and of course this is equally true the other way around.

There are, therefore, disagreements that irritate marriage partners and that will gradually be better understood as the motivations behind them become clear. This not only takes time, but it also calls for the exercise of that great virtue tolerance.

Tolerance is, unfortunately, a greatly misunderstood virtue, because it is nearly always interpreted passively. To be tolerant is not to put up with the intolerable. It is to explore more deeply, in order to understand more clearly. It is a virtue akin to patience, which Clement of Alexandria defined as "the knowledge of what is to be endured and what is not."

It will be clear, however, that coexistence as a way of dealing with disagreement is an option open only to marriages that have built up at least a modest reserve of love, of trust, and of mutual goodwill. Without this, the chances of living with deep disagreements that remain unsettled are not very good. In such situations—and every marriage counselor is familiar with them—differences tend all too easily to escalate into strong disagreements, which either touch off violent conflicts or lead to progressive alienation.

This in itself is one of the most persuasive arguments for providing couples, as soon as possible, with the tools and skills that they need to cope with the complex task of mutual adjustment. Every marriage freely entered into presumably begins with expectations and hopes that generate an initial fund of mutual goodwill; but if the couple lack the necessary competence to appropriate their potential, this initial reserve can soon be exhausted, and alienation and disenchantment will then soon destroy motivation and lead to progressive degeneration of the relationship. This can happen as early as the first year of marriage.

I have tried in the foregoing chapters to describe resources that can be used by any couple to safeguard and build upon the precious resources with which a marriage begins. Learning to cope with the complex task of living together in marriage is far from easy, and the sooner we all recognize this the better. Because we have failed so dismally to make these skills available to couples, we must face the fact that most of the disillusioned men and women whose marriages are breaking up around us today are not failures, but victims—victims of our corporate irresponsibility. But this needn't continue any longer. A better way is opening up before us.

12

AREAS OF ADJUSTMENT
IN MARRIAGE

IN this chapter I will examine, in practical terms, the tasks that confront couples when, starting out together on their wedding day, they begin to shape the raw materials at their disposal into what is perhaps the supreme work of art: a mature marriage. This involves two personalities making a long series of interpersonal adjustments. It has been said that a human personality is as complex as a universe; so what we are dealing with is the interaction between two universes. It would be hard to think of anything more complicated than that!

It is little wonder, therefore, that our forefathers judged it unwise to embark on any such task as this and roughhewed the traditional marriage into a relatively simple mechanism designed to fulfill two important cultural objectives: the begetting, and early socialization, of children; and the establishment of social units to provide the human community with a stable substructure.

Consequently, interpersonal adjustment in marriage was viewed in those days largely as a steady state of mutual tolerance, supported by religion and enforced by law. The intrusion of such concepts as love and equality, as we have seen, was frowned upon as dangerous. Adjustment was a crude process that required no fine tuning.

Our new concepts of marriage have changed all that. The result is that couples now go into the shared life with expectations so high that most of them have not until recently had the means to achieve their goals. So it becomes a matter of urgent necessity that we make it clear to all concerned that a truly satisfying marriage can be achieved only by enlightened and sustained effort. It is in fact no different from the other dazzling prizes that life has to offer. So long as we persist in believing that success in this area of human life is a matter of luck or of fate, rather than the reward of hard work, the blind will continue to lead the blind, and the casualty list will be heavy.

I have tried, in this section of the book, to describe the kind of equipment a couple will need for success. I have called it a "primary coping system," which should provide them with what Nelson Foote called "interpersonal competence." It consists of a clear sense of direction—seeking ongoing growth and the achievement of inherent potential—together with the learning of certain skills, sometimes called "tools." To be precise, two kits of tools are required; one to establish and maintain effective communication; the other to manage conflict creatively, so that it is used to promote relational growth.

It is quite understandable that many persons will not want to be bothered with all this. Some will settle for a traditional type of marriage, which is relatively easy to manage if both partners fully accept the arrangement. Others will be content with a relatively superficial relationship of equals who maintain sufficient distance to avoid serious disagreements, and consider that they do not need, or do not want, intimacy. Yet others will settle for the single life and limit their interpersonal skills to the smooth management of relatively superficial transactional relationships.

In other words, some people do not need marriage enrichment because companionship marriage is not their goal. Marriage enrichment does not claim to offer a panacea for all human ills. Its message is simply and specifically to those couples who want an intimate, loving, and tender relationship but have not yet, in spite of every effort on their part, been able to achieve it. For them, we have much to offer. We can provide them, if they are serious and ready to work, with the means to achieve interpersonal adjustment.

Areas of Marital Adjustment

I have referred in an earlier chapter to the many studies that have been made of areas of adjustment in marriage. We now need to look at these more closely.

The outstanding pioneer in the field was Lewis Terman. He carried out ambitious research with a large number of couples and reported his findings in 1938 in his book *Psychological Factors in Marital Happiness*.

Included in his report is a large table of complaints—fifty-three made by wives about their husbands, and fifty-seven by husbands about their wives. The complaints, which were reported separately by the spouses concerned, are listed in the order of their frequency of occurrence. For convenience, I will take only the first twenty from each list. This should give us a rough indication of what was bothering those husbands and wives in the 1930s.

Only four general areas of marriage adjustment are listed, all by both partners and in the following order: money, in-laws, friends, recreation. There is no reference to sex in the first twenty items, though it occurs later in veiled form—some husbands and wives complain that their partners are too interested in other women and men, and a few plainly accuse their spouses of unfaithfulness. In those days it was probably not easy to refer directly to sexual dysfunction in one's marriage.

It is interesting also that parenting does not appear in the top twenty complaints. Further down the lists, however, some wives complain that their husbands spoil or neglect their children, or are harsh toward them; and some husbands accuse their wives of spoiling or neglect.

All the other top complaints involve personal objections to the behavior of spouses. There is no neat way to categorize them, so the list is in random order: impatient, easily influenced by others, complaining, too conventional, manipulative, too emotional, interfering, oversensitive, critical, nagging, quick-tempered, bored, argumentative, fussy, down-putting, complaining, not affectionate, jealous, selfish, dominating, touchy, uncommunicative, inconsiderate, weak, addicted to drinking.

This catalogue of twenty-five items could be expanded considerably from the remainder of the list. It provides an interesting selection of behaviors one partner found objectionable in the other. A few of these deficiencies would obviously make the persons concerned hard to live with. But most of them represent behavior differences beween the partners that could surely have been adjusted by open, honest communication and the use of the procedures I have described in earlier chapters. Some of them could clearly be reactive behaviors stimulated by the complaining partner, which could be cleared up by some change of attitude on his or her part. They represent, in short, situations that should be capable of being resolved by any loving couple committed to growth and open to behavioral change.

Now let us look at some areas of marital adjustment listed by later writers. None to my knowledge produced a list comparable in size with that of Terman. I have selected three who reported in the 1940s and 1950s.

Judson Landis, in the *American Sociological Review* of 1946 (pp. 666–67), listed six areas of marital adjustment he had investigated: religion, social life, mutual friends, in-laws, money, and sex.

W. J. Goode, in his book *After Divorce* (1956), identified the following areas, in which couples he studied had experienced adjustment difficulties: drinking, desertion, triangles, relatives, nonsupport, money, value differences, authority, and idiosyncratic characteristics. Since all these marriages had ended in divorce, several of the complaints were not surprisingly about gross behavior in their former spouses.

R. O. Blood and D. M. Wolfe, in their book *Husbands and Wives: The Dynamics of Married Living* (1960), selected eight areas of adjustment that occurred frequently in the couples they studied: money, children, recreation, personality, in-laws, roles, religion, and sex.

It is not easy to make precise comparisons between separate and unrelated studies, because terminology differs. However, I have attempted to estimate roughly how far these investigations agree.

All three studies included the following as areas of high frequency: in-laws, sex, religion, and social life or recreation. Two of them referred to roles and behavior of the spouse. Only one referred to value conflicts and only one to parenting.

In order to include some reference to contemporary couples, I would like to add the ten areas listed in the Marriage Potential Inventory, which were selected as the topics most frequently placed on the agendas of all marriage-enrichment groups led by my wife and myself during the 1970s. These are: values, couple growth, couple communication, conflict resolution, affection, roles, cooperation, sex, money, and parenthood. These couples were, of course, a select group, people who were actively seeking enrichment of their marriages. Their items were not complaints about their partners, but obstacles they were encountering in their joint quest for love and intimacy.

Taken together, however, all these otherwise diverse findings may serve to give us a rough idea of the areas of interpersonal adjustment that have confronted many couples in the period during which the companionship marriage has been emerging as the preferred pattern.

We have to begin with a great variety of difficult behaviors in spouses. As I have pointed out, these are hard to categorize; but most of them appear to be differences that *could* be adjusted between two persons eager to achieve a harmonious relationship. The grosser behavior patterns, described by Goode as "idiosyncratic characteristics," would fall into the category of personality disorders, for which the best remedy would be professional therapy. There are certain individuals who have suffered traumatic injuries in earlier life that have made them incapable of intimate relationships, and who may have to be viewed as unmarriageable. It is hard to estimate how many fall into this category; however, my long years of marriage counseling would suggest that the great majority of persons willing to seek help for marriage difficulties fall well within the normal range, even though their extreme behaviors under heavy stress might suggest the contrary.

Turning now to the specific adjustment areas that have been listed, we find a few that recur in all the sources to which I have referred.

Critical Adjustment Areas

I have tried in Table 2 to put together the areas that seem to play a critical role in marriage adjustment in all of the five lists under consideration. Omitting the wide diversity of personal complaints against the spouse, we find that the following seven areas seem to represent the main sources of trouble: money, sex, in-laws, values (religion), social life (friends, recreation), roles, parenting.

Terman's study has only four of these among the first twenty complaints made by husbands and wives respectively. Sex is omitted; but as I have already suggested, this probably represents the taboos that still lingered in the 1930s.

Parenting is omitted, probably because at that time this was seen mainly as the wife's function. Roles are omitted; but many of the personal complaints reflect dissatisfaction with the role performances of the partner.

TABLE 2

MAJOR ADJUSTMENT AREAS IN MARRIAGE

↓Area↓ Reporter →	Terman	Landis	Goode	Blood and Wolfe	Mace
Money	√	√	√	√	√
Sex		√	√	√	√
In-Laws	√	√	√	√	
Values, Religion	√	√		√	√
Friends, Social Life	√	√		√	
Roles			√	√	√
Parenting				√	√

Landis omits roles and parenting. His list is, however, a short one, and all items on it appear in the table. If he had added more items, he might well have included the missing ones.

Goode is dealing with divorced persons looking back to the causes of their marriage failures. We have noticed that their list emphasizes gross behaviors—drinking, desertion, nonsupport—which in retrospect may have served to eclipse lesser issues that would trouble marriages in which there was relative stability and tranquility.

The list of Blood and Wolfe exactly corresponds with the frequently recurring items cited by the other reporters. Their eighth item, personality, probably represents the broadly diverse area of complaints we have omitted, since it is not really a definable area of marital adjustment.

The Mace list is from a select group of couples who were thinking positively in terms of their marital growth. The missing factors representing outside pressure on their lives—in-laws and social activities—were apparently being well handled. On the other hand, they were concerned about quality issues within their relationship—growth, communication, conflict resolution, affection, cooperation—which hardly occur in any of the other lists. This contrast almost suggests that in the earlier lists the couples were doing their best to *tolerate* each other, while the couples in marriage-enrichment programs were eagerly seeking to explore new ways to *enjoy* each other!

What emerges from this inquiry is that there seem to be four areas of interpersonal adjustment in marriage that particularly bother couples today:

Money: It is worth noting that not only in professional investigations, but also in popular newspaper and magazine polls, the primary "problem area" in marriage almost invariably turns out to be the management of money. Why should this be?

Particularly in American culture, money is the acknowledged index of an individual's worth. The hallmark of "success" is to be surrounded by evidence of wealth: to own an elegant home, to drive a quality car, to move in prestigious (which usually means wealthy) circles. The person who represents the peak of upward social mobility is the millionaire.

It can be argued that what money buys does not necessarily bring happiness, and that most of the things that really matter are free. But the fact remains that our main measure of self-worth is the extent to which we receive the esteem of others, and that the possession of an unlimited supply of dollars almost invariably produces that esteem.

Consequently, when we enter into a shared life with another person, our ability to use money to maintain personal esteem becomes a critical index of the fulfillment the relationship brings us. But the very nature of marriage is that it drains off money, which you could otherwise spend on yourself, to pay for the corporate obligations you have now jointly assumed: a home, furniture, raising and educating children, insurance and savings to meet future contingencies. And when stresses over differences and disagreements develop in the relationship, you easily become offended and even outraged at what seem unwarranted expenditures by your partner, or unfair deprivations imposed on yourself. Fights over money obviously don't concern dollar bills, which are only pieces of paper; what they do concern is the symbolic meaning of these pieces of paper in terms of your worth as a person, and the recognition of that worth in terms of your right to spend in accordance with your concept of your needs.

The management of money is, therefore, an acid test of what Fritz Kunkel called the "we-feeling" in a marriage, the sense of "togetherness" that the partners have achieved through the establishment of common goals and values. Once a couple have achieved the ability to share their hopes and fears openly, to assure each other of their mutual trust and caring, and to give each other understanding, support, and mutual affirmation, they should be able to manage their money without serious conflict. In every fight over family finance, the partners are in effect saying to each other, "You don't understand and love me enough to see and hear where I am in this situation."

In-Laws. When we marry, we take with us into the new relationship a vast complex of beliefs, habit patterns, tastes, preferences, points of view, loyalties, standards, and values that we have been continuously accumulating, and putting together into a system of guidelines, since the day of our birth. For most of us, the vast majority of these items, and often the ones to which we are most stubbornly attached, come from our "family of origin," as the sociologists call it—from our parents and the "significant others" who imprinted upon the plastic clay of our highly impressionable young minds the fundamental values that motivate us.

Soon after the wedding, if not before, these two vast piles of raw materials get raked together into one heap as the couple begin to share life at a variety of levels. As we have seen, there are highly gratifying similarities that enable them to reinforce each other, and some differences that obligingly turn out to be complementary. But there are also plenty of differences that simply clash head-on and produce the "collision of wishes" that signifies conflict.

These frustrated "wishes" are not just our individual differences of opinion. They are part of a sacred tradition that commands our loyalty to people we are expected to honor and respect, so that anyone who challenges these wishes is in effect insulting the honored parents who planted them in our personalities. Against this kind of insult we fight back with an almost holy zeal.

So it is not just the visible and present in-laws who disturb a marriage. They are also there, invisible but potent, in a host of petty disagreements or major controversies.

Nowadays, the in-law situation may seem less threatening because the youth culture has "liberated" teenagers and weaned them away from parental control. But this may only introduce a new subtlety, because it can create opposing feelings of pride and guilt, of loyalty and rejection, which contend for recognition within us.

All of us had parents, and all of us must come to terms with what their relationship to us has done to us. There are three possibilities: they may have controlled us, and may still be doing so; we may have voluntarily identified with them; or we may have rebelled against them and freed ourselves. In most of us, all three processes have been at work to varying degrees.

One of the primary adjustments of marriage is to establish our individual identities in relation to each other. And a major part of that task is to disentangle the strands of influence that still link us to our parents, and to determine what these mean to us now. For example, self-esteem is often tied to unfinished business with parents, dead or alive. This is a process both partners need to work on together, with understanding and compassion. Only when it is completed will the continuing role of the in-laws in our life together be clarified and accepted.

Sex. If it were not for sex, there would be no marriage. So the coming together sexually of husband and wife is profoundly symbolic as well as, it may be hoped, deeply satisfying. But we live in the era of emancipation, and sex has changed many of its meanings, in marriage as well as out of it. In the traditional marriage, the sexual power of the husband over the wife, which gave him "rights" over her body, was the symbol of his dominant role. Equally, the sexual surrender of her body to him symbolized her submission to his will in the entire range of their relationship.

Nowhere has companionship marriage brought more revolutionary change than here. It now seems incredible that within living memory the female orgasm was still scarcely recognized, and for the wife to initiate sexual intercourse was viewed as improper and even presumptuous. That she may now do so is taken for granted. Like other aspects of a two-vote system, however, the new sexual freedom has brought its complications.

Even though I have played my part in welcoming the new positive attitudes toward human sexuality, the flood of new knowledge about sex has been a mixed blessing; and it seems that my good friends William and Virginia Masters, and some other pioneers in the field, share my concern to some extent. What I see is that the pendulum has, as often happens, swung from one extreme to the other.

Let me be explicit. In my earlier years as a marriage counselor, couples couldn't enjoy their sex life because they were ignorant and embarrassed about their sexuality, and this created anxiety that paralyzed a natural function. Now I find by contrast that couples know so much, and expect so much of themselves and each other, that they may become obsessed by what has been called "performance anxiety," which again robs a natural function of its spontaneity. So we still have a good deal of sexual dysfunction in marriage, but for a quite different reason.

Sex has also, in our liberated era, become both entertainment and sport. Ignorance about the orgasm has now been replaced by so much sophistication about it that merely having an orgasm is a rather routine event. Consequently, expectation can become geared to multiple high-powered orgasms, and the spouse who can't maintain this pace may feel, or be made to feel, a failure.

There is no doubt that in our culture sex was for a long time given far too little attention; and if it is now getting too much attention, that should perhaps not be so surprising. It is, however, unfortunate that for some people today the word *intimacy* means nothing more or less than *sexual* intimacy, and the implication is that sometimes this is the essential ingredient for success in marriage. That is far from the truth.

For the average married couple, what seems important to me is that their sex life should be a natural and deeply satisfying function of their love relationship. What particular form it takes matters little, so long as both husband and wife can honestly and openly make their needs known to each other and use the procedures I have already described to find out the best ways of meeting these needs. If all their efforts to do this leave them frustrated and unsatisfied, then it may be necessary to seek professional help; and the source of that help should be chosen with care.

Values. The truly happy and fulfilled men and women are those who have a sense of vocation and are service-oriented, that is to say, they have pursued throughout their lives goals and purposes beyond themselves, seeking to make some significant contribution to the well-being of their fellows. And the truly happy married couples are those who pursue common goals and share common values.

Time was when just keeping alive and raising a family were tasks demanding enough to unite husband and wife in a shared struggle. In those days it was almost certain that the partners had both come from identical, or closely similar, cultural backgrounds, and that they therefore shared common values.

Today we live in an open society where couples choose each other with almost total disregard for the traditional barriers of class, religion, and race. This mixing process is to be welcomed, because it ends the irrational prejudices that have mocked our democratic ideals.

However, the more value differences a couple bring to their marriage, the more complex is the task of interpersonal adjustment. I am not saying this by way of discouragement. I suspect that those stable homogamous marriages in the past were sometimes very dull, and that a reasonable amount of difference between partners can generate creativity and growth. All I am saying is that this complexity in the adjustment process must be realistically faced as the couple get to work on building a marriage.

Conclusion

In this second part of the book I have tried to examine carefully the marital interaction process, in the light of what we know today about close relationships. As I look to the future, I find reason for much encouragement and hope. It is true that never in our history have marriages been in so much trouble as they are today; yet against this we must set the fact that never in our history have we made such rapid and promising advances in our understanding of the dynamics of marital interaction. As the situation worsens, the answers begin to come.

It must be clearly understood, however, that the days in which happy marriages just happened, if those days ever existed, are now over. In the adjustment process that is vital and essential to the companionship marriage, we shall often have to draw on such resources as our commitment to relational growth and the full acceptance of our capacity for behavioral change. There are of course disagreements that are based on misunderstandings about our supposed differences, and are not too difficult to clear up. There are other disagreements, however, that call for some restructuring of the relationship—of our roles, our coping skills, our habit patterns. With wisdom and patience, these are changes of which most couples are capable; but only if they understand the process, possess the tools, and are motivated to use them.

I would like to close this part of the book with two of my favorite quotations about marriage. They are deliberately selected from writers who lived before the clear emergence of the companionship model; but both writers were visionaries who saw far into the future.

The first is a passage from Edward Carpenter, an English social reformer whose book *Love's Coming-of-Age* was first published in 1896:

That there should exist one other person in the world toward whom all openness of exchange should establish itself, from whom there should be no concealment; whose body should be as dear to one, in every part, as one's own; with whom there should be no sense of mine or thine, in property or possession; into whose mind one's thoughts should naturally flow, as it were to know themselves and to receive a new illumination; and between whom and oneself there should be a spontaneous rebound of sympathy in all the joys and sorrows and experiences of life; such is perhaps one of the dearest wishes of the soul.

The second quotation is from Felix Adler, the founder of the Ethical Culture Movement. His book *Marriage and Divorce* was published in 1905, and includes this moving picture of a couple in the later stages of their married life:

Together they have traveled the road of life, and remembrance now holds them close; remembrance of many hours of ineffable felicity, of a sense of union as near to bliss as mortal hearts can realize, of high aspirations pursued in common, of sorrows shared—sacramental sorrows. And now, nearing the end, hand in hand they look forth upon the wide universe, and the love which they found in themselves, and still find there to the last, becomes to them the pledge of a vaster love that moves beyond the stars and the sun.

PART THREE

~~~~~

Marriage Enrichment: The New Frontier

In the following chapters the marriage-enrichment movement is described. Its historical development is briefly summarized. Ways in which couples interact in enrichment groups are discussed. Different patterns of marriage-enrichment events, demonstrating wide structural differences, are described in some detail. Effective means of recruiting couples, and the use of support systems for followup, are reported.

13

HOW IT ALL BEGAN:
A BRIEF HISTORY

ON a winter day in January 1962, a group of married couples (twenty-eight in all) assembled for a weekend retreat in Barcelona, Spain. They were not sure what was going to happen, but they had come to respect and love the young priest who had invited them. Assigned at first to work with youth in a city parish, Father Gabriel Calvo had soon concluded that teenagers were very much what their families had made them during their earlier impressionable years. So he had switched his assignment to working with families. Then, after a time, he had further decided that families function effectively only when the parents are a truly loving couple. So he had switched his emphasis again. Years later, he was to explain his actions in these words: "I began to realize that . . . I would have to go to the heart of the family—the couple. They are the key to the love revolution the world needs. . . . In many families I could see a characteristic, something special they had that was lacking in other families. I tried to discern what these special qualities were, and I concluded in time that the unique quality was the confidence and trust these couples had in each other."

In October of the same year, as the autumn leaves were falling in the mountains of eastern Pennsylvania, Vera and I drove one Friday afternoon from our New Jersey home to Kirkridge, a religious retreat center, to spend a weekend with a group of eight married couples. We were at that time serving together as joint executive directors of the American Association of Marriage Counselors (now the American Association for Marriage and Family Therapy) and were probably invited for that reason. We had no clear ideas about how to lead a retreat for married couples, because extensive inquiries had failed to identify anyone else who had done it and could offer suggestions. But we were ready to make the experiment. We knew how difficult it was to help, through counseling, couples who had already drifted into a state of alienation, and we were

121

curious to find out whether there might be ways of *preventing* trouble at an earlier stage.

Despite our lack of experience, we all had a good time that weekend. For one husband, it proved to be a turning point in his life. A pastor, he became convinced that helping marriages was the most important work he could do. After years of training, he became a qualified professional marriage counselor and later wrote a book on how to strengthen marriages.

We were invited back to Kirkridge. At this second retreat a crisis arose. The Kirkridge rule for retreats was that silence must be observed from the conclusion of the evening program until breakfast next morning. The couples were in open rebellion about this. "Why," they exclaimed, "just when you help us to open up to each other, you tell us we mustn't talk!" The rule was promptly waived for our particular retreat.

Two letters came later from participants in this second retreat. One wife said, "As a result of the weekend under your guidance, I feel we now have a mutual means of communication. It has been helpful for us to reevaluate certain aspects of our marriage, such as the quality of our time together, and for me to see the importance of being a companion to my husband, rather than merely a mother to his children." We felt encouraged by this; it seemed we were on the right track.

The other letter was a challenge. "We have been taught and talked to a great deal," it said, "but I could have welcomed briefer presentations, briefer comments by the leaders, and more sharing in the group. It was altogether too structured." We have taken that early warning to heart in all the years since!

We began to receive invitations to lead couples' weekends for various groups and organizations. We had to decline many of these requests; but we accepted them where we could and began to gain experience. Vera was also involved in leading retreats for mothers of small children, wives of pastors, and similar special groups; but it became more and more clear that what was really important was to bring husbands and wives together, and for us to lead them together as a couple.

We had no awareness, when we led those early weekends, of the far-reaching implications of our pioneer efforts. We have since sought diligently to find out whether other couples had done this before us. Of course, we know that all sorts of programs for married couples had been in operation before 1962. For example, Herbert Otto, the well-known pioneer in the field of human potential, had been investigating the possibility of improving the quality of relationships, including marriage relationships. But we have not found another couple who worked together leading enrichment weekends for couples before 1962, and who have continued to do so through the years, as we have done.

The next significant step was taken by Leon Smith, who in January 1962 had been appointed by the United Methodist Church in the U.S.A. to direct special ministries in marriage: preparation for marriage, marriage education, and marriage counseling, as well as some other aspects of family ministries. He had been my first graduate student when I came from England in 1949 to teach at Drew University in New Jersey. I had helped him get started on his doctoral program, and later opened up the way for him to take clinical training at the Marriage Council of Philadelphia. He had been working with couples in various churches since the mid-1950s.

In September 1964 Leon, teaming up with his wife, Antoinette, put together a suggested program for a two-and-a-half-day retreat for Methodist pastors and their wives, with twelve sessions on different topics. After experimenting with this, he persuaded Methodist Church leaders to finance a training program to prepare carefully selected clergy couples for leadership of such retreats. Announcements about this were sent out in October 1965, and the training program took place in February 1966 at Warwick, New York. The workshop lasted for five days, and there were fourteen trainee couples enrolled. The training team, in addition to Vera and myself, consisted of a specialist in group dynamics and a husband-wife team who were serving the Methodist Church together as evangelists. Leon himself was taken ill at the last moment, so he and Antoinette were unable to come. His colleague Edward Staples, with his wife, Ethlyn, filled in at the last moment.

As far as I am aware, this was the first training workshop for marriage-enrichment leadership. It was a lively event, with some disagreements arising in the leadership team, and among the trainees themselves. This was not a misfortune; it compelled us to clarify a number of issues.

The Methodist events were at first only training workshops for pastors and their wives, to equip them for leadership. The events they then led were called "retreats" in the beginning, using the term by which our original weekends at Kirkridge had been described. Later, the Smiths developed their own program model, and in 1967 called it the Marriage Communication Lab. Our own program, first called Marriage Retreat, was later expanded into Marriage Enrichment Retreat.

Development of the Three Models

Returning to Father Calvo, his first weekend in 1962 was called the Encuentro Conyugal. The Spanish word *encuentro*, like its English equivalent, *encounter*, can mean a confrontation or fight, but it more commonly describes two people meeting each other and finding or discovering each other. It is this latter meaning that Father Calvo had in mind. He had prepared a series of questions that would enable husbands and wives first to reflect on who they were as individual persons; then on their relationship to each other as a married couple; then on their joint relationship to God. Through this searching examination, the hope was that the couple would lay aside their defenses and be totally honest with one another. By this process, it was believed, they would reach the deepest levels of their relationship and become a truly loving couple.

Once started, Marriage Encounter weekends spread rapidly throughout Spain. Then the Christian Family Movement, following an international meeting in Caracas, Venezuela, introduced it to a number of Latin American countries, and to Spanish-speaking couples in North America. It was offered for the first time in English at a Christian Family Movement conference at Notre Dame University in August 1967. I happened to be one of the speakers at that conference, and I heard the announcement about Marriage Encounter; but I didn't understand what it referred to, so I didn't attend! I didn't actually meet Father Calvo personally until 1974, twelve years after we had developed separate movements with similar objectives.

At a meeting in Elberon, New Jersey, in January 1969, the North American Marriage Encounter was formally launched and a national executive board was appointed. At this time Marriage Encounter detached itself from the sponsoring Christian Family Movement and became independent. It grew swiftly, specially in Long Island, New York, where Father Charles Gallagher assumed leadership.

With rapid growth, variations on the original format of Father Calvo naturally emerged, although the basic objectives remained the same. By 1971, Father Gallagher insisted that his New York program was unique, and that it alone offered the greatest promise of advancement. It was controlled by a rigid and strongly centralized organization, in contrast to many of the other regional groups, to which the national board had given considerable freedom to develop their own interpretations of the original concepts.

Some controversy ensued, and it came to a head in May 1973, when Father Gallagher declared that the purpose of the Marriage Encounter was the renewal of the Catholic Church, and that non-Catholics could have only limited participation in the organization. This was resented by those who saw the movement as ecumenical, and thousands of these couples, with some priests, rallied round the National Executive Secretary Team to create the National Marriage Encounter, centered in Chicago, to distinguish it clearly from the New York organization. The national headquarters office moved in 1974 to Minnesota and established its identity more clearly by publishing the monthly journal *AGAPE*, now renamed *Marriage Encounter*. The New York organization later moved its headquarters to Saint Louis and took the title Worldwide Marriage Encounter, so that there were now two quite separate organizations. Attempts to heal the breach between them have, up to the time of this writing, been unsuccessful. The Worldwide Marriage Encounter organization has now, presumably in order to meet the challenge that it was not ecumenical, helped a number of Protestant Churches, including the Episcopal, Lutheran, and Methodist, to set up their own independent "expressions" of Marriage Encounter. In association with National Marriage Encounter, a Jewish expression was established in 1974 by Rabbi Bernard Kligfield.

Let us now return to the other models. The Marriage Communication Labs, under the leadership of Antoinette and Leon Smith, have spread extensively through the United Methodist Church and have been adopted also by other Protestant denominations, for example, the Christian Church (Disciples of Christ) and the Reformed Church. All of these have now linked up with the Association of Couples for Marriage Enrichment (ACME). The Smiths, who have served as ACME officers, have continued to play a leading role in the development of training programs to prepare selected couples to lead marriage-enrichment events.

The development of our own model, following our first pioneering efforts, took place within the Society of Friends (Quakers), of which we are members. In recognition of the development of our marriage-enrichment concept, I was invited to deliver, on October 6, 1968, the Rufus Jones Lecture, given each year to honor an outstanding American Quaker of this Century. I took as my subject *Marriage as Vocation: An Invitation to Relationship-in-Depth,* and the lecture was later published (Mace, 1969). Following its delivery, Vera and I were invited to spend a weekend with a selected Quaker group, to discuss what could be done to implement our ideas. The group was able to secure a foundation grant that enabled us, at the retreat center called Pendle Hill near Philadelphia, to train two successive batches of carefully chosen Quaker couples from across North America; these then returned and led retreats for their own yearly meetings. The training workshops were held in May 1969 and October 1971, respectively, and the experiment is described in a printed booklet (Mace and Mace, 1972). Some of the couples involved are still active in marriage-enrichment leadership.

Through these training experiences, and with the help of the very capable couples involved, we were all able to develop a model of marriage-enrichment leadership that reflected our basic Quaker concepts. This is much more flexible, and much less structured, than the other models. (I will later discuss, comparatively, the principal characteristics of all three.) We still use the term "Marriage Enrichment Retreat" for our weekends; and our particular style, used by most of the couples we have trained, is generally called the Quaker model.

Some Further Developments

As we entered the 1970s, the term "Marriage Enrichment" came to be more and more widely used. I do not know precisely how or when it started. (The phrase "How to Enrich Your Marriage" occurs in the subtitle of an earlier book of mine [Mace, 1952], but I am not aware that I had any conscious intention at that time of coining a new term.)

With the spread of the new idea, there have inevitably been other people who started all kinds of programs. Many of these were described in Herbert Otto's book *Marriage and Family Enrichment* (1976). So, in addition to the three main streams, there were many smaller tributaries helping to swell the broadening river. And it seemed to me and to others, as we saw all this happening, that a state of chaos might result unless the boundaries of that river were clearly established.

It was in 1971 that I first became convinced that marriage in our culture was heading for very serious trouble; and that at the same time, some of us were making exciting discoveries, which held the hope that the trouble might be reduced if not averted. It has not been an accident that the marriage-enrichment movement has been almost entirely launched by, and through, religious groups. These have been the people who really cared, and were really concerned, about the future of marriage and family life.

However, it seemed clear to me that the new movement must not be confined to religious circles. What marriage enrichment has to offer is for *all* couples who are seeking better marriages. It should therefore be a major concern, not just to church leaders and to professionals, but also to ordinary married couples.

Vera and I, after much thought, arrived at the conclusion that marriage enrichment was not yet of sufficient interest to the professionals to command their strong support. We knew that some kind of organization must ultimately emerge to coordinate the programs that were developing, and we were ready to get it started; but the question was: What form should it take?

We finally made out decision and launched the new organization in July 1973, on the occasion of our fortieth wedding anniversary. We called it the Association of Couples for Marriage Enrichment (ACME) (see Appendix 1 for further details). Our slogan was: "To work for better marriages, beginning with our own." The idea was that couples who joined us would seek to develop the full potential of their relationship (the Greek word *acme* means the top, or peak, of the mountain).

Progress was slow at first, but with the aid of a foundation grant we got ACME established. Our hope was that it might be quite neutral (with no direct religious, political, or professional connections of any kind) and might, therefore, become a coordinating agency for other organizations that were developing programs in this new field; that it might undertake the task of setting standards for leadership; and that it might encourage the development of local chapters, which could promote in their communities the cause of better marriages. It was also our hope that ACME might in time gain enough strength to be able to influence public policy concerning marriage and family life.

All these objectives have been, at least in part, accomplished. In the spring of 1975, we convened in Chicago a meeting of various organizations that were offering marriage-enrichment programs on a national scale, in order to provide a forum for exchanging ideas and sharing experiences. This group has met every year since, and is now the Council of Affiliated Marriage Enrichment Organizations (CAMEO), which ACME officially coordinates (see list of these in Appendix 2).

In addition, ACME set up a Committee for the Selection, Training, and Certification of Leader Couples, which has established standards for marriage-enrichment events that are now being widely accepted. (These standards appear in Appendix 3 of this book.)

ACME has meanwhile been seeking to influence public policy, as far as lies in its power. It played a central role in persuading President Carter to plan the White House Conference on American Families in 1980, and in bringing together the principal national organizations concerned with family life, in order to encourage them to form coalitions that can take united action.

ACME's own growth has been slow but steady. It has enrolled member couples in all fifty states, in most Canadian provinces, and in some twenty other countries. It is in the process of building local chapters in towns and cities across North America. It has established affiliated organizations in Britain, Australia, and South Africa.

Support from Family Professionals

Family professionals were at first disappointingly slow to recognize the importance of the new approaches to marriage and the family that are implicit in the word *enrichment*. They have not appeared to be as much concerned about the breakdown of marriages, and the fragmentation of the family, as might have been expected. Instead of making an agonizing reappraisal of their policies and services, they have responded by intensive studies of the new alternative life styles, and by the stepping up of their counseling services to meet the swelling tide of marriage and family disruption.

However, there is now evidence of an accelerating awareness of the need to make a shift in our emphasis—to augment the provision of remedial services by the development of effective preventive approaches. Marriage counselors are now beginning to see the value of promoting relational growth in addition to, or even instead of, probing for pathology. Family-life educators are becoming aware of the relative ineffectiveness of didactic as compared with dynamic programs, and we are hearing more and more talk about "experiential education." Family researchers are increasingly focusing their attention on relational growth and potential. So we may reasonably hope that soon a slow revolution will be manifest, one which will aim to keep families out of trouble, rather than wait till they are in trouble and then rush to their aid.

Some examples of new professional initiatives may be cited. My esteemed former colleague Clark Vincent has written convincingly about marital health (Vincent, 1973) and established a marital-health clinic at the Bowman Gray School of Medicine in Winston-Salem, North Carolina. Important work in the marital-health field has also been done by Robert and Patricia Travis at the University of Alabama Medical School in Birmingham.

I have already referred to the Couple Communication program developed by

Sherod Miller and his colleagues at the University of Minnesota, and the one Bernard Guerney and his colleagues have pioneered at Pennsylvania State University. Both of these have been based on careful research and have been rigorously tested to establish their effectiveness. Closely parallel to these is the well-known Parent Effectiveness program developed by psychologist Thomas Gordon.

At the University of Minnesota, David Olson, with a team of colleagues and graduate students, has been investigating programs of marriage preparation and helping to develop new techniques. Edward Bader of the University of Toronto and Claude Guldner of Guelph University, Ontario, are experimenting with programs of prevention in early marriage.

A steady stream of important books also testifies to our growing awareness of the need for a focus on relationships. David Olson has edited a symposium on *Treating Relationships* (1976); George Levinger and Harold Rausch have edited another symposium on *Close Relationships: Perspectives on the Meaning of Intimacy* (1977); and Bernard Guerney has written a significant book on *Relationship Enhancement* (1977). Larry Hof and William Miller have produced a definitive work on *Marriage Enrichment: Philosophy, Process, and Program*. These are only a few publications representative of a rapidly increasing volume of literature. Fortunately, Kenneth Sell, Sarah Shoffner, and their associates have now provided us with a comprehensive guide to these new materials in *Enriching Relationships: A Guide to Marriage and Family Enrichment Literature* (1980). Articles on marital interaction seem to be appearing with increasing frequency in the professional journals, and topics related to marriage enrichment are listed more and more often in the programs of professional conferences.

More Recent Developments

All evidence suggests that interest in what marriage enrichment has to offer is steadily growing. The churches are becoming more and more involved in providing marriage-growth experiences for their member couples. Pastors and their wives are increasingly seeking to equip themselves for this task, often by becoming involved themselves in marriage-enrichment experiences. Here and there, interest is growing in providing marriage enrichment as a service at community levels. Kansas City has established the Living Center for Family Enrichment, strongly supported by a vigorous ACME chapter. The Aid Association for Lutherans has developed a nationwide program of marriage enrichment as part of its offerings in the field of family health.

These enterprises are mainly motivated by the growing recognition that, with American families in such serious trouble, there is an urgent need to begin to supplement our remedial services with equivalent preventive services. At this point the marriage enrichment movement is expanding to join forces with already existing groups that are developing preventive programs in parenthood enrichment and whole family enrichment. A national conference has already brought some of the leaders in these fields together under the title *Toward Family Wellness: Our Need For Effective Preventive Programs*. (We shall return to the question of future policy in Part IV of this book.)

We are only at the beginning; the movement is still in its infancy. But the incentive for continuing to explore the dynamics not only of marriage, but of all close dyadic relationships, is likely to be sustained. The behavioral sciences, now at last coming of age, have the resources to explore the field much more deeply. We are all becoming aware that scientific technology alone is not going to make this world a paradise; and that the critical issue for our human future is whether or not we can all live together on this planet in peace, harmony, and creative cooperation. Unless we can manage to do this first and foremost in our marriages and families, that is going to be a hard question to answer.

14

COUPLES IN GROUP
INTERACTION

W E saw in Chapter 7 that the goal in a marriage-enrichment event is to create an environmental setting that will enable a couple to receive significant new information, process it as knowledge, use it to gain deeper insight into their interpersonal relationship, try this out in terms of new ways of interacting with each other, and together make a commitment to achieve further relational growth through the necessary behavioral changes. Although this seems a great deal to accomplish in a short time, the steps involved can in fact follow each other in rapid succession—provided the appropriately supportive environment is made available. In most existing environmental settings in which married couples normally find themselves, the possibility of this series of events taking place is remote.

The critical question is therefore how to create the necessary environment. Although, theoretically, it would seem that a determined couple could achieve all this at home alone using a self-help book or a set of cassette tapes, in practice this very seldom happens. The built-in behavior patterns the couple have established over the years simply inhibit the necessary motivation to initiate significant change. Even the joint decision to enroll in a marriage-enrichment program is hard enough to achieve. The weight of evidence suggests overwhelmingly that the stimulus of an outside agency of some kind is necessary.

Outside help *can* be provided by a marriage counselor, if the couple are willing to commit themselves to his or her care. However, the motivation to take this step normally develops out of a condition of pain and desperation in one or both partners, and this is likely to occur only when the marriage is in quite serious trouble. There is no reason, however, why couples should not seek professional help simply because they are dissatisfied with their marriage as it is and want to improve it. It is my hope that one day this will become a normal and widely accepted practice. We shall examine this possibility more fully in a later chapter.

Up to the present time, experience has shown that the most effective medium for marriage enrichment is the weekend retreat, on a residential basis, whereby a group of couples can share the experience together. Let us therefore examine this more closely.

Models for the Couples' Weekend

As we have already seen, three main models for the couples' weekend have developed. To describe all of them in detail would take up a great deal of space, so I shall simply summarize their main characteristics and indicate the principal similarities and differences between them. Since they are all highly experiential, however, it must be recognized that descriptions always seem inadequate. It is simply not possible to understand fully what occurs except by participation.

The Catholic Marriage Encounter model is basically *supervised self-help*. A group of couples—their number can vary widely—go through a fairly standardized program led by a team consisting of two or three leader couples and a priest. The weekend consists of a series of sessions, with all participants assembled together, in which the team couples, who have already been "encountered," give talks and testimonies. The object is to challenge the participants to examine their attitudes toward themselves as individuals, toward their marriage partners, toward God, and toward the outside world. Following each session, husbands and wives separate to write down, as honestly as they can, their personal answers to searching questions that have been presented to them. Each couple then, in the privacy of their own room, exchange notebooks, read and talk about what they have written, and "encounter" each other at a deep level of openness and honesty.

During the weekend, the priest and the other team members are available to help individuals and couples. However, no open sharing takes place on a couple-to-couple basis, except at social and religious levels. In other words, the intermarital taboo (described later in this chapter) is maintained. No special knowledge and skill are required in the leadership team. The process of facilitation is confined to providing the participating couples with seclusion, stimulus, and support. The major new procedure offered to the couples is the opening up of communication-in-depth by the writing down, and later sharing, of very personal thoughts and feelings that in most mariages are seldom if ever exchanged.

Second, let us look at the *Marriage Communication Lab.* I would characterize it as *experiential education*. The pattern varies from one Protestant denomination to another; but it consists ideally of eight to ten couples plus two leader couples, meeting for six successive periods of three hours each. For half of each period there is an experiential learning session in the total community, and for the other half two small groups, each with four or five couples, meet with a participatory leader couple. In the small group, a couple may spontaneously dialogue together about any marital issue of their choosing and may receive feedback on their communication process rather than suggested solutions. Often another couple will then identify a similar issue in their marriage and dialogue about it, again spontaneously, with other members of the group helping them with their process.

As indicated, variations of this basic model have been developed experimentally by different religious groups. Some are tightly structured, others much less so. In all of them, however, the experiential education emphasis is central.

Third, let us examine the so-called *Quaker model,* often described as the *Marriage Enrichment Retreat.* It possesses a minimum of structure, and can best be typified as focusing on *couple-group interaction.* The group is invited to take responsibility for itself and to make its own agenda. The major process is the sharing of experiences of marriage through the couple dialogue, which takes place openly in the group, thus relaxing the intermarital taboo that the Marriage Encounter maintains. Leader couples, therefore, require some training in group process. Their role is defined as "participating facilitators." In contrast to sensitivity training and encounter groups, however, the ground rules allow no confrontation. All participation is voluntary, and feedback to the dialoguing couple is offered only if and when requested. Some teaching may be given when relevant, and some exercises are used; but the main process is learning and experiencing through dynamic interaction between the participating couples. (A more detailed description will be given in Chapter 15).*

Experience and observation over the years suggest that all three models are effective in initiating growth and change in the participating couples. A number of research projects involving pretests, posttests, and followup have found evidence to support this. However, only one comparative study of different models has yet been made.

Experienced leader couples tend, over time, to experiment, and not to be tied to the use of any particular model. Vera and I, for example, have experienced all three models ourselves, and in leading a particular group we use flexibly whatever combination of procedures seems best suited to the needs of the couples concerned. (This will be illustrated in the next chapter.)

The field is therefore open to the development of new forms, and this is encouraged by ACME, which is not committed to any particular model. The "Growth Group," instead of being a cncentrated weekend experience, incor-

---

* More information about the Marriage Encounter may be found in the books by Antoinette Bosco (1972) and Don Demarest (1977). In Herbert Otto's symposium (1976) there are several descriptions of both the Marriage Encounter and the Marriage Communication Lab. The only description of the Quaker model that has to my knowledge appeared in print is in the booklet *Marriage Enrichment Retreats: Story of a Quaker Project* (Mace and Mace, 1972).

porates the same procedures in a series of six to eight weekly meetings with a qualified leader couple. The "miniretreat" is a shorter form of the weekend experience on a nonresidential basis, intended to give a larger group of couples, often in a church setting, a taste of what a full retreat would be like, in the hope of recruiting them for a fuller experience later. 'Enrichment Groups" have met, in communities where no trained leaders were available, to work through a book or to use a set of cassettes together—and this seems to be much more effective than when an isolated couple use such materials alone. In addition, "support groups" are widely used in ACME chapters as a followup for couples who have made a commitment to growth and need the continuing support of other couples for their ongoing growth. "Image groups" in Marriage Encounter serve the same purpose. ACME has now produced detailed manuals describing the miniretreat and the support group.

The Dynamics of Couples' Groups

Up to now, interaction process in couples' enrichment groups has been poorly understood. Since my own extensive experience of leadership has been almost entirely confined to such group interaction, I will discuss some of my findings.

It is necessary to make clear at the outset that a group of married couples is something very different from a group of individuals. This explains why people who are highly trained in group dynamics sometimes have difficulty in dealing with married couples who join groups otherwise composed of individuals, or in leading groups composed entirely of couples.

We need to understand that a couples' group is made up of established social units, with a shared past and moving toward a shared future. Each individual is there with his partner, as part of a family system; and any personal change that occurs in him or her will involve, inevitably, a corresponding readjustment of that system. To treat the group participants as separate entities is to risk disrupting the systems to which they belong and may deny them the main benefits they have come to seek.

For this reason, the interaction process in a couples' group is much more complex than that in a group of individuals. Within the group, the following interactions may occur:

1. between an individual and his or her spouse
2. between an individual and another unrelated individual
3. between an individual and another couple
4. between an individual and a coalition of individuals
5. between an individual and a coalition of couples
6. between a couple and a coalition of individuals
7. between a couple and another couple
8. between a couple and a coalition of couples

By contrast, interactions in groups of individuals are relatively simple and are confined to those between individuals and coalitions of individuals.

Further complications arise when, as is normal, the group of couples is jointly led by a leader couple, who may interact with the whole group or with various component segments of the group, either separately or together.

Yet another complication arises when the leader couple accept the participating-facilitator role. As facilitators, they act as quasi-authoritative figures, at least to the extent that they monitor the group's observance of the ground rules or intervene in a crisis. Yet as participators they function fully as members of the group, leaving it temporarily leaderless. Indeed, one of the most rewarding experiences in this type of leadership is to be able to sit back and watch the group literally running itself.

The two sections of Diagram 6 will illustrate the difference between this kind of leadership and the continuously authoritative role adopted by most professionals in leading counsel-therapy groups. The first section of the diagram shows the participating couples in a closed group (continuous line), but open to sharing with each other; with two co-leaders who though in the group, are *not* open to sharing their own experiences of marriage (dotted line) either with the group, or with each other in the group. The second part of the diagram shows all group participants, including the leader couple, open to sharing with each other.

Diagram 7 uses the same symbols to show the difference between married couples in a typical social group, where the several couples maintain defensive barriers, and a similar group of couples in a marriage-enrichment group, where the couples are open to sharing experiences of marriage with each other, but within a closed group. Each sharing group must make this transition from the first situation to the second, by the process of moving through the barrier erected by the intermarital taboo. As the group moves in this direction, some anxiety inevitably develops, and the resulting tension is easily recognizable by a characteristic type of high-pitched nervous laughter. Once through the taboo, however, the group undergoes a marked change to a state of comfortable relaxation, with rapidly developing trust and warmth. It is when the group has made this transition that we witness the dynamic process of couples really learning from each other and helping each other. Loving bonds develop between the participating couples that resemble kinship bonds in many respects; and I have often noticed that, even when couples who have undergone this experience together do not meet again for years, they can immediately resume the close, confiding relationship they had earlier established in the group.

In most marriage-enrichment models, but particularly in the less structured group where open sharing is achieved, it is possible to observe a characteristic sequence of events. Almost invariably, the participating couples begin in a state of *anxiety*. They are entering into an experience that is new and unknown, one that concerns an area of their lives in which they often feel highly vulnerable.

If the group is well led, however, this anxiety will soon be followed by

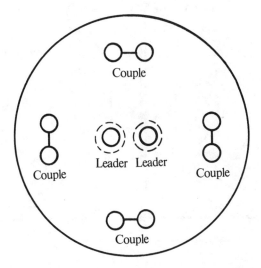

Leadership—Two Nonparticipating Co-Facilitators

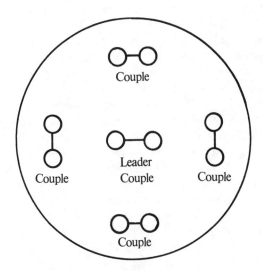

Leadership—Participating Facilitator Couple

DIAGRAM 6
Marital Therapy and Marriage Enrichment Groups

Defensive Social Interaction ⟶ Taboo ⟶ Open Sharing Interaction

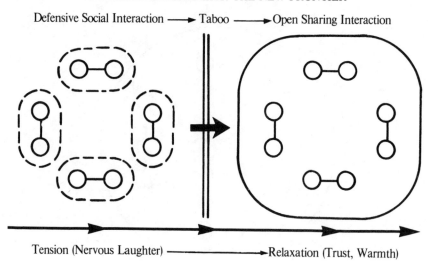

Tension (Nervous Laughter) ⟶ Relaxation (Trust, Warmth)

DIAGRAM 7
Process in a Couples' Enrichment Group

feelings of *reassurance,* as the participants realize that other couples have "problems" too, and that no pressure or compulsion will be placed upon them. They now know that they will not be made to feel uncomfortable, and that in fact the experience is going to be pleasant and rewarding.

Reassurance prepares the way for the development of *trust.* One couple in the group (and often this is the role of the leader couple) voluntarily, will open up their relationship by acknowledging their humanness and sharing with the others some of the struggles they have been through, or are presently experiencing. Their willingness to make themselves vulnerable may then encourage other couples to take the risk of self-disclosure. As this process continues, the sharing of experiences in the group moves progressively to a deeper level. All this should happen naturally and spontaneously and should not be in any way forced. Couples' groups differ widely in the rate at which they develop trust, and in the depth of sharing they ultimately achieve.

As trust in the group leads to deeper levels of sharing, a process of *cross-identification* takes place in which a given couple will relate to other couples who are going through, or have already gone through, significant experiences in marriage very like their own. They are now able to eliminate the protective distance that, under the power of the taboo, they have hitherto maintained between themselves and other married couples. As this happens, a warm, comfortable feeling of friendliness and closeness pervades the group.

Out of cross-identification comes a highly creative process of *experiential learning*—the means by which we shape our behavior patterns by identification with significant others in our lives. An obvious illustration of this is the fact that in most areas of common interest, people tend to get together naturally in order to exchange experiences and to learn from each other. This happens not only in the maturation process, but also in fields like work and hobbies. Unions, clubs, and associations are formed between stamp collectors, gardeners, photographers, and indeed in all activities in which people share a desire to learn and to become more proficient. To this general principle of human behavior, marriage, because of the taboo, has been a striking exception. The married couples in our culture are expected to "go it alone." By relaxing the taboo, however, the dynamic power of experiential learning is enabled to operate in this highly complex field of interpersonal relationships.

The final process in the couples' group is the development of *loving support,* in which the couples affirm each other in their commitment to ongoing growth. The sense of growing and changing together generates hope and confidence, and the dream of marriage as a loving, tender, creative relationship, which seemed to have been destroyed by personal disappointment and the pervasive social climate of cynicism, is renewed as a powerful dynamic in support of the new commitment the couples have made to each other.

We see this *commitment* as vital. Vera and I never conclude a retreat without giving the couples the opportunity, in a private time together, to make a growth plan for the following year—for growth in their shared life, and in their individual lives as well. This is put in writing and signed by both of them; it is not necessarily shared with the group, but is taken away as a tangible reminder of the experience.

I offer these observations about what goes on in marriage-enrichment groups, in the hope of encouraging more intensive study and research. Some basic principles for the leadership of *therapy* groups for married couples have already been established, but most of them represent the application of general marital-therapy procedures to a group form of practice. It is my impression that the enrichment group operates on somewhat different principles, and that these need to be examined and clarified.

A good illustration of this difference is the ground rule that there should be no confrontation in the group. Professionals who are qualified in group leadership have often challenged this, sometimes quite vigorously. In the early days of our development of the Quaker model, Vera and I replied to this criticism in the booklet referred to earlier in this chapter. On rereading our reply, written in 1972, I find that my thought on the subject has undergone no significant change in the meantime. I quote from it without further comment:

> Encounter groups provide opportunities for the participants to secure cathartic release of their pent-up hostilities, including hostilities engendered by, or projected upon, the group leader or one or more of its members. We recognize that many people in our culture are pregnant with suppressed hostility or rage, and that the

provision of properly controlled opportunities for its release may constitute a commendable service; and since the group members are generally strangers who will not be personally and socially involved later, no entangling complications are likely to follow.

For our married couples, the situation is different. We do not mean that they do not have hostile feelings toward each other. They often do, and this comes out clearly and unmistakably. We do not mean, either, that healthy discharge of these feelings might not be good for them—in our therapeutic work with individual couples in conjoint interviews, we make full use of such controlled opportunity for cathartic release with ensuing interpretation. It is our considered opinion, however, that in the particular context of our enrichment retreats, unrestrained discharge of hostile feelings should in general not be encouraged.

Our reasons? One, the shortness of the available time might not permit the proper resolution of such episodes. Two, a couple who have openly discharged rage against each other may well react later with deep feelings of humiliation that are not easily assuaged. Three, coping with this kind of explosive emotional discharge could be alarming for lay leaders not accustomed, as the therapist is, to the expression of deep feelings which normally are not displayed in public. Four, other members of the group could be similarly disturbed and diverted from full participation in the main purpose of the retreat. This complaint has actually been made, and we think justly, by participating couples in a group where a violent and prolonged emotional episode took place.

We have been criticized for taking this position, but have not been persuaded to change our considered opinion. That opinion is reinforced by another conclusion; namely, that when genuine positive interaction is promoted, negative emotion, even when it is strong and intense, tends to dissolve and wither away. Couples have told us how their fierce hate melted in the atmosphere of warm and loving support engendered in the group, and with the stirring of compassion within them, they began to see each other in a new light. We are inclined to the view, after hearing such testimonies, that in deploying our therapeutic repertoire we have often given short shrift to the power of love not only to cast out fear, but also to turn away wrath (Mace and Mace, 1972, pp. 11–12).

The Intermarital Taboo

We must now consider a vitally important issue related to couples' groups—what I call the "intermarital taboo." I have never come across any reference to it in either the psychological or the anthropological literature. I have myself given it a name, because I have encountered it so often in working with married couples.

A taboo is defined as "a prohibition excluding something from use, approach, or mention." The word comes from the island of Tonga in the South Pacific. In our language of today, it is something that just isn't done, or just isn't mentioned, as a matter of social custom.

Imagine a group of married couples having dinner together. They are good friends, and they talk quite freely among themselves about most subjects. Quite suddenly, Fred mentions something very personal that happened between him and Peggy last Tuesday evening.

A sudden silence falls on the group. Peggy catches Fred's eye and frowns at him. Everybody feels uncomfortable. Then Jim, the host, quickly changes the subject; and Peter, who always knows how to cope, makes a joke. Everybody laughs loudly, and the crisis is over.

The intermarital taboo is an unwritten rule that married couples should never, never talk to other married couples about what is going on in their interpersonal relationship. Why not? No clear reason is stated. it just isn't done.

Of course, there *is* a reason. There always is. A taboo is generally a useful device, and often with a long history.

How did this one get started? Someday I hope the anthropologists will tell us, if they haven't already done so. My own theory is that it all goes back to the time when groups of families lived together in small, isolated villages, and married couples needed to have some protection from curious, prying neighbors.

But today we no longer live in rural villages. We live in vast, sprawling urban complexes. And we often feel more threatened by the detached indifference of those around us than by their idle curiosity. What married couples need today is close friends to whom they can open up their inner perplexities and anxieties, with whom they can share the issues with which they grapple, and from whom they can learn better ways of coping. But an ancient taboo, no longer relevant, blocks the way. If you want help from another couple about growing lettuce or fixing the furnace or what to do when the dog is sick, you just ask for it. But if you need some guidance about interacting with each other in a difficult situation, that is taboo. You have to struggle with that alone. And if, for want of the help your married couple friends might have given you, but can't, your marriage breaks down, all they say is, "Well, well, just fancy that! We had no idea they were in trouble."

The time has come to relax this taboo. I don't want to see any couple's privacy violated. Vera and I would not be justified in asking you probing questions about your marriage if you give us no indication that you want to discuss it. But if we as a couple need some guidance or support or help in a crisis situation we're going through, why shouldn't we call on our married friends to help us?

I have, therefore, come to the conclusion that in marriage-enrichment events, the intermarital taboo can justifiably be relaxed. Cutting off from couples the opportunity to exchange experiences, and so to learn from each other, is depriving them of getting help they greatly need, for reasons that no longer have enough weight to justify such a policy. In my twenty years of leading marriage-enrichment groups, I have seen hundreds of couples learning a great deal from being able to observe the inside functioning of the marriages of other couples;

I cannot recall a single instance in which harm was done. Isn't it time we asked ourselves seriously whether this excessive privatism about marriage needs to be sustained?

The Couple Dialogue

A relaxation of the taboo would open the way for much wider use of open couple dialogue in the group. Couples' groups are, as I have pointed out, made up of social units and are normally led by a social unit of the same kind.

When we first began to lead groups of couples, we found that we knew of no effective way in which the participants could interact with each other *as couples*. One couple might wish to share with the group the need they felt to improve their communication. The husband would make a statement. Then the wife would break in and amend it. Each, quite naturally, saw the situation somewhat differently. So what the group heard was something like two accounts of the same event from two different reporters. Sometimes these were not in agreement, and we were left guessing at what the true situation was. Worse still, on occasions we might hear one partner (usually the husband) describe assertively to the group what was going on in the marriage; but we had no inkling of the way in which the other partner, who declined comment, might be viewing it.

For years we were puzzled to know how to deal with this situation. Then a Quaker trainee couple introduced a dialogue technique in which the partners faced each other and talked back and forth, slowly and reflectively, together. Now it was quite clear what the situation was, because *it was the marriage that was speaking*. This was an exciting discovery for us as group leaders, and we have used the couple dialogue, not exclusively, but as one important form of group interaction, ever since.

The benefits have been beyond all reckoning. The couple dialogue demonstrates and affirms the nature of the group as composed of social units rather than of individuals. In this way, marriages can literally talk to each other. It also keeps the discussion firmly focused at the level of sharing experiences and effectively prevents the group from drifting into theorizing and generalizing. It insures, too, that the feelings and thoughts of both partners get full recognition.

Our usual practice as group leaders is to demonstrate the couple dialogue ourselves, early in the retreat, and then to encourage its use by other couples. However, dialogue should be entirely voluntary, and the couple should *both* be willing to volunteer. Other ways of communicating within the group are of course equally open. All we want to emphasize is that the dialogue is an available resource.

However, there is no doubt that it is also a very *effective* resource. Good friends of ours in Marriage Encounter have sometimes argued that couples can communicate with each other much more effectively in private. We have not found this to be the case. Couples often report that it was only with the support of the group that they were finally able to get through to each other. They pay special tribute to the *restraint* the group makes possible for them. Alone, they say they would have been at the mercy of strong negative emotions that would have blocked their communication.

I should point out, however, that we also make use of the private dialogue, giving couples "time alone together" after writing down their thoughts and feelings on critical issues. Indeed, in our extensive use of couple dialogue, we have identified a variety of forms. Table 3 indicates what these forms are, and the situations in which they may be appropriately used.

TABLE 3

COUPLE DIALOGUE—FORMS AND SITUATIONS

Form→ Situation↓	Reporting	Exploring	Working	Affirming	Demonstrating
Private	—	√√	√√	√	—
Group Sharing	√√	√	√√	√	√
Public	√	—	—	√	√√

The different forms of dialogue are shown in the horizontal column. A couple *reporting* will talk to each other about some experience that is now in the past: a rough time that they went through together, a learning process, an area of significant growth. A couple *exploring* will search for a better understanding, or a clearer perspective, about some aspect of their relationship. A couple *working* will be trying to reach a sense of common purpose about some issue, or to resolve a disagreement by negotiation. A couple *affirming* are expressing appreciation of, and affection toward, each other. A couple *demonstrating* may be showing a group how the dialogue operates; or sharing something of their relationship in a public gathering in order to model the dialogue process for people to whom this is an entirely new concept.

The vertical column indicates in what kinds of situations these forms of dialogue would be most appropriate. A dialogue designed for reporting or demonstrating obviously couldn't be private! All forms of dialogue could take place in the sharing group, but the reporting and working dialogues are especially appropriate (double checks). Likewise, most exploring and working dialogues take place in private, and the demonstrating dialogue has special value in a public meeting; they are therefore double checked in those situations.

Couples in their first experience of a sharing group sometimes feel uncertainty about using the dialogue, although they would like to try. We can ease them into it in a number of ways. One would be to invite them to turn to each other and discuss together just why they feel hesitant to dialogue! Another would be to suggest that they talk together about exactly how they are feeling right now. A good positive way of beginning is for them to exchange their views about what they like most about their marriage. Sometimes couples are more comfortable about dialoguing for the first time with one other couple, and for this purpose the group can be divided up into foursomes.

The use of couple dialogue in the group, in that it opens deep levels of sharing by the couples, adds something to the responsibilities of the leader couple, so that they require some training in the management of couple group interaction. This leads us naturally to the subject of the training of leader couples.

Training for Couple Group Leadership

Although Vera and I began to lead marriage-enrichment weekends in 1962, it was not until Leon Smith invited us to serve as trainers for his first group of leader couples in 1966 that we had to ask ourselves how to set about this task. It is my impression that we did a pretty poor job on that first occasion!

It was not until three years later, in 1969, that we trained our first Quaker group of prospective leaders. Our policy then was a very simple one. We took them through a retreat experience and allowed plenty of time for questions and discussion about what was happening. They then went off to lead retreats of their own and returned six months later to report. This second period proved to be a most profitable exchange for all of us. Looking back, I am inclined to think that the couples we had "trained" taught us more than we taught them! Concerning the process of training, it is certainly true that we all learned it together.

Meanwhile, however, Antoinette and Leon Smith were involved in training in a big way. They must be recognized as the pioneers in this field. When we started ACME, and the need for extensive training programs arose, it was to the Smiths that we turned, and we owe them an incalculable debt. They gave a generous amount of time during a five-month study leave to share our early training workshops with us. Later, other couples who had had considerable experience as trainers joined us on the ACME Committee on the Selection, Training, and Certification of Leader Couples, which in six years of work has hammered out standards based on extensive experimentation. After frequent revisions these standards are now being tested out thoroughly over an additional period of years (see Appendix 3).

I am aware that the training and certification of lay couples to lead couple-growth groups raises some questions in the professional community. Actually, very few of our trained couples are strictly "lay." Almost always, at least one member of the couple belongs to one of the helping professions. And where this is not the case, we require some basic knowledge of human development, of marital interaction, and of group dynamics.

It must also be remembered that marriage enrichment, as we presently understand it, is *not* a professional function. We go out of our way to discourage couples with serious difficulties from coming to our weekends; we urge them instead to seek professional help. Even so, a few get in under the wire. When that happens, our leader couples are expected to assume the responsibility for getting them into counseling if at all possible. So, in intention at least, ACME-trained leader couples are performing essentially an *educational* task. It must be remembered, too, that they have to undergo a quite searching process of *selection*.

It is in any case doubtful, at the present time, whether professionals would wish to be deeply involved in marriage enrichment. The couples who come to retreats do not see what they are doing as seeking professional help, so they would not be disposed to pay anything like a professional fee. Also, the demand for marriage enrichment is not high, though it is steadily increasing. The churches are the main providers at this stage, and they are not accustomed to charging fees for their services.

This situation may change in time, and I shall discuss the issue further in the chapter on marriage counseling. Marriage enrichment is at present only in its infancy. But already exciting possibilities are opening up, which could lead to revolutionary developments in the future. These possibilities must be fully explored and taken into account as we try to assess the outlook for marriage.

15

A MARRIAGE ENRICHMENT
RETREAT

In the last chapter I discussed, mainly in theoretical terms, the dynamic processes that seem to take place when married couples are involved in enrichment groups. However, no detailed description of an actual couples' weekend was included; and, since many readers of this book have probably never participated in such an event, it occurs to me that a step-by-step account of what actually happens might help them to visualize the process more clearly.

This chapter offers such a description. I will report on a retreat led by Vera and myself, closely following our original Quaker model, but introducing also a few components from other models. A small group of only six couples (twelve persons plus two leaders) is involved; the program is highly flexible; and there is a minimum of rigid structure, although a clear sequence is followed. The style is the one that best demonstrates the practical application of the principles discussed in the last chapter.

This, however, probably is not typical of most marriage-enrichment events, and it will therefore have to be supplemented by a description of a much more structured program involving a much greater number of couples. This follows in the next chapter. The two descriptions together should give an effective picture of the wide range of marriage-enrichment events today.

In order to make the description seem realistic, I shall describe the process in the present tense.

Friday Evening

(The six couples who signed up for our weekend retreat have now all arrived. We planned a dinner together at the conference center at 6:00 P.M. We find that this provides a pleasant social event to get us started;

144

and it also has the great advantage of making sure that all couples will be present in time for the beginning of the opening session, which we are now about to start. It is 7:15 P.M., and all fourteen of us are sitting in comfortable chairs, in a wide circle, all partners next to each other. We are wearing name tags with our first names only, in big letters. The room is quiet and comfortable, and in the daytime it looks out on a pleasant rural scene.)

DAVID: We want to welcome all of you to our marriage-enrichment weekend. We have come together here for a purpose, and we want to explain it clearly to you. But first, to set you at ease, let me recognize the fact that nearly all couples come to their first retreat with mixed feelings. On the one hand, we are looking forward to the weekend and to what it can do for us; we hope it will be enjoyable and profitable. But because this is going to be a new kind of experience, we have some anxiety, too. I wonder if any of you, right now, are having what we sometimes call "butterflies in the stomach"? Perhaps you wonder, a little apprehensively, what's going to happen. All right, let us tell you right away.

VERA: Our weekend will have *three objectives*. They're all on this sheet of newsprint that I'm going to put up on the wall. They are:

1. to take a sincere and honest look at our marriage *as it now is*
2. to decide together the *new directions in which we want our marriage to grow* in the next twelve months
3. to develop some *new insights,* and to gain some *new skills,* which will make it possible to achieve the goals we set for the future growth of our relationship

So there it is. The first two objectives are for you as a couple to work on privately. You'll have opportunities to share some of this with the group if you wish, but there's no obligation to do so. The third objective is *our* responsibility. As your leaders, we'll try to see that you get whatever resources you need to do the work that lies before you.

DAVID: As well as the three objectives, we also have *three ground rules*. They will go up on the wall, too, so that we can check from time to time to make sure we're keeping to them. They are:

1. *There will be no confrontation. All participation in the group will be voluntary.* We won't even go around the circle and "take turns"—we regard that as confrontation! If we suggest some activity, and nobody volunteers, we just won't do it. Actually, it would be possible for a couple to go through the whole weekend and take no part in anything! Of course, we very much hope that *won't* happen! But we want you to know that you do have that right.

2. *We are here to share experiences, not to exchange opinions.* Discussion

groups certainly have their value. But that isn't our purpose this weekend. We find it much more helpful to tell each other about what is actually happening to us, because we learn much more from each other that way.

3. *Marriage enrichment is not therapy, so we shall not diagnose or analyze each other.* We are not here as couples because we are in trouble, but because we want to make our good marriages even better. So when you tell us about your relationship, we won't start counseling you or giving you advice. However, you *can* ask for feedback from the group if you wish, and in that event we'll do our best to help you.

So, we are here to learn from each other, to help each other by sharing experiences, and to give each other encouragement and support as we plan our future growth. It is the joint responsibility of all of us to see that we keep to these ground rules.

VERA: We also want to say something about our role as your leaders. We would really prefer you to think of us as "participating facilitators." That means that we want to be fully members of the group—ready to share *our* experiences of marriage, and ready to learn from other couples. To make that clear, we'd like you to call us by our first names, so that we don't sound like authority figures. However, we are also facilitators. That means we'll try to guide the group so that it makes the best possible use of the time we spend together. But please understand clearly that if you don't like anything we suggest, you can turn it down. You, the group, are in charge of the weekend, and we shall make all decisions together.

DAVID: To make sure that everyone is comfortable, we shall start every session by asking if any of you have any "concerns." A concern can be anything that is bothering you—about yourself, about someone else, or about what is happening in the group generally. A concern always has priority, and we stay with it until we clear it up. You can even interrupt the sessions and say you have a concern. It will be dealt with right away. We believe that the group won't function really effectively if any members are feeling uncomfortable or unhappy, so we beg you to share your concerns, whatever they are, as soon as you become aware of them. Incidentally, we think this is a good thing to do in married life as well!

Has anyone got a concern now?

(A pause for concerns to be shared)

VERA: There's one last thing we want to add. Because people participate in marriage-enrichment groups as couples, it sometimes happens that one partner comes much more willingly than the other. A special name has been coined for the less willing partner. The word is *dragee*—the one who was dragged here! Now, we don't on any account want to *identify* any dragees who may be here this evening! But we do, without identifying you, want to *honor* you. If you are a dragee, you have done a very kind and loving thing by enabling your partner to participate in this experience. We want to thank you for this, and to express the hope that you will soon cease to be a dragee, and feel glad you came after all. We have never to our knowledge had a dragee in any of our groups who remained a dragee for long!

DAVID: These are all the explanations we wanted to give you at the beginning. Is there anything that isn't clear?

(A pause here to answer questions)

Now we want you to join us in what some people call a "guided fantasy"; we prefer the description of the wife who called it "a trip down memory lane." Will you please settle into a comfortable position in your chair, close your eyes, and let all your body muscles relax as much as you can.

(A pause while the group members settle themselves)

Now we'd like you to go back to the first time you two met each other. Can you remember when it was, and what happened? Try to recapture the experience.

(Pause)

Now move on to the first time you acknowledged to each other that you loved each other enough to want to marry someday. Remember, if you can, what was said and how you felt about it.

(Pause)

Move on through the courtship, and now recall your wedding day. Flash the picture on the screen of your mind, and think of the place, the time, the assembled family and friends, and yourselves.

(Pause)

Follow on now to the first time you were alone together in your own home. Recall how you felt about it—the joys, the hopes, the expectations.

(Pause)

Now pick out one or two peak experiences in your early married life—a moment of great joy, the birth of your first child, some significant new beginning.

(Pause)

Now move on to what happened when you first heard of this retreat. You talked it over together and finally decided to come. How were you feeling then?

(Pause)

Come now to the experience of leaving home and making the trip here. What did you talk about? What positive feelings did you have? Any negative feelings?

(Pause)

And now you are here, sitting side by side, with a group of other couples who have come for the same purpose. Think lovingly of your partner, and of all that he or she has meant to you in the years that have passed since that time when you pledged your love to each other. And think lovingly of the other couples, your new friends, who are going to share this weekend experience with you.

(Pause)

Now open your eyes, turn to your partner, and for the next ten minutes share with each other some of the memories you have just relived. Do it warmly and lovingly. Hold hands if you like—or even put your arms around each other.

(The couples are talking eagerly to each other, as we are. They look as if they are enjoying this experience. There are smiles and loving gestures.)

VERA: We hate to bring these happy exchanges to a close; but now we must start the pleasant task of getting to know the other couples in the group. We consider this to be very important, because we hope we will be sharing each other's lives quite deeply this weekend.

There are many ways in which people can get to know each other. One that we especially like, and that we want to suggest now, will also have the advantage of giving you a little break. We want each couple to take a sheet of newsprint and some colored crayons. Then get some coffee and go off together for ten minutes and draw a picture of your marriage. No further instructions! Just do it in any way you like. We'll tell you when your time is up.

(The couples go to work on their pictures. We also prepare a picture. When time is up, the group comes together again.)

DAVID: What we suggest is that, one couple at a time, we spread out our pictures on the rug in the center of the circle and then explain to the group what the picture is all about. Why don't Vera and I volunteer to start, and then others can volunteer when they feel ready? After each couple have interpreted their picture, we'll give them five minutes to answer any questions the group may wish to ask them.

(One after another the couples volunteer to spread out their pictures, explain them, and answer questions from the group. We are now getting to know each other by name, and getting a sense of each other's identity as persons, and as couples. It is all very pleasant and relaxed, and the couples are quickly making friends with each other.)

VERA: Now we all know something about each other, and we are no longer strangers. When our session is over, we suggest that you put your marriage pictures up on the wall, with your names added, as a sort of picture gallery.

Our time is running out, and we want you to get to bed early and have a good rest, because we have a full program tomorrow. But before we end tonight's session, we have a simple exercise for you to do. We're going to give each of you a sheet of paper and a pencil, if you don't already have one. David will tell you what to do.

DAVID: This exercise will give you a start in taking a look at your marriage. Each partner should do it separately, without collaborating. You should write down, first, three things about your marriage that you especially like; then three things in your marriage that are good, but could be even better than they are, areas where there is room for improvement; finally, three specific things that you personally could do, but are not now doing, to make your life together better and happier still.

Don't make a big issue of this—you'll be looking at your marriages much more closely tomorrow. Just jot down whatever comes into your head. We'll give you about five minutes.

When you're through, turn to your partner, share what you have written down, and talk about your reactions for about another ten minutes. Finally, team up with any other couple in the group, and exchange your impressions of the exercise. When you've done this, the session will be over. We won't close it formally. We hope you'll all have a very good night!

Saturday Morning

(It is 9:00 A.M. and we are all back in the group.)

VERA: We hope you all feel rested and refreshed. Do any of you have a concern you would like to share with the group?

(A pause while concerns are shared and dealt with)

DAVID: As you took a look at your marriage last night, you may have found some areas where there was room for improvement. Or there may be aspects of your relationship that represent growing edges—issues that you don't feel clear about, that cause you confusion or uncertainty; perhaps some areas where you could use some help. What we want to do now is to put these issues together and make an agenda for the weekend.

We told you that you, the group, are in charge; and of course that includes the program. There are all kinds of aspects of our relationships that *could* be discussed; but we want to build an agenda together, with the focus on our particular growing edges.

So we're going to give you ten minutes now for each of you as couples to decide on items you'd like to put on the agenda. Please turn to each other and identify together any items you want to contribute.

(The couples talk privately to each other for about ten minutes.)

VERA: Now we're ready for our agenda. Please call out your items,* and I'll write them down. Don't bother to go into any details now. Just identify any areas you're particularly interested in. All right, who'll begin?

(As the items are called out, Vera puts them on a sheet of newsprint. We end up with a list of ten.)

1. wives working
2. need to be alone
3. expressing affection

---

* Some leaders prefer to have agenda items submitted anonymously in writing.

4. quarrels
5. different expectations
6. making decisions together
7. gender roles
8. financial policy
9. use of time
10. sexual attitudes

DAVID: Now you can see what we mean by the group making the program. You have chosen the areas *you* want to explore. Of course, we don't have to stay rigidly with this list. Someone once called it a "rolling agenda"—items roll on and roll off! So we can change it at any time if other issues arise that seem more important.

We're going to ask the group to take charge again. We'd like you to pick out an item to start with. We suggest you might choose something that will be likely to concern *all* of us. And it's a good idea to hold sensitive issues—such as sex and anger—until the group has settled down and developed a comfortable level of trust.

So go ahead and choose your first item.

(*The group members hesitate and seem confused. They didn't take us seriously when we told them they were in charge. But we want to make this point very clearly, so we wait. A few suggestions for suitable topics are offered, and we help them to reach agreement. The subject selected is "gender roles."*)

VERA: All right, we're going to talk about gender roles. But remember we're not going to exchange opinions, but rather share experiences. What we need is one or two couples who would be willing to start us off by sharing with us how *they* see their roles in marriage as man and woman, husband and wife. A good way to do this is to use what we call the "couple dialogue." The idea is for one or two couples to discuss the issue with each other first, very much as you talked about your growing edges; but do it this time so that we can all hear you. This may seem a bit strange to you, to talk to each other while the others listen. Maybe David and I could do it now to show you what we mean.

(*We turn to each other and talk together about how we have worked on the issue of gender roles in our own marriage.*)

DAVID: Now can you see what we mean? If I had talked to the group from *my* point of view, or Vera had talked alone from *her* point of view, you wouldn't have seen where we are nearly as clearly as you did when we talked directly to each other.

Of course you don't have to dialogue unless you're willing to try it. And you should *both* be agreed before you volunteer. Would you like to talk privately together as couples now and see whether we *do* have any volunteers?

(*The couples consider this privately for a few minutes.*)

VERA: Now let's see how you have reacted to David's suggestion. *Do* we have any volunteers? Or have any of you any questions to ask about it? Remember, we understand that this may be something new to most of you, and all we want is for you to consider it. We hope some of you at least will try it out during the weekend, but you may not be ready now.

(Two couples volunteer to try the dialogue. We encourage them to go ahead, and explain that when a couple are dialoguing, the rest of us don't interrupt, but wait till they have finished.)

(The couples dialogue, one after the other. They seem quite relaxed and comfortable about it.)

DAVID: We want to thank you two couples for getting us started. Now you've heard three dialogues about gender roles, and a lot of aspects of the subject have come up. And notice that they are all practical issues that come out of the actual experience of couples here in the group. As the rest of you listened, I wonder if any of you identified with something the dialoguing couples talked about? Are there some questions that have been raised that we can look at now in a general discussion?

(A brisk conversation now gets going in which most of the members of the group take part. The time passes quickly and by 10:30 we are ready for a coffee break. When we resume, two further agenda items are taken up, and two more couples volunteer to try out the dialogue. At 11:40 we intervene to make an announcement.)

VERA: We need to interrupt you now because there's an exercise we'd like you to do before lunch. David will explain it to you.

DAVID: This exercise gets you into the second of our weekend objectives. After lunch, as you will see on the timetable we've put up, you're going to have an hour alone together for private dialogue. When you have finished lunch, we ask that you do no more socializing with other group members, but just go quietly off together to your room. We want you to have at least an hour of time alone together, without interruption. This is a very important stretch of time. Let me explain why.

You've already been looking at some of your growing edges. And now we want you to do this much more thoroughly, with the help of what we call the Marriage Potential Inventory. It's a kind of test each partner should do quite separately, and we're going to ask you to do it now. So please take a sheet of paper and a pencil. And it might be a good idea for you to change to another chair so you are not sitting next to your partner.

We want you to understand clearly that this test is something you do *privately* between yourselves. You don't have to turn it in to us, or to anyone else. It's just a way of enabling you to look together, very specifically, and in very positive terms, at the directions in which your marriage has the potential for new growth.

VERA: All ready? We're going to give you a list of ten areas of marriage, and they should be written one below the other; you should also leave a small space on the right of each item to enter a score. Let me now read the items so you can take them down. We prefer you to write them down yourself rather than giving you a handout.

(Vera reads the list of items, and explains how to score the test, as already described in Chapter 4. She tells the couples that, when they have finished, they should put the test away and go to lunch.)

Saturday Afternoon

(It is now 2:00 P.M., and the couples reassemble. Several concerns are shared.)

DAVID: We hope you found your private dialogue helpful. You know that, of course, there's no requirement for you to report what happened; but if any couples would really like to share something arising out of your time alone together, or need some help about an issue that came up, the group would be glad to hear from you now. Take a minute to talk to each other about this.

(Three couples respond. One couple ask a question about how they scored their items. Another report that they decided they were doing very poorly in the area of money management and have now made a commitment to try out an entirely new system. The third couple had realized that they have been unable to communicate in any meaningful way about negative feelings and ask for this subject to be put on the agenda. A discussion follows in which we as leaders provide some teaching on communication and conflict resolution, which is followed by several couples dialoguing on the subject and deciding to modify some of their policies and practices. The rest of the afternoon session is taken up with discussion of further agenda issues.)

Saturday Evening

(No concerns are expressed as we reassemble after dinner. The trust level of the group has grown steadily, and the decision is made to get into the subject of sexual fulfillment. Three couples volunteer to dialogue on this, and some very honest sharing follows. Further agenda items are then picked up. At 9:30 we intervene.)

VERA: We'd like to make a suggestion for the closing part of this session. We have already stressed the importance of positive affirmation between married partners, and we suggest that we now do a very simple exercise in which we express our appreciation to each other. Would you be agreeable to this?

(The group supports the proposal.)

DAVID: All right, let me explain the exercise. A romantic atmosphere is helpful, so we're going to light some candles and turn off the main light. We'll also rearrange ourselves so that as couples we can face each other directly and hold hands.

Vera and I will begin the exercise, and then you will all join in privately. The idea is to tell each other, warmly, what we appreciate about each other. It will be a dialogue in which we take only one turn each. In my turn I will say to Vera, "I love you because . . ." and reflectively share, one by one, the things about her that bring me joy and fulfillment. In her turn she will do the same.

So, we will begin, speaking so that you can all hear us. When we have finished, we will signal to you, and each of you will turn to each other privately and begin. When you have finished, please leave quietly together. The last couple to leave should blow out the candles.

Sunday Morning

(We reassemble at 9:00 A.M. Concerns are dealt with.)

VERA: This is our last session. For the first hour, we can talk about any agenda items that we feel we need to clear up. Then, before our coffee break, we have an exercise for you to do, to help you prepare for making a growth plan for your next year together.

(Several agenda items are taken up. At 10:00 A.M. we intervene.)

DAVID: Now it's time for our exercise. Each of you should write down a list of items under the title "What I want." There are three sections. First, "What I want for me." Second, "What I want for you." Third, "What I want for us." The idea is to look ahead to the next twelve months and to consider the desirable things you would like to see happen—for each of you separately, and for both of you together. We'll give you ten minutes to write down all you can think of.

Then we'll have a short coffee break, and after that you'll have forty minutes of time alone together. You can go to your room, or find a place where you won't be interrupted, and work together on a growth plan for your next year. Do it in any way you like, but here are our suggestions.

Take some paper with you, and try to draw up what we call a "Declaration of Intention"—just a general statement of goals you want to achieve, as separate persons and as a couple. Be sure that you agree on the wording of the statement, and then we suggest you both sign it. It's your own private document, to be kept for future reference.

You may want to add some contracts. Contracts are specific things you agree to do. They can be helpful to married couples, but they can also be dangerous. If you make contracts, we suggest you keep them separate from the main statement. And we suggest that they be reasonably possible things that you *could* carry out. We also think that contracts should be made for a short time only—

for instance, one week is a good way to start—and then renewed or renegotiated. It's demoralizing to have contracts around that you have failed to keep, so renew them or change them from time to time.

We'll expect you all back here again at 11:15 for our closing session. Then lunch, and you're on your way home.

(The couples complete the exercise and soon go off to prepare their growth plans. At 11:15 we reassemble.)

VERA: For the last time, we're giving you each a sheet of paper—each individually this time. What we want you to do is to write a ten-minute "spontaneous evaluation." This one *is* to be handed in. We want you to write down just how you feel about the experience you have had in this retreat. It should be anonymous, so you can be quite candid. Don't bother about style, spelling, or punctuation. Just jot down what you liked about the weekend and what you didn't like; what was helpful, and what wasn't. We always ask for these evaluations, because they help us to be aware of what is happening. We like appreciation, of course; but we also learn a lot from constructive criticism. So feel quite free to say whatever you feel or think.

(The participants write their evaluations, and they are collected.)

DAVID: We now want you as couples to prepare a brief report to be given verbally to the group. Decide on what you want to say, and decide which of you will say it. If you want suggestions, consider what you have learned or experienced here that has been new to you. Also, what you can do to follow up the experience. If there's anything special you want to say to the group, this is your last chance to say it. We'll give you ten minutes to prepare your report.

(The couples confer together. We then call the group to order.)

VERA: We'll follow our usual custom of not going around the circle! Who would like to start?

(In random order, one member of each couple, including one of us, report to the group.)

DAVID: For our final act, we suggest spending a period of silence together. Groups of the same religion like to close with some formal act of worship, but since we are a very mixed group, no particular form would necessarily suit us all. So we shall observe the Quaker custom of silence, which we can each use in any way we wish. If during the silence you have a thought you'd like to share with us all, go ahead and do so. We'll continue in relaxed silence for about five to ten minutes. Then we will stand up, and each couple will go to each other couple in the group and affirm them in any way we wish.

(The silence is observed, and the retreat ends with mutual affirmation all around.)

Some Further Comments

What I have described is typical of scores of retreats, perhaps hundreds, which we have led over the years. Of course the basic description is like bare bones, and all the interesting human detail has had to be left out. Something of that will appear in Chapter 17, when I quote some typical evaluations.

There are three aspects of the retreat about which a less experienced couple might feel some apprehension. They deserve some comment here:

The Absence of Structure. I admit that it takes some courage, and experience, to meet with a group of strangers and trust them, in the course of some fifteen to eighteen hours, to form themselves into a close, trusting, united, and sharing group. Yet for us a vital principle is at stake: that it is only when the group takes full responsibility for itself that it can function at the deepest possible level. In order to achieve this, we are prepared to take the risk of letting it flounder at times, and of asking for help when we don't know what to do next. We are even prepared to allow a crisis to develop, because we have found that there is nothing like working through a crisis to achieve group identity and solidarity.

However, I recognize that less experienced leaders may at first feel the need for a more structured program, and for the security they feel as a result of being "in charge." I will respond to this in the next chapter, where a much more structured model is described, one that can be viewed as an alternative.

The Use of the Dialogue. Again, inviting couples to get into dialogue early in the group process may seem premature. I will admit that it doesn't always work. However, if it *does* work, the progress the group makes is usually much more rapid than if dialogue was introduced later; and it is my invariable experience that, from the point when dialogue is accepted and used, the group stays "on course," and real sharing begins to take place, at increasing depth.

So I am willing to invite dialogue at this early state. If there are no volunteers, we do not press the matter; we offer alternatives, such as open discussion and exercises, to move the group along. But we always demonstrate the dialogue at an early point, indicate our hope that most couples will give it a try as we proceed, and explain that some couples might be more comfortable making a start in a smaller subgroup, or in a "foursome" with one other couple. If there is a response, we then act accordingly.

The Absence of Specific Teaching. Although I have made it clear that information giving alone is of very limited value, I have also stressed the importance of understanding our new concepts. In the retreat experience, we are ready to include short minilectures as they become relevant. But rather than putting them formally into the program, and treating the group as a class, we much prefer to offer knowledge informally as "teachable moments" arise. For example, if a couple explain to the group that they are having difficulty with communication in some areas, or are not handling anger effectively, or cannot reach agreement on some vital issue, it may be highly appropriate to let in some light through a brief explanation, and if possible the use of a diagram. Even then, however, the learning process is much more effective if the teaching can be given experientially, either through a report dialogue from the leader couple, or in response to an exploring or working dialogue from another couple or couples for whom the issue is a relevant one.

Next Steps for Participating Couples

There is obviously no way in which we can predict how the couples in any group will react to the retreat experience. They may come in very different states of readiness, ranging from some who are doubting and critical, to others who are in a highly "teachable moment." To some extent we can, with a flexible program, assess any special needs the participants may have and try to meet them. But in the end we cannot know precisely where they really are, or what they really need. All we can offer them is an environment that positively encourages experiential learning, experimental action, and commitment to future growth and change.

Likewise, we cannot predict what will happen to them after the retreat. We know for certain that the weekend can be for some the beginning of a new life of growth and creativity. We also know that, for others, good intentions formed during the retreat can soon evaporate.

It has been our custom, in the retreats we have led, to ask couples to consider seriously three particular "next steps" for following up the weekend experience:

1. Set aside about twenty minutes each day for keeping close to each other by the honest sharing of inner thoughts, feelings, and intentions.

2. Whenever an emotional crisis or conflict develops in the relationship, clear a period of "time alone together" to find out what is really happening and if possible to work it through.

3. If at all possible, join a support group of other couples committed to ongoing growth, who will meet at least once a month and make themselves accountable to one another. If no such existing group can be found, try to start one.

The experience of many couples with whom we have kept in touch indicates that, if they keep up this regimen for a year or so, their marriages reach and maintain high levels of creative relationship.

On our side, we take responsibility for the couples who have been in groups we have led. We tell them they can count on our further help if they ever need it, either directly or by referral to a qualified professional helper. And we assure them that they need never feel that nobody cares, because we do.

16

A MEDLEY OF MODELS

$\mathbf{A}$ GOOD deal has happened, in the way of development, in the twenty years since the marriage-enrichment movement began. Creative leaders have experimented with many options. This has been all to the good, because it has taught us a great deal. And of course, there is much that we still have to learn.

In the previous chapter, I described the kind of event that Vera and I, as pioneers, first developed and have continued to lead ever since. In this chapter, by way of contrast, I will outline briefly a very different pattern, which we have used extensively in recent years. Comparisons and contrasts will then enable us to evaluate the various criteria we will need to use in our attempt to improve the effectiveness of the services we are trying to offer.

Evolution of the Miniretreat

As interest in marriage enrichment began to spread, we realized that, if all concerned couples had to come, eight at a time, to a residential weekend retreat, the spread of the movement would be greatly delayed. At first, this didn't particularly bother us, because we needed time to test out both our theory and our practice. But as we became more confident about what we had to offer, it was obviously desirable to make it more widely available.

Out of this concern came the idea of an event that would take less time, involve a greater number of couples, and enable the participants to go home overnight. We realized that all these changes were likely to diminish the effectiveness of what we could achieve; yet it was clear that this was the price we must be prepared to pay in order to reach more couples.

When we had accepted this, we also found that a further disadvantage was involved. These new requirements would compel us to use a much more closely structured design, and to lose much of the flexibility to which we had become accustomed.

We went ahead, however, and what emerged was the miniretreat. It seemed to fall short of what the full retreat offered in so many respects that we chose to consider it as "an introduction to marriage enrichment," and express the hope that those who participated would be motivated to follow it up by fuller and deeper involvement in other events. This would still, I believe, be desirable. However, I now have to acknowledge that experience has shown the miniretreat to be a very meaningful experience for almost all couples who participate in it; and for some, who came in a state of considerable readiness for the experience, it has had a powerful and lasting impact.

I will defer further discussion until later and proceed now to describe what happens. There will be no need to go into the same amount of detail as I did in the last chapter. I will outline the program by reporting on an actual miniretreat Vera and I led quite recently, with a few variations to fill out the picture.

An Event for Seventy-one Couples

In response to an invitation, seventy-one couples gathered in a retreat center that belonged to a religious organization. Most of the couples stayed overnight, though some went home and returned in the morning. We had at our disposal one large auditorium, where we not only held all the retreat sessions, but where all meals were also served by the kitchen staff. The food was prepared while our sessions were proceeding and was brought in on trays and trolleys at the appropriate times. All food was eaten at tables for six persons each, scattered about the auditorium.

Dinner began at 6:00 P.M. on Friday evening, after which the tables were quickly cleared. Promptly at 7:00 P.M., the retreat began. Vera and I sat on a slightly raised platform at one end of the room, with clip-on microphones so that we could be clearly heard without the need to raise our voices.

We began with a welcome to the group and some basic instructions. The three objectives were explained, and we made it very clear that the event could proceed smoothly only if we all observed strict punctuality. We checked our watches to make sure of this.

We then asked the couples to relax and close their eyes, while we led them in the guided memory fantasy I have already described. They then turned to each other as couples and shared some of the happy memories they had recalled.

Next we introduced ourselves, taking ten minutes to answer what we have called the "eight questions." These incorporate the questions most often asked about each other by the couples who have been with us in retreats through the years. Every couple in the miniretreat had a copy. Here are the questions:

1. Where do you come from?
2. How did you first meet?
3. How long have you been married?
4. Have you any children?
5. What are your vocations?
6. Why did you decide to come to this retreat?
7. What are your *hopes* for this experience?
8. Do you have any *fears* about this experience?

We then explained that, since it was impossible for seventy-one couples to get acquainted in any realistic fashion during the weekend, we would arrange them in groups of three couples each, using the numbers they had already been given during dinner. We indicated the location of each of the twenty-four groups, and quite quickly these got together and pulled chairs into circles. Each group was asked to appoint a timekeeper. The total allowed was thirty minutes, so each couple had ten minutes to introduce themselves, using the eight questions. Since one group was one couple short, we joined that one.

Long experience has taught us the fantastic appropriateness of the three-couple group for the four half-hour meetings the miniretreat provides. With four couples, one seems always to be left out of the inner circle. We have also learned never to appoint "leader" couples in the group—they talk too much and tend to be viewed as authority figures. We have also learned not to go around "visiting" the groups, because we find we only interrupt what they are doing.

After the groups, we took a fifteen-minute break, with coffee and tea available. Then, reassembled, we all took ten minutes to write the "three-things" exercise as already described. Vera and I then openly shared with each other what we had written, by way of "modeling" the exercise. The couples briefly "checked in" with each other, to decide whether the exercise had raised any issue in their relationship that they would not be comfortable about sharing in the small group. The groups then met together for another half hour, each couple having ten minutes to share the things they had written down about their marriage. This brought us to 10:00 P.M., our closing time.

We had now, in three hours, introduced the couples to the plan for the weekend and introduced ourselves to them all. Each of them had similarly introduced themselves to two other couples. They had reaffirmed each other as couples by reviving happy experiences from the past. They had begun to take an honest look at their marriages and shared what they comfortably could with two other couples. We, for our part, had demonstrated the leadership process of teaching, modeling what we had taught on our own experience of marriage.

We reassembled on Saturday morning at 9:00 A.M., after the 8:00 A.M. breakfast had been cleared away. Our beginning exercise for all was to write down all the feelings we could identify in ourselves as we relaxed and listened to our "inner voices." After ten minutes of this, Vera and I, by way of modeling, took a further ten minutes to share openly the eight or nine feelings we had identified in ourselves. For yet another ten minutes, following our example, the couples shared privately their lists of feelings, and then checked, as we had already done, how many of their partners' feelings they would have known about, or guessed, if they had not been told.

With this leadin, we were ready for the first teaching session, taking about twenty minutes, on "couple communication." We told them about the importance of being open to each other, and of being able to communicate effectively. We explained some of the new knowledge couples can use in improving their communication systems: the importance of self-awareness (already demonstrated in our opening exercise); the value of self-disclosure as an essential step toward attaining intimacy; how to avoid misunderstandings by completing communication cycles; how to learn to understand our use of the four communication styles; and the vital importance of affirming each other.

Following this minilecture, we asked them to join us in an exercise to take a closer look at our own communication systems. We all wrote down:

1. areas in our relationship where our communication is very good and clear
2. areas where we *are* communicating but there is room for improvement
3. any areas where we are not communicating at all.

We then modeled for five minutes and they went back to their groups for ten minutes of sharing for each couple, having first "checked in" on any issues not to be shared.

After all this, there was a fifteen-minute break, with coffee or tea available. We then reassembled for a short talk about marital growth (about fifteen minutes), after which, explaining that growth in our relationships is basically the claiming of our potential, we explained the Marriage Potential Inventory (MPI) and asked them each to check this separately, without any collaboration.

We had already explained to the couples that the hour after lunch was set aside as their private time together, to look in depth at their marriages as they had rated them in terms of their relational potential. We explained that, after they had left the lunch table, there would be no talk with others, and no socializing, until they both returned together for the 2:00 P.M. session. In that private hour, they should go to their rooms, or to someplace where they could not be interrupted, and share how they had each scored the MPI, discussing how they could work together for future relational growth.

At 2:00 P.M., we moved into the area of conflict and anger: first a minilecture for about thirty minutes, after which we as leaders dialogued about how we learned to process anger in our own relationship. Following this, we all did the anger exercise, writing down responses as follows:

1. *Causes*. What kinds of situations make me angry with you?
2. *Feelings*. How do I *feel* when I get angry with you?
3. *Actions*. What do I *do* when I feel angry with you?
4. *Wishes*. What do I *wish we could both do* when we get angry with each other?

After "checking in" together, they then all joined their groups for thirty minutes of sharing, as before.

Following a fifteen-minute break, we now explained the making of a growth plan and contracts, as already described. We all did the "I want" exercise; then they scattered as couples for some forty minutes, each couple working on their "Declaration of Intention" for their next year together.

When they reassembled for closing, we modeled the positive affirmation exercise, and then they responded privately. Finally, after a closing period of silence, all couples affirmed the other two who had shared in their small group (usually with a group hug); and, with warm and tender farewells, we went on our way.

Some Criteria for Evaluation

On the basis of this somewhat sketchy account, we may now consider briefly the wide range of differences that can exist in events, all of which answer to the general description of "marriage enrichment." It would require another book to explore all the comparisons and contrasts between the many models that now exist. Here we will confine ourselves to five obvious criteria.

1. *Length of the Event*. The ACME standard requires the involvement of the couples for a minimum of fifteen hours to define a valid marriage-enrichment experience, and in my judgment this represents a wise standard to set. Even that is too brief for some couples who are unaccustomed to group interaction. It takes some time for the new couple to grasp the basic principles of marriage enrichment, and to feel comfortable enough in the unfamiliar environment to begin to benefit from the experience.

This minimum implies fifteen hours of *planned activity*, viewed as a continuous and cumulative experience.

The essence of a "retreat" is that you are away from your normal day-to-day activities. The Marriage Encounter firmly insists on no telephone calls and no radio or TV for the participants while the event continues.

2. *Number of Participating Couples*. I have already indicated that, where open sharing in the group is involved, our experience clearly indicates that eight couples represent the outside limit; five or six is the ideal number, and four the minimum for a full retreat or growth group. If the number registered falls below four, we normally cancel the event.

If there is no couple-to-couple sharing, of course, these limits don't matter. This is true of the Marriage Encounter, which allows only social and religious interaction; so, as we have seen, fifteen couples represent a desirable group. And the miniretreat is very flexible as to numbers—the largest group we have led consisted of 150 couples. It is possible, however, as I have demonstrated, to provide for couple-to-couple sharing, on a limited basis, even with large numbers involved.

3. *Residential or Nonresidential*. Here we are concerned with events that allow the couples to go home overnight. As the cost of hotel rooms has risen higher and higher, it has become increasingly difficult for some couples to afford participation in marriage-enrichment events. So some other answers have had to be found. We have personally led retreats in which the couples used tents or travel trailers. We have known of some couples who had their children farmed out to grandparents or friends, so they could return home without involvement. In one instance, the couples swapped homes for the nights concerned, so they wouldn't have to take phone calls or be accosted by neighbors. But it is hard to remove all distractions.

Of course, ACME has recognized an alternative in the "growth group" with a series of weekly meetings, considered fully equivalent to a retreat when led by a qualified leader couple. Continuity is indeed hard to resume between one weekly meeting and the next, and we recommend a longer total period together in such events (six to eight weekly meetings). On the other hand, a compensating advantage is gained, because the couples have time to do extensive "homework" between meetings. One careful study made a comparison between a retreat and a growth group, matched as closely as possible, and found that in terms of pretests, posttests, and followup the growth group couples made significantly greater progress.

4. *Structured or Unstructured*. One of the major differences in retreat patterns is concerned with the extent to which a structured program is or is not employed. By structure, I mean a closely planned pattern predetermined in advance. I can think of one model for which a detailed manual is used by the leader couple, and this tells them exactly what they should be doing at any and every moment after the couples are assembled.

Such closely structured designs are often welcomed by leaders who have received limited training and experience, and who would feel very insecure if they had to cope with any diversion from the precise instructions they have been given. I have met couples for whom participation in such events has been beneficial, so they cannot be dismissed as inadequate. However, ACME's unwillingness to accept events in which the participating couples have no part in program planning is probably wise. Since unexpected situations inevitably arise when couples interact, departure from the planned program should at least be accepted as a possibility.

5. *Type of Leadership Involved*. In all the three original patterns of marriage

enrichment, leadership by married couples has been the invariable rule. Marriage Encounter has developed team leadership in the form of several couples and a priest. These are selected with care, but are not required to be trained in marital interaction or group dynamics (the programs they lead do not involve them in facilitation, since no group sharing is permitted). In the Marriage Communication Lab, normally only clergy couples are trained for leadership, and at least one spouse is expected to be a professionally qualified helper. In ACME, a carefully designed process of selection, training, and certification is required for all leader couples (explained in Appendix 3).

A few marriage-enrichment events are led by an individual, usually a professional, and occasionally two professionals as co-leaders. This of course excludes the possibility of a modeling and sharing leadership, and would seem to me to be a decided disadvantage.

It is clear that, with the passage of time, our understanding of what is most effective in marriage-enrichment events will steadily improve. Wide experimentation with different methods and approaches should increase our understanding, and none of us can at this stage in the development of marriage enrichment be dogmatic about what works best. (We shall return to this subject in Chapter 21, "Testing the New Product: Research.")

17

RECRUITMENT AND FOLLOWUP

HOW do couples react to the retreat experience? Here are a few excerpts from typical anonymous evaluations—all from one group of six couples.

"My horizons have widened, there is yet more that we as a couple can experience, and I am feeling a great deal of excitement about it. I feel in the company of the 'enlightened few' who reach beyond their dreams and expectations to find there is more and more."

"I feel like another light bulb has been turned on. I have achieved a greater understanding of my self and my spouse. But most of all I have experienced a deeper level of experiencing our relationship."

"I have learned new ways to be with the person I love most. I have experienced growth. I have made commitment. I have felt love, warmth, acceptance, joy, comfort, and peace."

"This weekend has brought a new commitment between my spouse and myself, to work on areas of our relationship that need attention. We are taking home a specific plan for continuing growth. I am very excited about it all!"

"I feel good, warm, and cleansed. I have experienced insight into my marriage that will enable me to be a loving, giving spouse in a new way."

"I have always felt that my wife and I had a great marriage, and now with the skills we have acquired this weekend, I know that we can grow and make our relationship even greater than we ever thought possible."

"I'm glad I came, and I am the richer for what I have experienced. The retreat was very meaningful for my spouse and me. We had no big breakthrough, but that was not where we were. It was more of a time to reflect on where we want to be, and this proved very helpful.''

"This time together has been a major turning point for me personally and for our marriage. Through sharing with other couples we were all brought close together, and the group really became a community."

"I've experienced a closer relationship with my spouse, and we are now committed to develop our relationship in greater depth than ever before. Above all, we now feel that we know how to deal with conflict creatively."

We have accumulated hundreds of testimonies of this kind, from four continents. They demonstrate beyond doubt that the couples' weekend proves to be, for most of those who participate in it, a significant experience. However, the anonymous evaluations turned in by these couples do not hesitate to respond also to our invitation to offer candid criticism. We welcome this, and we get it. But we find, again and again, that the criticisms cancel each other out: there was too much teaching, there was too little; the pace was too slow, it was too fast; there were too many exercises, there were not enough; the leadership was too assertive, it was not assertive enough. These differences simply indicate that couples have different needs and come in different states of readiness. We monitor the complaints carefully; and as long as they roughly cancel each other out, over time if not in a particular group, we assume that all is well. If on the other hand a particular criticism keeps recurring, we take it seriously and make the necessary changes in our procedures. We encourage all leader couples we train to follow this process, developing a flexible style that is comfortable for them, and that seems best to meet the expressed needs of those with whom they work.

In all the years Vera and I have been involved in leading retreats, I can recall only one person who was completely and openly negative. He previously had been deeply involved in groups that used a great deal of open confrontation, and he regarded our procedures as so low-key that he considered the weekend a waste of time. Interestingly enough, his wife went out of her way to tell us that she didn't agree with him!

Over time, as our corporate experience grows, we shall find better and better ways of achieving our goal: to create an environment in which the three objectives of the weekend can best be met. No doubt now remains that the marriage-enrichment group represents a powerful medium for growth and change in many married couples.

The weekend experience in itself, however, does not represent the totality of marriage enrichment. In some quarters there has been a tendency to assign to the weekend miraculous qualities, as though it represented a passage from darkness into light.

Although we understand the enthusiasm that leads to such optimistic judgments, we cannot agree with them. Growth and change are processes that take place over time, and they cannot happen in one weekend.

What then *does* happen to cause people to be so enthusiastic about the retreat experience? The couples experience *attitudinal change,* which may or may not be transmuted later into *behavioral change,* depending on how far the couples put what they have learned *into action.*

This does not diminish the value of what happens during the retreat. I believe that a change in attitude is always needed to provide the dynamic for a subsequent change in behavior. The dynamic for change is *hope;* and what happens in the retreat is that it reawakens the dream with which most couples enter marriage, but which so often ends in disillusionment as the stern realities of life are confronted, without the insights and skills that are necessary to process them so as to make the dream come true.

It is therefore necessary to put the central experience of participation in the couples' weekend into a much broader perspective. We need to understand where couples have been *before* the experience, and what motivated them to seek it. We also need to know what we expect to happen to them *after* the experience. In this chapter we shall consider these two critical questions: recruitment and followup.

Recruitment for Marriage Enrichment

The average couple, when invited to a marriage-enrichment weekend, react by becoming defensive. What their behavior is saying is, "Look, *we* don't need that kind of thing. Our marriage is all right." Everyone who has seriously tried to enlist couples is very familiar with this reaction. It is a discouraging experience, and many who begin with great enthusiasm for "spreading the word" ultimately give up the task as just being too difficult.

It *is* difficult. The couple who themselves have discovered new fulfillment in their relationship feel a strong urge to recommend this exciting and rewarding experience to their friends and associates; and when they meet evasion, or even a sharp rebuff, it seems almost as if they had offered a precious gift and had it rudely rejected. As one couple expressed it, "We are offering other couples what they want most of all in the world, and they are treating us as if we had insulted them."

What lies behind this negative reaction? Let us try to analyze what is happening. There must be many components of this defensive attitude. I can think immediately of four of them:

1. "This is an invasion of our privacy. What you are asking us to do is to open up areas of our lives that concern us alone, and are nobody else's business." Here we have, of course, the intermarital taboo. In our urban society today, this taboo can with advantage be relaxed a good deal; but I also hold very strongly that the relaxation should take place entirely voluntarily in a group of couples in which trust has developed. Unfortunately, the average couple have never experienced this kind of warmth and trust, and consequently have no understanding of what it could do for them. Their attitude must therefore be sympathetically understood.

2. *"If we went to a retreat, we might have to take off our masks and be revealed as we really are. What would this do to our self-esteem?"* This is simply another aspect of privatism. The need for privacy is in itself healthy and legitimate. But it gets mixed up with a less creditable need to maintain our self-esteem by projecting a false image of ourselves upon our friends and associates. We have all heard dramatic stories of persons who, like the Doctor Jekyll and Mr. Hyde of Robert Louis Stevenson's famous story, lived a double life. But we are not so comfortable about admitting that to some extent all of us do this. In order to conceal the less creditable aspects of our behavior, we wear masks (the literal meaning of the Latin word *persona*) in the presence of those upon whom we want to make a good impression. We do this particularly as married couples. The result is that to acknowledge what is really going on in our relationship may literally mean a "loss of face." This is one reason why it is easier to go to our first marriage enrichment retreat with total strangers, rather than with other couples we know socially.

3. *"If we become involved in this marriage enrichment business, we might get into painful areas of our relationship—conflicts we haven't resolved, issues we're too uncomfortable to talk about. We prefer to let sleeping dogs lie."* This is of course a defeatist attitude; but most of us are cowards at heart when it comes to facing up to areas of deficiency in our lives. And I suspect that there are a few "skeletons in the closet" in most marriages. It is of course tragic that these unresolved issues don't get cleared up, because doing so could bring so much happiness that otherwise will be missed. But this is simply a fact about people that calls for our compassion rather than for harsh judgment.

4. *"You are suggesting that we may have 'marriage problems,' and that is somewhat of a insult and makes us feel inadequate and inferior."* Unfortunately, our culture has created a climate in which any expressed wish to improve your marriage may be interpreted as an indication that you are "in trouble," which carries a subtle suggestion of incompetence and humiliation. This was dramatically demonstrated at an interprofessional workshop Vera and I conducted in which no lawyers took part. When we asked why, we were told that the local bar association had declined the invitation with the comment, "We resent the implication that our marriages could be better than they are." They would not, surely, have reacted in this way to an invitation to improve their golf, or even their professional practice of law!

We must, therefore, accept as reality the discomfort that couples generally feel when offered an experience of marriage enrichment. Nearly all couples who are now committed to the cause have acknowledged that when they attended their first retreat, they did so with a good deal of apprehension.

As I have pondered this situation, I have come to see clearly that we need to provide these people with "stepping stones." The concept is of a couple standing on the bank of a stream and being invited to take part in something interesting on the other side. But there is no bridge, and crossing the stream would mean getting wet and uncomfortable. It is too broad to get over with a single leap; yet a few flat rocks, suitably placed, could make it possible to get over dry-shod.

So we can best help these hesitant couples by providing intermediate steps—experiences that will enable them to observe what it is all about and even to get a little taste of what it feels like, without any extensive commitment on their part. This is of course achieved to some extent when a couple who have been through the experience tell their friends, in the form of simple testimony, what it has meant to them and invite their friends to try it for themselves. Provided this is not done in a coercive or aggressive manner, it has the power of personal recommendation and may be all that is needed. One simple way of doing this is to invite a few couples into your home, with the express purpose of telling them about marriage enrichment and answering their questions, with no further obligations. In ACME's early days we prepared two cassettes that could be used by couples for such informal meetings in their homes.

Explaining What Enrichment Means

More recently, a two-step process has been developed. The first step is what we call an E and D meeting—explanation and demonstration. In every community there are organizations—churches, PTAs, and the like—which have regular programs and which welcome speakers on topics of general interest. It is much easier to attend a regular meeting to which you might go anyway from time to time, and hear a talk about marriage enrichment, than to go to a specially organized gathering on that subject, where people might ask themselves, "I wonder why the Joneses came to this? Is it possible they are having marriage problems?" The E and D meeting, however, is not just a matter of making a speech. In the first place, the organizers should make it known that it will last for at least two hours, preferably with a coffee break in the middle. It should also be announced that the speakers will be one or more married couples. The first half of the meeting should be an explanation of what marriage enrichment means. Vera and I have found it helpful to use diagrams, to include some personal testimony, and to do some informal dialoguing with each other. In the second half, we ask the audience to imagine that they are a group of about six couples spending a weekend together, and that we will demonstrate, without involving them personally, some of the things that might happen. For example, we might ask the audience to suggest subjects for an agenda and then we could choose a topic and dialogue it briefly. We may invite them to write down a simple exercise, which they might consider doing experimentally later at home with their marriage partners. We often close by positively affirming each other, and suggesting that this is a nice thing for a couple to do privately at home.

These demonstrations go over very well. Participants don't need to come on a couple basis. They can ask questions, and they often do. The atmosphere is very relaxed, and people tell us they enjoy it. Often they say, "Now we see what you do, and we realize there's nothing to be afraid of."

We always invite participants to leave their names, addresses, and phone numbers on a sheet of paper, to indicate that they would be interested at some later time in coming to a miniretreat or a full retreat. We assure them that this involves no obligation; it just means that we'll inform them of further programs. Those who attend generally talk about the meeting later among their friends, and the word gets out to many more people.

The second stepping-stone is the miniretreat, which I illustrated in the last chapter. As its name implies, it is a shortened version of the weekend experience and usually covers three hours on Friday evening and all day Saturday, omitting or including the evening. A good place to meet is a church, which seldom has other major programs on Friday night and Saturday. Couples usually go home overnight, but they take some meals together: supper on Friday (mainly to enable us to start on time); lunch on Saturday; and supper if we are going on into the evening. Sometimes we arrange child care so that parents can come.

The miniretreat introduces the couples to all the major components of a full weekend; but no deep involvement takes place, because time for group interaction is very limited and occasionally it may be omitted altogether. It is explained to the couples that there is an inevitable sense of pressure because of the large numbers involved and the shortage of time, and that this would not occur in a full weekend retreat. Of course, the participants are invited at the end to sign up, if they are willing, for a full retreat later. My own experience has indicated that many of them may do so. Those who don't sign up usually explain that the miniretreat has been helpful, and that it has met their needs for the time being.

These recruitment procedures have been found useful in providing stepping-stones for couples who would not be ready at once to move into the full weekend experience. These and other similar methods and procedures are described in greater detail in the ACME handbook *Toward Better Marriages* (Hopkins and Mace, 1978). Other ways and means will no doubt be developed; and, as marriage enrichment becomes widely understood, the need for these intermediate steps may not be as great as it has been up to now.

Followup: What Happens after the Event?

In 1974 Myrle Swicegood, a Ph.D. candidate at the University of North Carolina, completed her doctoral dissertation. It was a careful, competent piece of work, based on a series of marriage-enrichment retreats led by Vera and myself. Myrle and her husband, George, had first attended two of our retreats themselves and studied our procedures. She then prepared pretest and posttest instruments, which were completed by the couples before and after the retreats for which the evaluation was made.

Of the forty-six persons who completed the forms, forty-two definitely reported that their marriages had been improved, and most of the tests confirmed that significant changes had taken place in their relationships. This was a gratifying result then, and is even more so now, because, in the years that have since elapsed, our procedures have been greatly improved.

However, there was one disappointment. Followup inquiries addressed to some of the couples, though not undertaken as thoroughly as the original investigation, showed that the changes that occurred as a result of the retreat had not always been maintained over time. Some of the couples had found that, without continuing support from other couples, they had lost some of their incentive for ongoing growth.

This of course was not surprising. However, faced with the fact in this realistic way, we decided that it must be taken seriously. ACME was at that time just one year old; and retreats were being organized on a wide scale, since this seemed the obvious course to follow. We actually maintained a fairly lengthy waiting list of couples seeking to get involved, because we did not have enough trained and experienced leader couples to meet the demands.

The decision made at that time was that we had an obligation to provide "support systems" for the couples who had made their commitment to growth. Since then, the major function of the local ACME chapter has been perceived as being the provision of such support systems. The way this is done is described in detail in the ACME Handbook.

The followup process, when fully carried out, occurs in three directions (see Table 4). The first is the steadily increasing quality of the couple's own relationship until it blossoms into full flower in the enriched marriage. The second direction is the sharing of their new experiences with their children or other close relatives, finding its culmination over time in enrichment of the life of the total family. The third direction is involvement in service to the community, leading ultimately for a few to full accreditation as leader couples skilled in facilitating marriage-enrichment events. Let us trace the stages through which a couple would move if they achieved all of these goals.

For most couples it is desirable to follow up the weekend with further shared experiences. In the Marriage Encounter this can be done by joining an Image Group or taking part in a Marriage Reencounter weekend. ACME strongly recommends couples to take the full twelve-hour Couple Communication course, although ideally we would like this to be done *before* the retreat. ACME also provides special followup weekends or growth groups in such areas as sexual enrichment, conflict resolution, money management, handling of anger, gender roles, and similar issues that frequently are featured in the programs of chapter

TABLE 4
Followup Activities for Couples

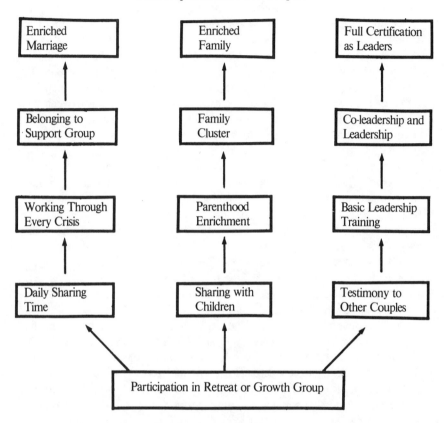

meetings. The principle is to provide whatever the couples seem to need for their continuing growth. Some couples like to move from the weekend directly into a growth group meeting on a weekly basis, and in fact this can be the full equivalent of the weekend itself, with certified leadership.

For their own personal followup, I have found it to be very helpful for couples to establish the daily sharing time, when they open up their inner thoughts, feelings, and needs to each other, in order to keep in touch with what is happening to them day by day. The Marriage Encounter considered this so important that the "ten and ten" (ten minutes to write down your thoughts and feelings, ten minutes to share them with your partner) was at first a rigid requirement for "encountered" couples. Although obviously it is not wise to impose this, I must admit that my own marriage would soon begin to deteriorate if we gave up our established habit of starting the day with a period of sharing. It is disturbingly easy, without this daily reopening of the channels of communication in depth, to lose touch with each other and begin to drift apart.

Another vital element in continuing growth is a firm commitment that every marital crisis will be thoroughly worked through until harmony has been reestablished in the relationship. By a "marital crisis" I mean any conflict, any situation involving anger against each other, any important decision or major adjustment. What I mean by "working through" is arriving at a positive solution that is acceptable to both partners and can turn the situation into a growth experience. Failure to do this is to reject the raw materials out of which constructive change comes about, and to allow barriers to build up between husband and wife. This can only be surely avoided where a solemn contract has been made to work everything through together, seeking outside help if necessary.

These commitments can best be carried out if the couple are members of a support group. This consists usually of five or six couples who agree to make themselves accountable to each other, which means keeping the group informed of their progress and seeking or rendering any help or encouragement that may be needed. Support groups do not need certified leaders. They meet informally, usually in each other's homes, once a month at least, and normally contracting to do so for about a year at a time. At one meeting of a long-established ACME chapter, couples who had been involved for as long as five years testified, over and over again, that the key to their real relational development had been the support groups to which they had belonged.

The second level for followup is the expansion of marriage enrichment into family enrichment. It begins when the couple, following the weekend, gather their children together and share with them the new commitments they have made to each other. I have heard many moving accounts of this experience; and Vera and I, at the invitation of the couple concerned, actually shared in one of them. I hope that someday a study can be made of the impact on children of their parents' marriage enrichment experience. We have observed on many occasions the warmth and openness of communication that exists in the homes of ACME couples.

Here is a testimony from one ACME couple, taken from an issue of the ACME newsletter. The wife writes:

> Today we celebrated the marriage of our first daughter. She watched as Jim and I moved from a painful marriage relationship, and as we became involved in marriage enrichment. She watched as we experienced conflict, and as we struggled to learn to deal with it. She watched as we learned simple communication skills, and as we struggled to put them into practice. She hung in there with us as we turned a painful parent-child relationship into a close, loving relationship. She taught us the beauty of forgiveness—forgiveness of mistakes made as parents. And she taught us the endless love of the child-parent relationship.
>
> Marriage enrichment has helped us become what we are today. We celebrate that, and celebrate that we have been able to share with each of our children the

journey we have traveled through our marriage. We think their marriages, and their families, will be much stronger because of watching their parents grow—grow together as a couple, and grow together as a family.

Today we celebrate the marriage of a daughter—and again we celebrate our own marriage. How blessed we are to be able to love—and to be loved.

A natural step for a couple to take after the marriage-enrichment experience is to sign up for a parenthood-enrichment course. The best-known program is Parent Effectiveness Training (PET), an excellent course devised by psychologist Thomas Gordon and fully described in his book *Parent Effectiveness Training* (1970). But there are other similar courses. One is the Positive Parents Program developed by the Family Communication Skills Center of the National YMCA, 350 Sharon Park Drive, A-23, Menlo Park, California 94025. Another program is Systematic Training for Effective Parenting (STEP), developed by Dr. Don Dinkmeyer and Dr. Gary McKay. A special program is the Minnesota Early Learning Design (MELD), 123 East Grant Street, Minneapolis, Minnesota 55403, which is like ACME in that parents who have had their first child form groups for new parents expecting their first child. And there are other programs; information can be secured by writing the Parent/Early Childhood and Special Programs Office, U.S. Department of Education, 400 Maryland Avenue, SW, Washington, D.C. 20202.

Parenthood enrichment naturally leads to whole family enrichment. The major pioneer in this field has been Margaret Sawin, who has developed the family cluster movement, described in her 1979 book *Family Enrichment with Family Clusters*. It brings several families together in a cooperative unit in which, over a period of time, they contract to help and support each other in the achievement of more effective family living. For a number of years, training for leadership of whole family enrichment programs has been offered in June in North Carolina. This is a new field bound to develop in the future. Among others, Father Gabriel Calvo, the founder of Marriage Encounter, has now developed a new organization called Family Inter-Communications Relationships, Experiences and Services (FIRES), 1425 Otis Street, NE, Washington, D.C. 20017.

The third level for followup begins when the couple share their new experience with friends and associates. Beginning as simple testimony, this can develop into a number of outreach approaches to the community as a whole. Marriage Encounter invites suitable encountered couples to undergo team training with the object of sharing in the leadership team of a subsequent couples' weekend, where they give their testimonies in the form of carefully prepared "talks," which have been "critiqued" in advance by the other members of the team.

ACME has experimented with what are called "extension growth groups." Three ACME couples form a kind of nuclear team and join up with an equal number of persons from various categories: six young adults of both sexes; three engaged couples; three couples in marriage counseling (with the approval of their counselors); six recently divorced men and women. The idea is that the ACME couples share their marital experiences with the others in the group, providing models of healthily growing marriages and at the same time offering their friendship, help, and support. Not enough has so far been done to produce reliable data, but the experiments have had encouraging results. One very imaginative experiment was carried out with a group of men in prison who were soon due for release, and whose wives were permitted to participate.

Some couples, aspiring to become leader couples themselves, register for ACME basic training as facilitators. If they also meet selection requirements, they can then be given Provisional Certification by ACME, and proceed to co-lead retreats and then lead them alone, finally taking Advanced Training and receiving Full Certification after at least a year (see Appendix 3).

These three possible paths are open for the couple to follow after they have been through the weekend retreat or growth group. We need to see clearly that, although the weekend is a critical experience of major importance, it is also part of a long continuum that normally stretches out over a number of years— from the first awareness of the concept of enrichment to the point at which the couple are secure and happy together in a truly creative interpersonal relationship, surrounded by growing or adult children who have come to be part of an enriched family, and possibly involved in rendering services for the promotion of better marriages and families in their community and the nation.

PART FOUR

Enriching Marital Therapy and Education

An attempt is made to relate the new ideas and processes used in marriage enrichment to our existing ways of serving families. An account of the historical development of marital therapy suggests that it has the necessary flexibility to incorporate many marriage-enrichment concepts. Family-life education and marriage preparation are reviewed as attempts to provide preventive service, and their limitations evaluated. The promising possibilities of working with couples through their first critical year together are explored.

18

GROWTH-ORIENTED
MARRIAGE COUNSELING?

W HAT I have been presenting in the preceding chapters represents a new approach to the increasingly high incidence of marriage and family breakdown in our culture. It amounts to a major shift from a remedial to a preventive emphasis. As yet it is mainly experimental, but what has already been tried out seems to offer considerable promise.

We now need to examine the relationship between programs for marriage enrichment and the existing services we are offering to those who need help in managing their marital and family relationships. These existing services fall into two broad categories: marriage and family counseling, and education for marriage and family living. I shall try to examine these two fields, in relation to the perspectives I have so far defined in this book, in this and the following chapter.

Our Marriage Counseling Services

It may be considered an oversight that, so far in this book, I have said very little about marriage counseling. After all, the establishment of counseling services represents what is undoubtedly our most significant organized response to the widespread increase in marital breakdown that has developed in our time. In this country and in many others, a well-qualified corps of dedicated men and women now stand ready to help couples who are in trouble. Some serve in community agencies, some are in private practice. And in addition to those who have specialized exclusively in this field, tens of thousands of other professionals in allied fields, such as medicine, psychiatry, psychology, social work, the ministry, education, law, and nursing, take time out from their other duties to render at least first aid, and often much more than first aid, to marriages in distress.

I am neither uninformed about, nor indifferent to, these important facts. I have, in fact, spent the major portion of my professional life in developing marriage-counseling services across the world. I wrote the first book that was ever published (*Marriage Counselling,* 1948) on the subject. I devoted seven full years of my life (1942–49) to developing the marriage-counseling services in Britain, and another seven (1960–67) to building up the American Association of Marriage Counselors (now the American Association for Marriage and Family Therapy) in this country. In addition, I was actively involved in the initiation of the marriage-counseling services in Australia, New Zealand, and South Africa, as well as in a number of European countries. For fourteen years I was chairman of the International Commission on Marriage and Marriage Guidance, set up by the International Union of Family Organizations, a consultative body of the U.N. and of UNESCO. All this I did because I was deeply convinced that these services were greatly needed and would enable us to weather the crisis in marriage through which I believed we were about to pass.

Have I then changed my mind about the importance of marriage counseling? My reply is an emphatic no.

I am still deeply convinced that marriage-counseling services are very much needed. I vividly remember spending a full day in a Moscow divorce court in 1960, listening to the stories of the couples who came before the troika of judges. As they unfolded their sad tales of conflict and stress, and the judges struggled to make wise decisions, again and again I wanted to say, "Look, you can't deal with this kind of material in the setting of a court of law. Why don't you refer these couples to marriage counselors who would have the time and the skill to sort it all out?" Then I realized that there were no marriage counselors as such in the USSR at that time, and what a tragic lack that was. So I am profoundly grateful that we have well-qualified marriage counselors at our disposal, and proud to know that I had a share in making this possible.

I am very happy, too, to know that good marriage counselors today are very good indeed. Our knowledge of the field has expanded vastly since my little book, now no more than a museum specimen, was written. Our training procedures are being continually refined and upgraded, and professional marriage counselors today fully deserve the hard-won recognition they are now at last receiving. Elsewhere in the world, too, I see everywhere the maturing of this new professional specialty.

What I have now come to recognize, however, is that however good they are, marriage counselors alone, with their present almost exclusively remedial orientation, do not provide a sufficient answer to the grave crisis marriage is passing through in our culture. Let me try to make this very clear.

All too often, the marriage counselor represents a last resort for the couple in difficulty. Again and again I have listened to couples describing the degeneration of a relationship upon which they had embarked with high hopes and strong motivation. It was all too easy to trace the course of events that had brought these couples relentlessly to their final state of misery. Some of these events were the unavoidable consequences of innate incapacity in the individuals concerned, or of hostile factors in their environment. But far more often, the cause was the gross mismanagement of the relationship through tragic ignorance and the lack of the coping skills I described earlier in this book. As I listened, I was saddened and frustrated to think that it might all have been very different if these people had had the kind of experiences marriage enrichment is now learning to provide.

Of course it was possible for me, using knowledge the couples did not possess, to explain all this to them, and try to help them to start all over again and do it right this time. That's what successful marriage counseling is all about. But this doesn't always work. Often one or both of the partners have become so hurt, so alienated, so disillusioned, that they simply cannot summon up the motivation for so arduous a task. It may seem to them more attractive to get out of the atmosphere of strain and pain the relationship has come to mean, in order to gain a haven of peaceful detachment in which a battered ego can slowly recover. Or it may seem more sensible to ditch this relationship, around which so many negative feelings have developed, and to start afresh with someone else and hope it will turn out better (as it sometimes, though not always, does) the second time around.

In other words, much of our marriage counseling has to be done in circumstances that represent almost the worst possible strategic opportunity to use the knowledge and skill we have spent years in accumulating. At any earlier time in the history of the relationship, if these people had only been motivated to seek our help, we could have achieved much more in much less time.

All counselors have to cope with this awareness. Some become quite philosophical about it, and reset their goals, giving up hope of doing anything about seriously damaged marriages; focusing instead on improving the mental health of one or both of the partners individually, helping to terminate the relationship as tidily and painlessly as possible for all concerned, and hoping to reorient the partners to the deficiencies that caused them to mismanage this particular relationship, so that they may stand a good chance of doing better next time.

Counselors have also, of course, tried to find ways of getting couples to come to them earlier. But the recent trend toward easier divorce has probably counteracted these laudable efforts. Divorce is so readily accepted and so easily procured today that public opinion imposes little restraint on the couple; while cynical attitudes to marriage, widely disseminated in our culture, have cut the nerve of effort for many couples who in another cultural setting might have invested a great deal of energy in the attempt to achieve reconciliation before giving up. I have heard counselors in social agencies say, with a touch of cynicism, "Oh, the couples today just make a stopover at our office on their way to the divorce court."

This raises another question. When we started marriage counseling forty or fifty years ago, marriage breakdown appeared to be comparatively rare, at least as measured by the divorce rates. What we confronted then was a situation in which most marriages seemed to work out all right, but a few here and there got into difficulties. Of course no one in his or her senses really believed that *every* marriage could be successful, so a certain modest failure rate was inevitable and had to be tolerated by society. The idea was that, by providing marriage counseling services, the ratio of failures could be maintained at an acceptable level.

There is an obvious parallel here to the medical profession. All people can't expect to enjoy continuous good health throughout the life cycle. But provided the physicians can patch up enough of the ill and disabled to keep most members of the community functioning reasonably healthily, they can be considered to be doing all that can reasonably be required of them.

For marriage counselors, this is no longer possible. The number of marriage breakdowns has reached epidemic proportions and there are simply too few counselors to handle them. We could, of course, as a desperate measure, try to increase rapidly the number of marriage counselors available. But that would take some doing. A gynecologist of my acquaintance once estimated that, if all the members of his specialty were conscientiously to refer for marriage counseling all their patients who needed it, it would take nine thousand marriage counselors to do the job! But that represents the entire membership of the American Association for Marriage and Family Therapy. And of course, if the members of all the other branches of medicine, not to mention all other professions, and not omitting bartenders, were to refer people with marital difficulties to the proper source of help, the situation would be totally unmanageable.

In other words, we have to face the fact that, thankful as we are to have competent marriage counselors in our communities, they are currently working with only a tiny fraction of the couples suffering from marital dysfunction. A British study of separated couples showed that the vast majority of them had never been in touch with qualified marriage counselors; and an investigation in a small Minnesota community (Grand Rapids) found that the great majority of broken families on welfare had had no contact with either the churches or any other source of responsible community aid at the time the marriage broke down.

Even if we could greatly increase the number of marriage counselors, this would only reverse the state of dysfunction in some marriages already in trouble. Of course this would be possible only for those who would be willing to submit to therapy; and the therapy would not always be successful. This would not, however, protect new marriages, of which there are over a million a year. Increasing the number of marriage counselors would only increase the chances of couples whose marriages become seriously disturbed to receive the necessary repairs to get them working again. And inevitably this would be achieved at heavy cost in both time and money. Might it not be better to expend some of that money and effort to keep as many couples as possible out of trouble, so that they would not need counseling at all?

Even if this were to cost just as much time and effort, it would be a more humanitarian approach, because it would save millions of husbands, wives, and children from needless distress and pain. But of course a massive preventive program would in fact cost far less in time and money than a massive remedial program. The amount of professional time involved would be much less; and a sizable part of the effort could become a process of couples helping couples, which would cost nothing at all, but could be a very rewarding experience for all concerned.

From Remedial to Preventive Counseling

It may be instructive to examine the obstacles that might block the way when we consider a transition from marriage counseling as primarily remedial service to a new kind of service that would be primarily preventive. I am not saying that this would be easy, or that it could happen quickly. What I am asking is whether, and under what conditions, it could ever happen at all.

Since I have lived through, and been closely involved in, the entire history of marriage counseling since its early beginnings, I am in a position to sketch the various stages in its evolution. When I try to do so I find that there has been nothing monolithic about it. The goal—to help marriages function more effectively in terms of what couples needed and wanted—has never changed. But there has been a succession of quite significant changes in the ways in which this task has been perceived. Let me trace a few of them.

The earliest identifiable pattern was the *legal model*. The courts were compelled to deal very directly with marriages in trouble when all other professionals preferred not to be involved. The concept of the "matrimonial offense" was used to decide which partner had broken the established rules. When this had been decided, appropriate penalties were prescribed. The probation officers, however, acting in their role as troubleshooters, tried meanwhile to persuade the parties to be "reconciled"—which meant that the offender expressed regret and promised not to do it again, and the offended party forgave the fault and accepted the pledge of better behavior in the future. This has been an almost universal process in human communities. I have seen it used by the assembled elders of an African tribe, dealing with a marital situation.

Marriage counseling proper never really used this system, though its implications had to be taken into account. It was replaced by the *medical model*. The counselor had to find out not "Who's wrong?" but "What's wrong?" The implication now was that the marriage was no longer healthy, but afflicted with some kind of malady; and the all-knowing counselor could diagnose the trouble and prescribe an appropriate remedy. The couple didn't need to understand all the complexities of their condition. If they faithfully carried out the instructions of the counselor, all would be well.

This approach, which developed an approved formula for each identifiable situation, was found, however, to be too simplistic. It was therefore supplanted by the *psychotherapeutic model*, which recognized the great complexity of human behavior and called for an in-depth exploration of the personalities of the partners, using the standard psychoanalytic techniques. But few of those who were involved in dealing with marriages in trouble were versed in these complex arts; so referral to a psychotherapist was viewed as the proper course to take, though few couples could afford it. There was a time, as I recall, when all marriage counseling done with anything less than the full psychotherapeutic armamentarium was viewed as inferior treatment that bordered on quackery.

This dilemma was happily resolved with the advent of the *Rogerian model*. Carl Rogers appeared, like a new star in the firmament, to shed light in dark places. He argued convincingly that letting the clients talk it all out, and playing a supportive role as a responsive listener, was enough to bring insight that could point the way to a solution. In Britain, where lay marriage counselors are the rule, the Rogerian approach gave them a status they could not otherwise attain; and in North America, pastors took heart and became dedicated listeners to their maritally troubled parishioners.

There was, however, an inherent weakness about both of these approaches. They had been developed primarily for dealing with *individuals,* and not with relationships. The idea was to take a spouse, get him or her functioning again, and then return him or her to the marriage, and all would be well. In fact, this often didn't work; the personality change in one partner led to further alienation from, rather than reconciliation to, the uninvolved and excluded spouse.

Sociology now came to the rescue. Family sociology had been making steadily increasing use of systems theory to explain the complexities of relationships; and it was an article published by sociologist Gerald Leslie in the *Journal of Marriage and the Family* (February 1964) that ushered in the *systems-theory model,* which saw "conjoint counseling" with the couple as a primary operation of the marriage counselor. This was powerfully reinforced by the parallel movement in psychiatry and social work which led to the emergence of family therapy, which is now in its heyday. Conjoint therapy is so much the accepted practice today that a former president of the American Association for Marriage and Family Therapy told me that he would consider it almost unethical to work with only one partner in a marriage and call what he was doing marriage counseling.

The acceptance of marriage counseling as essentially relational opened the door to a number of innovations, most of which could hardly be called new models. It may be possible, however, to speak justifiably of a *behavioral model,* provided we give the term a broad interpretation. Certainly the recent welcome attempts to assess the effectiveness of marriage counseling by putting together the findings of a motley group of "outcome studies" is tending to suggest that the behavioral-change approach may turn out to be the most effective we have. Family therapy, as well as our new forms of relationally focused marriage counseling, seems also to point in the same direction.

Where next? It seems to me that our present focus on helping couples to readjust to each other by changing their behavior is taking us clearly in the direction of promoting relational growth and the achievement of relational potential. As I talk with marriage counselors and read the articles in the current professional journals, I gain the impression that there is a trend that may in time bring the practice of marriage counseling quite close to some of the marriage-enrichment concepts I have tried to describe in this book. It seems therefore not inappropriate to see the possibility of marriage counseling adopting a *growth-oriented model*.

Some Implications of Growth-oriented Marriage Counseling

It is obvious that a couple seeking to enrich their marriage, who put themselves in the care of a marriage counselor who is growth-oriented in approach, could make very rapid and effective progress, especially if the counselor and his or her spouse work together (as is now beginning to happen on an increasing scale) and include couple growth groups as part of their service. It seems reasonable to hope that this may become a trend in the near future.

Some marriage counselors have tended to be suspicious of the marriage-enrichment movement, and even to feel threatened by it. True, it must be a little disturbing to know that lay couples can be trained to give competent leadership to marriage-enrichment events, even if they see themselves as performing educational rather than clinical functions. And there is also the disturbing fact that couples can greatly improve their relationship without the need to pay out the kind of money that is required for counseling services.

On the other hand, realities have to be faced, and it might in the long haul be advantageous for some marriage counselors to get into the marriage-enrichment movement now and secure the goodwill of the increasing numbers of couples who are supporting it. Of course the counselor would have to bring his or her own spouse along and put his or her own marriage on the line; but I could hardly see evil consequences arising out of this.

A number of interesting developments worth watching are already taking place. Some experiments have been made that suggest that couples become better motivated to use counseling when, with the approval of their therapist, they are at the same time members of a couples' growth group. One counseling center is now automatically drafting all couples who have completed marriage counseling into marriage-enrichment groups, because it is recognized that these couples are now ready for a spurt of new relational growth. A prestigious center for training marriage counselors is now also experimenting with the use of marriage-enrichment approaches for what are called "clinical couples."

If couples are to be persuaded to go to marriage counselors for growth rather than for therapy, however, some changes in the image of the marriage counselor will have to take place. The barrier to seeking counseling earlier is not based only on our cultural taboos. These actually have been reinforced by the needless overemphasis on pathology in the language commonly employed in the counseling field. Growth-oriented counseling will need to find more positive and less forbidding terminology.

The medical model of marriage counseling lingers on in the concept of couples with "sick marriages," which are affected by some mysterious malady, or crippled by some injury, and must be healed or restored by applying an appropriate remedy. Another set of concepts sees the marriage as having "problems," a humiliating condition that must be "cleared up" or "straightened out" or "put right." A more graphic terminology sees the couple as in dire peril, needing to be "rescued" or "saved" from some awful catastrophe by a major intervention. Frequently, also, the static concept of marriage is reinforced by language that suggests that the relationship has fallen apart and needs to be put together again, or is damaged and needs to be repaired. This clearly suggests something that must be restored to its former state, or to some hypothetical condition of static normality.

This kind of language is subtly degrading, because it demeans the people who are being dealt with, casting upon them an aura of incompetence, failure, or inadequacy. As long as that kind of impression is given, people are going to hold out as long as they can before they accept the indignity of being counseled. There is a stigma attached to seeking the help of a marriage counselor, and the sooner it can be removed the better for us all.

By contrast, consider how much better people would feel if they saw marriage counseling as a learning process that would enable them to develop the hidden resources in their relationship, to clear away obstacles to their continuing growth, to sharpen their skills, to improve their coping system, and to enable them to realize their potential. Couples frequently tell us how refreshing it is, at a marriage-enrichment retreat, always to be thinking positively and in terms of growth. We even ask them, without conspicuous success it must be admitted, to try to avoid using the word *problem,* which has come to imply the idea of failure, and to speak instead of an "issue" or an "obstacle."

Even if the goal is a long way off, there is no reason why we should not begin now to make the shift from a remedial to a preventive emphasis in marriage counseling. Clark Vincent has given wide publicity to the concept of "marital health" and suggested that we should work toward a time when it would be as natural for couples to go to their counselor for their annual marital checkup as it is for them now to have an annual physical or dental examination.

And Herbert Otto has been challenging professionals to start the process of change by spending from 10 to 15 percent of their time in providing preventive service, whether they are paid for it or not.

The logic behind all this rests upon the concept that the best service we can offer to people in trouble of any kind is not to set right what has already gone wrong, but as far as possible to equip those concerned with the insights, and the resources, to manage their lives so that things don't have to go wrong at all. In marriage, this clearly means a concerted effort to insure that the couple begin by establishing sound foundations, especially in their critical first year together, upon which they can build a happy and healthy relationship in the years that follow. (We shall develop this concept further in a later chapter.)

19

CAN WE EDUCATE
FOR MARRIAGE?

THE great majority of all adults in our culture marry at one time or another, and since it is in the interest of all concerned that these marriages should if possible be successful, does it not seem logical that, as an integral part of their growing up, our children should be prepared in advance for the exercise of the roles and functions of married life?

We already take it for granted that all young people should go to school until they reach the age of sixteen. This means that, during at least ten years of their lives, a major part of their time is spent in the process of learning what they need to know in order to function later as responsible adults. In our society, any person who cannot read, write, or do elementary arithmetic, is seriously handicapped. Beyond that baseline, the general rule is that the more you know, the more options are open to you in the choice of your career, and, in general, the better salary you should be able to command.

Thousands and thousands of hours in the lives of our young people are, therefore, devoted to acquiring knowledge that is intended to make their later lives successful and rewarding. This involves a vast expenditure of money on the part of the community as a whole; but few would doubt that this is a public expense that is fully justified by the results.

Why, then, should we not provide a corresponding program of education for marriage? If it is important that young people be qualified for their future vocations, is it not equally important that they be qualified for their future roles as founders of families? We are surely not in any doubt about the contribution made to the community, and to the nation, of happy, healthy, successful family life. Is it possible to prepare young people for this as an integral part of our system of universal education? That is the question I propose to explore in this chapter.

Education for Traditional Marriage

Preparing young people for marriage is not a new idea. In fact, it is a very old one.

An anthropologist friend of mine once spent a period of years in Africa studying the educational systems of primitive peoples. Talking with him after his return, I asked him what he had learned. "My general conclusion," he replied, "is that the educational systems of these tribal peoples is exactly the opposite of our own civilized systems. Their policy is that they carefully teach their young people about the art of living, as their culture defines it; but they leave them to pick up information about the outside world in any way they can. By contrast, we carefully teach our young people about the outside world and leave them to pick up whatever they can about the art of living." He then went on to explain how, in the African tribe, the young people learn about living from their elders as they grow up; and then, at the age of puberty or soon after, the boys and girls separately go off into the bush, to be prepared, under the supervision of carefully chosen elders of the tribe, for the duties of adulthood. I have myself witnessed the concluding initiation ceremony for young men in a West African tribe, and I found it an impressive experience.

In traditional societies in the West, there has been in the past little possibility of making marriage preparation a part of the school system. Universal education is a relatively recent development; and the concept of using the schools for education for living is even more recent. In the traditional European school, what young people learned had little to do with their personal lives. A mastery of Latin and Greek, and a knowledge of the classics, was the mark of the educated man; and in these terms, educated women were few and far between.

Learning for living, therefore, took place primarily in the home. And this was not just the parental home. In preindustrial and early industrial Europe, large numbers of young people, from the age of ten upward, were sent out to become servants or apprentices in homes other than their own. Contrary to what has often been supposed, marriage for both boys and girls was seldom possible until the late twenties or even the early thirties, because a young man could not marry until he was independently established and could provide a home, and a means of support, for his wife and for the children who were then likely to appear in rapid succession.

The process of education for marriage and family living was, therefore, based on the continuous observation of the models provided by the homes in which boys and girls lived throughout their youth and early adulthood. The young girl observed the behavior of her own mother, the mothers among her close relatives, and the mistress in the home where she became a servant. We have seen how she internalized these role models through the years, and by the time she married she was thoroughly conversant with the functions of woman, wife, and mother, and able to perform these functions with little or no difficulty. The boy, likewise, was thoroughly familiar with the roles of man, husband, and father, which he had continuously observed throughout his life.

Since marriage in those days was in the main hierarchically structured, the roles of husband and wife were clearly defined and inflexible. Since these roles were also designed to avoid conflict, and did not attach much importance to love and intimacy, there was not much that could go wrong. The possibility of divorce was remote, so the relationship between the spouses had to be accepted for what it was. A husband who complained that his marriage was not satisfying might become a laughing stock, because any man worthy of the name should be able to manage his wife; and a woman in marital trouble would be told that she had made her bed and must lie in it. These attitudes have not entirely died out in our more sophisticated contemporary society.

If, therefore, the husband could keep his household under control, and could get his wife pregnant at regular intervals, those were all the skills that he needed. And if the wife could cook, sew, keep the home reasonably organized, be sexually available to her husband, and take adequate care of her children, she could measure up satisfactorily to what was expected of her.

There was, therefore, a system of education in traditional culture that provided all that was needed to enable marriages to do all that was expected of them.

Education for Companionship Marriage

The transition from the traditional marriage to the new companionship model has obviously involved a revolutionary change so far as educational needs are concerned. If whatever competence was needed for marital adjustment was adequately provided in the past, the situation today is very different. The kind of interpersonal competence we need today is hardly even understood, let alone provided for. It is, therefore, little wonder that marriages are in trouble on an unprecedented scale.

Our inability to understand this is tragic, because it leads the superficial observer inevitably to the false conclusion that marriage has failed; whereas the truth is that marriage has changed, and *we* have failed to understand this fact. People have said to me, "Why do you talk about education for marriage? Our forebears didn't need it, and they got on all right." The answer is that our forebears *did* have all the education they needed for the achievement of their marital expectations; whereas today, because expectations are so much higher and the task is therefore so much more difficult, young people have to embark on marriage either with the wrong kind of preparation, or with virtually no preparation at all.

Consider what should be covered in effective education for marriage in our culture today. It will be enough, for our present purpose, to take the eleven items included in the Marriage Potential Inventory, which represent the most frequently occurring areas in marriage that many groups of couples under our leadership contributed to their agendas:

1. agreeing about common goals and values
2. promoting shared growth and developing relational potential
3. achieving effective couple communication
4. negotiating disagreements and resolving conflicts creatively
5. expressing appreciation and affection through mutual affirmation
6. achieving congruent gender roles
7. sharing homemaking responsibilities and tasks
8. achieving mutual sexual fulfillment
9. agreeably managing the family income
10. becoming effective parents
11. making wise and acceptable decisions together

All of these are highly complicated skills that are essential for any two young people getting married today. None of them can be acquired in two or three easy lessons. Indeed, lessons as such are not enough.

The question is, therefore, could all young people possibly be trained to perform these operations competently *before they marry?*

What Can Be Done?

I wish the answer to this question were clear and simple, but it is not. The great difficulty, as I have already pointed out, is that relational skills are not acquired simply by receiving information about them. Many people will probably remain unconvinced of this, because the belief that the processes of learning for knowing and learning for living are basically the same is deeply implanted; and abandoning that belief is, as I myself know, a very painful process to anyone who has devoted long years of his life to being a teacher in the cognitive sense. Yet I cannot give ground on this point, because I am now deeply convinced about it.

I am therefore reluctantly compelled to take the view that the classroom offers limited opportunities for effective marriage and family life education. Its associations are strongly with the didactic approach, with academic requirements, with acquiring credit, with the teacher as authority figure, with the competitive quest for ratings. I know that some teachers have made heroic efforts to transcend all these pervasive restraining influences, and some have even succeeded in doing so. Yet the odds against us are so heavy that I believe that we cannot conscientiously continue to assume that this is the only medium to use, because adherence to this misconception would only cut the nerve of the effort we need to make to find better ways of doing the job.

We therefore need to admit humbly that education *about* marriage is not necessarily education *for* marriage. Much of our so-called family life education is of necessity undertaken with groups of *individuals* who happen to be members of families. Unless the other individuals with whom we are trying to help our students to relate in the family are also present and involved, the chance that those to-be-related persons can together, in a congruent process, go through the four stages from receiving information to behavioral change is quite remote.

But in education for marriage courses, generally the student is not yet involved in an existing relationship that could lead to marriage; so we're not even dealing with to-be-related persons. The student's future marriage partner is as yet a hypothetical and unknown figure. So there is no possibility of going further, in imparting knowledge about marriage, than the promotion of fantasies.

Of course, it can be replied that knowledge can be applied to *existing* relationships, and this is true. But the essence of what is needed for functioning in marriage is the ability to promote relational growth, openness, in-depth communication, affection, the management of conflict, and the negotiation of disagreements; and all these in a situation that represents a deep commitment to a shared life between a man and a woman. Other relationships entered into in the process of maturation cannot be other than pale shadows of the marital commitment; so many basic components are missing that it is rather like learning to swim by practicing the strokes on a piano stool. This might be a little helpful as a preparatory exercise; but it only very remotely resembles learning to swim when you are really in the water.

The French have made a helpful distinction in defining *preparation au mariage,* by dividing it into two successive stages: *preparation lointaine* (literally preparation "at a distance" before mate selection takes place) and *preparation prochaine* (preparation "close up" when a partner has already been chosen and the couple are moving toward marriage).

Preparation lointaine for marriage is actually a very complex process. Readiness to move successfully into the married state when the time comes depends on a combination of factors that have little or nothing to do with information about marriage as such. Some of these factors are: how marriage has been perceived as the couple have encountered married persons who have been significant others in their lives, and particularly their own parents; whether as family members, and in their friendships, they have experienced warm, positive, and affirming relationships and escaped traumatic and destructive experiences; what characteristic traits they have developed in the process of their personal growth—in particular, sensitivity to the needs of others, honesty and integrity, patience and perseverance in tasks undertaken, self-confidence and optimism, freedom to express love and caring, a comfortable and responsible attitude toward their own sexuality. All these are personal qualities that can be developed through active involvement in many life situations, but not to any significant extent in a classroom course on marriage.

I would have to say that by far the most positive educational experience young people can have, in terms of their preparation for future marriage, is to grow up in a truly happy home. So far as *preparation lointaine* is concerned, the true teachers are those who enrich marriages, and so enable the children of the couples concerned to see living models of a successful relationship in their own parents. If you really have a vocation to prepare youth for marriage, the best way is to get up to your neck in promoting the cause of marriage enrichment.

Let me try to be a little more positive. Although we may not be able to do much to prepare public and private school students for the intricate adjustments of later marriage as such, a great deal can be done to guide them in the management of real-life relationships in which they are currently involved—with their classmates of both sexes, with their teachers, in their family situations, and with other people in general. It is never too early for children to learn the basic skills for communication with others, for empathic acceptance, for handling anger creatively, for making creative use of conflicts, and for negotiating disagreements. Bernard Guerney has experimented with such programs within the school system, and there is a long and honorable tradition that sees the school as a powerful medium for character training. Youth organizations also play an important part in "learning for living" in this more generalized connotation.

Premarital Counseling

What about *preparation prochaine?* Here, in the engaged couple, we *do* have an existing relationship that is in the process of growing and developing, so there is really something to work on. Most of the areas of adjustment that will later become crucial in marriage are already operative: growth is occurring, a system of communication is being established, differences are producing disagreements and, to some extent, exploding into conflict. Sex is an issue, and strong feelings have to be dealt with. Some decision making is taking place. Goals and values are being explored and compared. Concepts of gender roles are being tested out in a process of mutual accommodation.

Here again, a promising opportunity has seemed to present itself. What the school has offered to the unattached youth in family life education courses, the church has tried to provide for the already paired couple through premarital counseling. Pastors have diligently arranged interviews, courses, and seminars for engaged couples. What have these programs achieved?

Unhappily, evidence now being accumulated suggests that the results of these efforts have been quite limited. I myself, over a number of years, made it a practice to ask married couples who had come for counseling whether they had received premarital counseling. Most of them had. I then asked them just what had happened; and invariably, the response was that the pastor had been friendly and concerned and had either talked to them or given them a book to read. When asked what the pastor had talked about, or what they had learned from the book, the response was generally an embarrassed acknowledgment that they could remember almost nothing. When further asked whether, in the course of struggling with the marital difficulties that had now become acute, the couple had at any time made use of anything they had learned in the course of the premarital counseling, the response was negative in all but one instance.

It gives me no pleasure to record this unproductive exercise. But much recent research, better carried out than my own rather superficial inquiry, has confirmed what I had begun to suspect. Let me summarize these studies briefly.

In 1971 Claude Guldner published a report of a careful investigation, which found that premarital couples generally were in a state of "bliss"—an emotional detachment from reality, which rendered them not very teachable. This condition, it was found, continued into the early months of marriage. Not until the sixth month after the wedding had most of the couples come to see themselves in very realistic terms. However, by that time they were ready to stretch out both hands eagerly for help, which they would previously have ignored. Moreover, these six-months-married couples agreed that the help they now needed actually couldn't have been provided before marriage, because they just weren't ready for it then. They needed first to have actual *experience* of married life.

A major four-year study has now been completed at the University of Toronto by Edward Bader and a team of colleagues in the Medical School, who have checked out the Guldner findings. Two dynamic programs were provided for a group of engaged couples, one premarital and the other six months after the wedding. The couples involved in the study were individually interviewed four times—before the wedding, six months later, a year later, and four years later—in all involving a total of over three hundred interviews. Although it was found that the premarital program did provide *some* help, it was the program offered six months later that was really effective. The couples who went through this made good progress, and at the end of a year, and thereafter, their relationships were much better developed than those of a control group of couples who were not involved in any program at all.

Meanwhile, another study, undertaken at the University of Minnesota and supervised by David Olson, evaluated five different premarital programs—each covering a weekend or providing weekly sessions extending through six to eight weeks. Using the best testing procedures available, the study found that the effectiveness of the programs generally was very low. The Bader study in Toronto, on a much smaller scale, arrived at a similar conclusion about didactic programs.

More investigation is needed, but it does now look as if we need to revise some of our assumptions about what premarital programs can achieve. What seems clear is that information-giving programs are by themselves of very low effectiveness. What couples can use before marriage is training (not just teaching) in couple communication; encouragement and guidance in looking at their own and each other's attitudes to and expectations of marriage; and opportunities to get together in group sharing with other couples. A number of evaluative instruments have now been prepared to alert couples to the areas in their relationship on which they need to work.

I am aware that this disappointing news about the programs some pastors have so conscientiously developed in the form of premarital talks to couples will not be welcomed. But facts must be faced; and the fact seems to be that these didactic talks have had little or no impact on the couples, and in some cases have even produced negative reactions.

It would seem, therefore, that the sincere attempts of pastors to prepare couples for marriage through premarital talks may have to be submitted to the same agonizing reappraisal as the attempt of the school to prepare the unattached through classroom teaching. We know in theory what we want to do, but if we are honest, we must admit that we don't yet know in practice how to do it really well.

It is not my wish to adopt a negative attitude to our well-meaning efforts in the fields of marriage counseling, of family life education, and of marriage preparation. However, the development of marriage enrichment has opened up new possibilities, which inevitably compel us to examine what we have been doing in comparison with the new possibilities that are now emerging.

In an article in *The Family Coordinator* (Vol. 28, No. 3; July 1979) I attempted to do just that; and to illustrate what I was trying to say, I included Diagram 8 (which I reproduce here with permission).

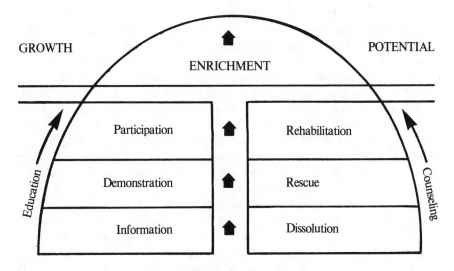

DIAGRAM 8
Relationship of Counseling, Education, and Enrichment

The arrows in the center represent our attempt to find effective ways to move couple relationships upward in the direction of achieving growth and appropriating their potential. The further the couple can move upward, the more effective is the service we render to them.

Beginning on the right, we look at counseling. At the lowest level, the counselor sometimes can do no more than guide the couple, as painlessly as possible, through the *dissolution* of their marriage. This need not be seen as a reflection on the counselor's ability. Some couples seek counseling only when the relationship is so far damaged that nothing could put it together again. In such circumstances, wise guidance can at least minimize the pain and distress that must be suffered by the partners, and often also by their children. What is done at this level is sometimes called "divorce counseling," and must certainly be recognized as a needed service, even if it does nothing for the marriage as such.

The second level is what I call *"rescue* counseling." It is well expressed in a famous series of articles that appears in *The Ladies Home Journal:* "Can This Marriage Be Saved?" The picture is of the couple drifting down the river—helpless, unhappy, and apprehensive—while the menacing roar of the cataract ahead sounds louder and louder in their ears. And then, as all seems lost, the counselor plunges in, takes his place beside them, and steers them safely to the river bank. Though this may seem a dramatic representation of therapeutic intervention, most experienced marriage counselors have been cheered from time to time by such an experience. Although "rescued" marriages may never rise to great heights, at least the family holds together, and that may be considered something of an achievement.

The third level is *rehabilitation.* Here the counselor works with the couple and has the satisfaction of seeing them confidently headed toward claiming their potential. This is what I call growth-oriented counseling. It is not simply clearing up problems, but moving ahead to new and exciting possibilities.

Notice, though, that rehabilitation counseling is taking the process to a level where it is indistinguishable from enrichment. So it can be said that, as our marriage counseling becomes more and more effective, it shades imperceptibly into enrichment as I have described it in this book. Indeed, one well-known marriage counselor made it a practice, when he terminated counseling that had been successful, to give the couple a year's membership of ACME as a parting gift, signifying that they were now ready for a new spurt of relational growth.

Now look at the area of education for marriage on the left-hand side of the diagram. The lowest level of achievement is represented by *information-* giving, as we have already seen. More effective than that is *demonstration*—enabling the couple to see, as in the marriage-enrichment group, creative interaction in process through the sharing, especially in dialogue, of another couple. But the most effective process of all is when the couple themselves *participate,* by becoming involved in a new experience and finding that it is rewarding to them.

These stages represent a scale of values widely recognized in educational theory today. And it seems that these concepts are by no means recent discoveries. A proverb dating back to ancient China sums it up: "When I hear, I forget; when I see, I remember; when I do, I understand."

Notice again that as we have moved up the scale from purely cognitive education to experiential education, we are now virtually in the field of enrichment. So we can say, concerning both the field of marriage counseling and that of marriage education, that the more effectively they are able to function, the closer they move toward identification with the enrichment approach.

An Additional Note

Before finally concluding this chapter, I want to add a postscript about a promising new development that has come to my notice.

There are now a number of experiments to use the classroom as a vehicle for effective experiential education. A pioneering effort in this new field, in the form of a college course in marriage enrichment, is that of Brent Barlow at Brigham Young University; a similar plan has also been approved at the University of Missouri in Kansas City, where the teachers will be Dwane Hartley and his wife. These experiments will try as far as possible to eliminate the disadvantages I have described.

It seems best that only married students (and possibly a few engaged couples) should be enrolled for the course; and where one spouse takes the course for credit, a decidedly lower cost can be made available for the other, who would audit the course. Scheduling the sessions in the late afternoon or early evening makes it possible for couples to come together.

Ideally, the instruction would be given by a husband-wife team who can model what they teach; in addition, other married couples can be brought in to dialogue about their own experiences of marriage. The teaching in class is further supplemented by giving the enrolled couples suitable exercises to be done at home, with the opportunity to report back from time to time.

By these means, a teacher couple can not only interpret the theory of marriage enrichment, but also open up their own marriage and share their own growth experiences, thus coming very near in the classroom to what a retreat or growth group would provide.

To my knowledge, the course at Brigham Young University in the spring of 1981, was the first of this type to be offered in an academic setting. One hundred and forty-one students were enrolled, and the general reaction was highly favorable. Fortunately Professor Brent Barlow kept careful records, including the pretests and posttests.

It now seems very likely that this new approach, embodying a decidedly more realistic introduction of experiential education into the classroom, marks the beginning of a promising new trend.

20

FOCUS ON NEWLYWEDS

SOME years ago I counseled a couple who were in serious trouble. It was a very difficult case, and for a time I was uncertain of the outcome. At last, however, I was able to get their full cooperation and see them start out together in new and promising directions. I got to know them very well, and as often happens, when the time came to end our association, it was quite hard for us to part.

When I finally shook hands with the husband, he hesitated, and then said, "As we leave you, there's something I want to say."

I encouraged him to go ahead. He cleared his throat and began, "You might feel it's a criticism. But really it isn't. I'm very sincere about it.

"You see, we've learned a lot through this experience—a lot about ourselves, and something about marriage counseling. And what we've learned leaves a question in my mind.

"It seems to me that when you try to help couples make a success of marriage, you do it in two ways. First, you get with us *before* the wedding and tell us a lot of things we ought to know. You do it very sincerely, but we can't really appreciate it then, because that's before we begin to have the experience of being married.

"Then off we go in our new life together. And of course it's all new and strange, and we make a lot of mistakes—just like Meg and I did. But you don't come near us then; you leave us to struggle on alone. And of course, some of us get into bad trouble—like Meg and I did.

"But then you make yourself available to us for counseling. Thank goodness you do, because some of us sure need your help. But here's my question: you offer us help *before* we've had the experience of marriage, then you offer us help *after* we've had the experience and made a mess of it. But why, oh why, don't you offer us help *while we're having the experience?*"

I have never forgotten that question. I have never seen Tom again, but if by any remote chance he should happen to read this, I want him to know that I went on pondering his question for days, for months, for years. And this chapter, indeed this book, finally represents my response.

Once Again, the Taboo

I have already described how the intermarital taboo pervades our culture. It shuts married couples up in lonely little boxes, denying them the understanding, support, and help they might otherwise get from other couples, also shut up in their lonely little boxes, who likewise have to struggle with adjustments and crises with which they are poorly equipped to deal. Some manage to cope, and some don't. If they get into enough trouble not to care any more about the taboo and they ask for help, we have well-qualified people to come to the rescue. But this seldom happens at the time when help would be most welcome and most effective—when they are beginning to have the experience. And when is this? It is the first year of marriage.

By a grim irony, that is the time when the taboo is most powerfully enforced. At the wedding ceremony we shower the couple with our good wishes for their future happiness and send them on their way. Then we surround them with a pall of silence. We say that we must respect their privacy; but what we are really doing is saying two things very clearly: first, that all normal people should possess all the resources necessary to make marriage work (it just "comes natural"); and second, that if by any chance you should ask for help in managing your interpersonal relationship, you are thereby acknowledging that you are inferior persons, stupid, and incompetent. This is what Clark Vincent has called "the myth of naturalism."

For several years now, I have been exploring this supposed need to "protect the privacy" of newlyweds. Increasingly, I am convinced that most of them neither want nor appreciate such protection. However, because we felt we had to honor the taboo, we have developed almost all of our marriage counseling services at the only two points at which we had some justification for breaking the silence.

The first of these points is when the couple come to register their intention to be involved in the wedding ceremony. Since this has traditionally been in the sphere of religion, it is the pastor who has acted to provide marriage preparation. This is especially a concern of the Catholic priest, because Catholics do not recognize divorce; and since there are so many divorced Catholics these days, one way to reduce the number is to discourage all couples who seem not to have what it takes to stay together for a lifetime. Indeed, some marriage-preparation programs have been justified by quoting the percentage of couples who, as a result, decided not to get married after all. I offer no criticism of this; it is much better to turn back than to plunge recklessly into a really doubtful venture. But it is only fair to recognize that marriage preparation is in part an attempt to weed out the unmarriageables.

The other point at which we can intervene in a marriage is when the couple (or one of the partners) break out of the lonely little box and cry for help. I remember a social worker saying to me, "You see, we can't help a couple with their marriage until they have gotten themselves made into a case." What she meant, of course, was that it would amount to an insult to *offer* them help; which is exactly what some of us have been made to feel when we have invited couples to participate in a marriage-enrichment retreat. This is a curious game: pretending that we all have great marriages, alhough we know quite well that this is far from the truth.

The time has come to give up this stupid posturing and to *offer help* to newlywed couples *when they are having the experience of marriage*. We have tested out marriage enrichment enough to be satisfied that it is effective, that this is precisely the best place to put it to use, and that the time has come to get on with the job.

The Critical First Year

There is plenty of evidence, including the findings of the Guldner and the Bader studies quoted in the last chapter, that the first year of marriage is a critical time. These and other American studies find strong support in an investigation of divorce carried out in Britain by Barbara Thornes and Jean Collard, who found that of all the divorced persons they interviewed, one-third admitted that their marriages were already in serious trouble by the time they reached their first wedding anniversary.

That first year together is a very important time. Once it is over, the best opportunity for flexible adaptation of the partners to each other is past. In these early months, everything is fluid and malleable; competent help offered then could significantly increase the number of successful marriages in our communities. If we miss this opportunity, we are failing to use the best chance we have to get marriages off to a really good start.

A Practicable Plan

Well, how do we go about it?

I can see three possible ways; and obviously others could be developed.

The first has already been put into operation in Kansas City, where Vera and I served as part-time consultants (to the city) for nearly three years. This gave us an opportunity to carry out a practical experiment, which is still being used. We were able to secure the support of a number of city pastors, who undertook to encourage couples they married to sign up for the Growth in Marriage for Newlyweds program. This entitled them to take part in a series of sessions for marriage enrichment—at first, once a week for a period of four weeks; but now extended, at the request of the couples themselves, to six weeks. Five or six couples take part in each series, led by an ACME certified leader couple who have also had additional training for this special event. The program runs consecutively in different parts of the city, and the couples, through the project director at the Living Center for Family Enrichment, choose a time and location to suit themselves, at any point in their first eighteen months together. The program is not of talks or lectures, but is an extended marriage-enrichment experience specially designed for newlyweds. This has been approved by the ACME Training and Certification Committee, and a manual for leaders is available from the ACME office.

The Kansas City pastors are free to do whatever they wish with their couples premaritally, but are urged to sign them up for this followup program. The cost of the program is forty dollars per couple. They, however, pay only fifteen dollars; the church in which they are married pays ten dollars; and a special fund raised in the city pays the remaining fifteen dollars. The couples, therefore, get a bargain, and are encouraged by the knowledge that both the church and the city wish to contribute to their future growth together. So far well over a hundred couples have been through the experience, and their anonymous written evaluations are enthusiastic. There seems to be no reason why similar programs should not be developed in other cities. Many inquiries have been received from communities in the United States and even some from overseas.

Another type of program that has been tried is to find mature, wise, friendly couples who are willing to serve as sponsors to newly married couples for their first year together. This has been done in churches, although I am not aware of any evaluations comparable to the data collected in Kansas City.

Yet another approach is for pastors, following whatever premarital procedure they adopt, to arrange for later sessions with the couples following the wedding. Six months later would be a good time; the Guldner study found this to be the point at which the postwedding couples were really ready for help, and the Bader studies strongly confirm this. Pastors who do this say that it has seemed to be effective. During my ten years as a professor in a medical school, I used this procedure with my medical students. I got to know the couples in a friendly way in the premarital interviews, but it was after they had been married six months that we really got down to business. At that time, some issues in the relationship, for which there had been no evidence earlier, had surfaced. One point I noted was that it was not a good plan to leave the couples to get in touch with me at a postwedding time of their own choosing, because they almost invariably failed to act. But when I took the initiative and called them for an appointment, they readily responded; in one case the couple were already in real trouble, and we only just saved the marriage in the nick of time.

Though these are illustrations of programs for newlyweds, the plan I think will really get this moving has yet to be initiated. I hope one day to see mar-

riage counselors get into this field. I know that some of them are already exploring it. But what I have in mind is a major effort that could begin to make
a real impaçt.

The plan would best suit a husband-wife counseling team, working together
and specializing in this field. They would contract with the newlywed couple
for a two-hour monthly session throughout their first year together, with the
added possibility of also getting them involved in a support group with other
newlyweds. Through these regular contacts, the counselors would keep in close
touch with the couple as they made all their early interpersonal adjustments,
and literally guide them into interaction patterns likely to produce sustained
growth.. The frequency of the interviews would make reasonably sure that all
aspects of the adjustment process were given whatever guidance was needed.
At the end of the year, close ties would have been established between the two
couples, and no opportunity for developing potential would have been missed.

The question that arises, of course, is how all this would be paid for. Talking
to a number of parents and other relatives of newlyweds, I have found that
weddings are not cheap and that they would have been willing, even if it involved skimping a little on the wedding, to deposit a sum of, say, one thousand
dollars toward guiding the young couple through their first year of marriage, to
make sure that the new relationship got off to a good start. I was not, of course,
asking for cash down; but I have not yet found close relatives who did not
respond positively to the proposition. The way I have put it was: "Would you
be ready to pay this money to a neutral source—an agency or church, for
example—from which the counseling fees would be paid as the sessions were
held, on the understanding that, if the money could not be used as intended,
or the arrangement broke down for any reason, the unused portion would be
returned?" In one instance an uncle of the bride said he would be happy to
raise the money from various family members and that this would be the best
wedding gift to his niece and her fiancé that he could possibly imagine!

I would even carry this project a step further. I can imagine the counselor
couple, at the end of the year, signing up the recently wed couple for an annual
marital and family checkup, with any special extra guidance they might need.
For example, a similar arrangement could be negotiated to prepare them for,
and guide them through, their first experience of parenthood.

This kind of marriage counseling would be a pleasant departure from the
problem-oriented concept we now have, with the stigma it tends to create. It
would be hard to imagine a more pleasant career than that of a husband-wife
counselor team, happily busy with the task of guiding their charges, who would
become close personal friends, through the growth and adjustment processes of
the life cycle, and ending up with something like a large extended family!

We are being told these days, as the divorce rate steadily rises, especially in
the younger age groups, that we are nearing the point at which half of all young
couples getting married will end up in the divorce court. I offer this plan as a

sound, practical answer that would in my judgment be the best possible way to turn the tide. This would indeed be marriage enrichment in action. I can see no practical reason why it should not be done, if the idea can be put to the test.

The Shift to Prevention

Working with newlyweds would, in my opinion, be the best way to make the transition from remedial to preventive services to families.

The logic behind this transition is unassailable. As my counselee Tom put it, why not make our new insights about marriage fully available to couples as soon as they begin "having the experience"? Working with them to promote their relational growth in their first year together is the obvious way to do it. Why have we not attempted this before?

In my opinion, there are two main reasons.

The first I have already referred to. It is that, because of the intermarital taboo, we have not looked logically for the best vantage point, but have concluded that we were entitled to intervene only at the points at which couples are obliged to make contact with us—either in order to arrange for the wedding ceremony, or to cry for help when they are really hurting. So we have built up our services—premarital and marital counseling—without even considering that any other approach might be open to us. It has not even occurred to most people that we might offer help at any other time.

The sad truth is that, our view of human need is conditioned in favor of a narrowly remedial approach, and we find it very hard to think in preventive terms. This is true of our medical services, where a mere fraction of money and effort is spent on prevention. In the field of mental health, I have been told that the figure 2 percent represents the proportion of our total resources that is devoted to planned prevention.

The second reason why our focus has been on remedial services involves what I call the pain-gain formula. A number of therapists to whom I have spoken have told me plainly that they couldn't make a living out of helping married couples preventively, because it is only when they are really hurting that they will find the money to pay the fees the therapist needs as a fair return for his or her services. No doubt this is true today, but surely it need not remain so. The whole concept of insurance, for example, is widely accepted in modern society; it is based on a principle very like that of prevention—making sure that if unexpected danger threatens, you will have the necessary resources to cope with it. After all, isn't the major difference between human beings (*Homo sapiens*) and the so-called "dumb animals" that we have the foresight to look ahead and to take the necessary steps now to avoid pain and misery later?

When you come to think of it, our lives are surrounded by protective devices designed to prevent us from getting into situations that could be dangerous and distressing: inoculation against disease, street lighting at night, road signs on our highways, traffic lights at busy street corners, protective railings beside railroad tracks, steel helmets for construction workers, masks for surgical teams, warning sirens for emergency vehicles—the list could go on and on.

The principle is simple and sensible. If evidence repeatedly shows that getting into certain situations, without the means to protect yourself from an accompanying danger, can be damaging to your health and happiness, it is simply a matter of plain common sense to take the appropriate preventive action. And surely, with our present rate of marriage breakdown, it can only be a matter of time before we learn to develop the necessary "interpersonal competence" to protect ourselves, and those who are near and dear to us, from the folly of letting something that should be a rich and rewarding experience turn out instead to be a cause of pain and misery.

I am deeply convinced that marriage enrichment, as widely applied as possible to all couples who have the sense to use it, is the wave of the future. It is only a matter of time.

PART FIVE

Implications for Social Action

In these closing chapters, the transition to the companionship marriage is examined from the point of view of our national policies and community services. The need for research to test the validity of marriage enrichment, the possibilities of overcoming indifference and opposition to new approaches, and ways and means of developing community programs will be examined and discussed. A specific plan will also be proposed.

21

TESTING THE NEW PRODUCT: RESEARCH

SOMEONE once described marriage counseling as "a practice in search of a theory." This was supposed to be a joke, though it was a rather grim one. Although it is no longer true, it is unfortunate, though perhaps unavoidable, that it was ever true.

It is my earnest hope that nothing like that will ever be true of marriage enrichment. Our new insights are much too important to be denied the validation that rigorous testing can alone provide. If we do indeed have a sound product, it could open up revolutionary possibilities. If the product is *not* sound, the sooner we know this the better, so that we can look elsewhere for something that *does* work.

My major purpose in writing this book, as stated in the Preface, is to offer at least a beginning in the construction of a theoretical frame of reference. I am now inviting the theorists to examine it, criticize it, tear it apart if they can—so long as they can put something better in its place. And I am inviting the researchers to move in and test everything we are doing. We surely all agree that family life in our culture is in deep trouble. We are looking for answers. I am offering what I think *is* an answer; and all I ask is to be told, by those best able to judge, whether it will stand up to their most searching scrutiny.

The Role of Research

Before I go further, let me clarify the role of research as I understand it. I am not a researcher; I have chosen to be actively involved in promoting better marriages and families all over the world and that has left me no time for much

205

else. But I have the greatest respect for what research can and must do in order to enable the behavioral sciences to come of age.

The scientific method, as I perceive it, is concerned primarily with a pragmatic task—to develop the vast resources around us, and within us, so that they can serve to make our ideals and goals practicable.

As we move in this direction, it is necessary constantly to maintain a balance between our three basic sources of information: the project or experiment, the theory that either launches the project or is derived from it, and the research that tests both. These three items can, in any given inquiry, operate in any order; but in most situations project and theory come first, often together; and research then examines the effectiveness of the project and the soundness of the theory. This may then lead to an improved project, a clarified theory, or both; and so on. The following diagram makes this clear.

DIAGRAM 9
The Role of Research

If we apply all this to marriage and family enrichment, where are we? For more than ten years (omitting the earlier period of very tentative exploration), we have been promoting experimental projects, and at the same time evolving theoretical concepts to explain them. We have now produced some programs that are apparently workable, because they seem, on the basis of experience and observation, to be having the desired effect. We are, in short, precisely at the point at which we need research to move in and check out both our projects and the theories we are evolving to explain them. Researchers therefore should now be able, unless they decide that we are on a wild goose chase, to enable us to improve our projects and to refine our theory. From that point onward, practice, theory, and research should move smoothly together in a process that should bring our programs to a high level of efficiency.

All this sounds very clear and simple. But alas, in our real world it does not often happen so.

In the *1979 Yearbook of Science and the Future*, Robert G. Sharrar has a fascinating article entitled *Legionnaires' Disease: Stalking a Killer Epidemic*. It records the steps that were taken, following the outbreak of the mysterious disease that broke out in a Philadelphia hotel in the summer of 1976, to track down the bacterium, hitherto unknown to medicine, that caused the deaths of twenty-nine people and threatened many others. As the story unfolds, we see the almost perfect articulation of the efforts of many investigators, ranging widely in their search for evidence, moving progressively from theory to experimental action, checking out all data secured against existing research and initiating relevant new research, until the mystery was cleared up, the cause of the trouble identified, and the necessary steps taken to keep the situation under control.

Of course all this could be swiftly and efficiently done because motivation was strong, money freely available, and the necessary teams of trained investigators on call. Medical science has the needed resources, and when a crisis arises it can move in swiftly and get the job done.

Reading this account stirred in me a tremendous sense of admiration. This was followed, however, by melancholy reflections as I realized how comparatively ineffective are our resources in the family field. The apparently needless death of twenty-nine people, and the possibility that many others might meet the same fate, was a clarion call for all-out action, which met with a full response. By comparison, however, I thought of the millions of broken marriages, fragmented families, and deprived children in our communities, and of our apparent indifference to the possibility that much of this might be prevented if we could only attack it with anything like the coordinated efforts that our medical services were able to apply to the challenge of Legionnaires' Disease.

And then I wondered whether something might yet be done to marshal our resources around a new, promising approach to family breakdown, such as marriage enrichment seems to offer. Could there not be some process of coordination, of uniting the efforts of many people—practitioners, theorists, and researchers—around a specific common goal?

Professional journals are now publishing more and more research reports on various aspects of family relationships. The major motivation behind many of these projects seems to be either the gaining of a coveted doctor's degree or the professional recognition that comes as a result of getting into print. Both of these are creditable goals. But might not many of these diligent investigators derive added incentive if they were doing work that, merged with the findings of many others, might in time lead to increasingly effective services being rendered to American families?

I am aware of the view of research purists who seek to maintain a scrupulous "detachment" from the possibly contaminating effect on their work of any direct association with ends and means. There is an important place for what is called "pure" research. But there is also a great need for what I would call "facilitative research," which continuously examines projects with the express purpose of enabling them to become more and more effective. Ernest Burgess held the view that family research should fulfill *two* purposes: to increase scientific knowledge, and to apply its findings at a practical level to the problems of marriage and the family. David Olson uses the terms "applied research" and "integrative research" to describe studies that fall into the second category.

There is a particular feature about marriage enrichment that should make it an especially favorable field for research: the ready accessibility of both the project and the subject. If you desired to make outcome studies of the effectiveness of marriage counseling, you would have to overcome one formidable difficulty: once the counseling episode is over, the couples concerned normally wish to close that particular chapter of their lives and leave it behind. Busy investigators, pursuing them in order to take their marital temperatures from time to time, would be decidedly unwelcome. By contrast, couples who have been involved in marriage enrichment are generally ready to be highly cooperative; and many of them are, or become, part of ongoing organizations through which they can be reached easily. The prospects for longitudinal studies should be particularly good under these circumstances.

Those of us who are deeply involved in marriage enrichment would be more than ready to offer an open door and all possible cooperation to bona fide researchers who are willing to examine the effectiveness of what we are trying to do.

Outcome Studies Already Completed

I have referred earlier to the 1974 report on Myrle Swicegood's research. That was by no means the first investigation in the field, however. I am aware of around a dozen marriage-enrichment studies carried out before that date. Fortunately for me, the outcome studies in this field have been carefully reviewed on three occasions by experienced investigators. First, Dorothy Fahs Beck, director of research for the Family Service Association of America, contributed a chapter to the symposium *Treating Relationships* (editor, David Olson, 1976) entitled "Research Findings on the Outcomes of Marital Counseling," which includes a short section on "Controlled Outcome Studies of Marriage Enrichment Groups" (pp. 458–61). Second, Alan S. Gurman and David P. Kniskern, at the University of Wisconsin Medical School, published an article entitled "Enriching Research on Marriage Enrichment Programs" in the *Journal of Marriage and Family Counseling* (vol. 2, no. 2, April 1977). Third, *Marriage Enrichment,* a book by Larry Hof and William R. Miller, has an excellent chapter on research, which analyzes no less than forty studies.

The reader who wants details is referred to these sources. In addition, the inventory *Enriching Relationships* (1980), by Kenneth Sell and Sarah Shoffner, lists about a hundred doctoral dissertations and ten masters theses on marriage enrichment, and the number may well have increased considerably since this publication. My own personal correspondence suggests that this is a field of inquiry that is particularly attractive to graduate students.

This research, as may be expected, exhibit considerable variety; taken together, they can provide only some general findings. Rather than analyze them in detail, I will summarize a few of the conclusions in the Gurman and Kniskern analysis, which raises more general issues than the highly technical discussion by Hof and Miller.

In all, twenty-nine studies are included. Ninety-three percent of all the programs used couples' groups for the enrichment experience. Three-quarters of them, however, consisted of series of weekly meetings, and not intensive weekends—probably because they were carried out with student couples in university communities. The groups averaged fourteen hours of meeting time. Little is known about the competence of the leaders.

The general comment of the analysts is that most of the studies "offer very striking evidence of meaningful change as a result of these enrichment experiences." However, the methods used in most of the studies come in for criticism on two counts. First, the majority of the studies (60 percent) measured change in the couples only in terms of their own personal responses after the experience; only 40 percent applied more objective methods of evaluation. Second, only four of the studies (including Swicegood's) made any followup investigations to see whether the benefits of the experience were sustained later.

All that these investigations tell us, therefore, is that most of the couples involved in these programs felt pretty good about their experiences immediately afterward; but we know very little about the further progress they made over time. Clearly, we need research that will include followup inquiries.

As I have already indicated, however, I am assuming that sustained growth after the enrichment experience cannot be counted upon unless we provide support systems, and this is the major criticism. So, while it is true that these studies don't tell us *all* we want to know, what they *do* tell us is highly encouraging and gives us good reason for confidence.

It must be realized, also, that some of the programs investigated in these studies were carried out years ago, when we lacked much of the knowledge and leadership skill we have gained since. If, therefore, those older programs were effective, we may reasonably expect that our more up-to-date ones will prove to be even more effective.

Areas for Future Research

I shall devote the remainder of this chapter to considering some of the areas in which I would like to see competent future studies carried out. I will follow roughly the order used in setting out the contents of this book.

I regard the major findings of Ernest Burgess and his colleagues as having been based on very thorough research, and as now established beyond serious question—namely, that marriage and the family are not failing or dying, but undergoing necessary changes in the course of healthy adaptation to a major cultural mutation. The rash of irresponsible propaganda about the impending "death" of the family, the grossly inaccurate descriptions of the nuclear family as a phenomenon of recent origin that is now about to end its brief sojourn on earth, and other similar sensational extravagances have I hope now had their day, and we may expect that sanity will prevail again. If so, it would be good to reexamine the trends Burgess saw so clearly and to discover how well the "companionship" model of marriage and family relationships is now being understood and accepted.

In particular, I would welcome searching investigations of my attempt to define Nelson Foote's concept of "interpersonal competence" in terms of a "primary coping system," and to confirm or modify my identification of the three essentials for a successful companionship marriage. Are three needed, or should there be more than three? And if so, what are the others?

A good deal of excellent work has already been done on couple communication and on conflict resolution; but I would like to see more attention given to what I consider a crucial issue: handling love and anger creatively in an intimate relationship. George Bach has written most on this subject, but I find his concept of "fight training" to be quite unsatisfactory.

I would also like to see further clarification of the process of "learning for living" as contrasted with "learning for knowing." This is somewhat out of my field, and I am aware that my four-stage concept may very well bring down the wrath of many educators upon my head; but I have been driven to it relentlessly by both experience and observation. Constructive criticism of this would be welcome.

It would be helpful to make studies of the process of marital growth, and of the concept of marriage potential. I have found almost nothing on these topics in the literature, yet I find that couples respond very positively to these concepts as I have tried to explain them.

I would particularly welcome further study of the dynamics of couples in groups. This is a subject of vital importance for marriage enrichment, and I think we cannot just apply our current knowledge of group dynamics to this very special situation.

Of great value would be an attempt to discover the origins of what I have called the intermarital taboo, to which I have never found any written reference. Possibly anthropologists might help us with this.

Several issues that apply to marriage counseling might profitably be investigated. One is the possible effect of examining a couple's "coping system" as a routine process at intake. Another is the use of the marriage-enrichment retreat with clinical couples; I have seen some promising results in the few experiments I am aware of. Some good results have followed also from putting clinical couples in growth groups at the same time as, or immediately following, the counseling process.

These issues fall into the category of testing out some of the theoretical concepts I have formulated, which are scattered throughout the book. I now want to focus attention upon the practical procedures used in our actual marriage-enrichment programs.

Investigating Marriage Enrichment Programs

Gurman and Kniskern offer six specific suggestions for future research, and I will include all of them here. For convenience, however, I will list the needed areas of investigation in the sequence before, during, and after the retreat experience.

1. *Before the Experience.* It would be valuable to make a careful study of the reactions of average uninformed couples to the idea of being involved in a marriage-enrichment weekend, by way of testing out some of the grounds for their fears, such as those I have suggested in Chapter 16. It would also be interesting to examine a question one study has already raised: Does marriage enrichment appear attractive to certain personality types, and forbidding to other types?

A closely related question is: To what extent can marriage enrichment be meaningful to couples belonging to our various subcultures?

It would also be helpful to have an objective evaluation of how couples react to such recruitment programs as the Explanation and Demonstration meeting and the miniretreat, and to know whether other approaches might serve better. Any increase in our understanding of the reasons why some couples respond to our invitations and others don't would enable us to structure our approaches to be more appealing.

Another question concerns readiness for the experience. We find that some couples seem to come for marriage enrichment at a highly "teachable moment" in their relational development. This seems not to be determined by age or length of time married, but by the internal climate of the couple's life together. Other couples, by contrast, seem capable only of low-key response. An attempt to find out what conditions these wide variations in responsiveness, and what kinds of programs are best for what kinds of couples in what kinds of relational climates, might yield some very interesting information.

2. *Types of Experience Offered.* While studies have so far found all the main models of marriage enrichment programs effective, few attempts have yet been made, to my knowledge, to evaluate their comparative effectiveness. Nor do we know what are the comparative impacts of the several components of a program—teaching, exercises, couple dialogue (private or open), and the like. It may well be that different components have value for different couples in different states of relationship. Certainly researching the issue would not be

easy, but it would be helpful to have *some* idea of what works best under what conditions. At present this matter is settled entirely by the subjective evaluation of the leaders and the observed responses of the group. These may in fact prove to be the most valuable guides; but it would be useful to have objective data to work with.

3. *Timing of the Experience.* Two different questions are involved here. First is the matter of *duration.* ACME standards require a minimum total of fifteen hours in organized sessions of one kind or another, because that amount of time seems to be required for the trust level in the group to develop to a sufficient point to make the experience really effective. On the other hand, extending the time much beyond this can lead to fatigue, and a falling off of responsiveness, in the participants. This criterion, however, has been determined only by leader-couple consensus, and may well be influenced by the fact that a weekend is a very convenient time slot into which to fit a program! The second consideration related to time is the value of *continuity,* which can be secured in a weekend program, but not in a growth group meeting at successive intervals. The growth group, however, offers the alternative advantage of enabling the couple to do homework between sessions and to report progress at later meetings.

4. *Size and Makeup of the Group.* In the Marriage Encounter, where no group interaction takes place, any number of couples could theoretically be accepted; though I believe Father Calvo favors about fifteen. The Marriage Communication Lab can take up to ten couples by dividing them into two small groups under co-leader couples for the sharing sessions. Where group interaction involving all participants together is basic, we find eight couples to be the outside number, with a minimum of four, and five or six best of all. These preferences are the result of subjective experience, but have never been checked out objectively. As to makeup, both homogeneous and heterogeneous groups appear to have their own special merits, and the question of what is best remains unsettled. The same can be said for educational, socioeconomic, religious, and age difference. Sometimes it seems good for the couples to be "all of a kind." At other times, having them mixed seems to lead to highly creative interaction. The fact that the couples come simply as married persons, use first names, and share personal experiences, proves to be a powerful leveling influence. However, objective investigation of these assumptions would be welcome.

5. *Group Process.* We very much need extensive studies of what happens to couples in group interaction. How can we best get off to a good start in terms of introductions and community building? How can the sequence of events during the weekend be arranged to make the "flow" of the experience match the needs of the couples? What signals from the group call for a change of pace? How far is it desirable to allow the group to make the program? Are

there established procedures for dealing with crisis situations? What are the best ways of closing an event—weekend retreat or growth group?

6. *Developing Trust*. Are we right in thinking that the trust level established in the group is the decisive factor in judging the effectiveness of the experience? How are couples motivated to be comfortable about opening up their relationships to the group? What conditions in the group best help the couple to initiate sharing? How can the group best respond to tentative attempts of the couple to share? Is willingness of the couple to dialogue a reliable index of their trust? Do we rightly avoid confrontation because it inhibits the growth of trust? These and other questions are open for investigation. Such investigation would be quite possible; we have experimented with groups observed, with their approval, through the one-way vision mirror.

7. *Modeling*. Just how does the modeling process promote experiential learning? Are we right in believing that modeling takes place automatically in groups of couples who are open to each other? Should the modeling process be contrived, or just allowed to happen? Can modeling have a negative effect—for example, when a person says, "Our marriage could never reach that level." Is it true that the deeper the level of sharing by a particular couple, and the more couples in the group participate in sharing, the more opportunity for modeling is provided? Such questions as these await more objective answers.

8. *The Couple Dialogue*. Since one of our central objectives is to get couples into effective communication with each other, we need to know what are the best ways to do this. We have some evidence that couple-communication training before the event enables couples more quickly and effectively to use opportunities to dialogue in the group. Are there dangers in the Marriage Encounter procedure of moving couples into deep private dialogue with no previous training or demonstration and no group support? What forms of couple dialogue in the group should be encouraged, and how can inexperienced couples be helped to get started? What are the relative merits, and the likely effectiveness, of reporting, exploring, working, affirming, and demonstrating dialogues? Are there any other forms? In what settings are these appropriate and effective?

9. *Leadership*. This offers a vast area for exploration. ACME has had a national committee of very experienced couples working on standards for leadership over a period of years, and Appendix 3 gives the latest version of what has been agreed upon. Many questions, however, remain open to investigation. Here are some of them: Are we right in our view that couples' groups are best led by a couple, or can an individual serve effectively? What are the comparative merits of leadership by one individual, man or woman; one leader couple married to each other; one leader couple, man and woman, not married to each other; two or more couples co-leading; a team of couples with a priest (Marriage Encounter)? What are the comparative merits of detached (nonparticipating)

leadership, as in a therapy group; facilitative (leaders as teachers and/or facilitators) only; or participating facilitators (functioning fully also as group members)? From answers to these questions we would then need to know whom to select as prospective leaders. Are ACME's present criteria adequate? Should the leader couple both be qualified professionals; at least one professionally qualified; or would a lay couple with unusual qualities be acceptable? If professional qualifications are considered necessary, how should they be defined? Further questions follow about the training of leaders. Are the ACME standards and requirements adequate? Should they be modified, or should further conditions be added? Another area of possible investigation concerns the effectiveness of the basic (Phase 1) and advanced (Phase 2) training workshops, and the processing system for certification. All these questions are under constant consideration by the ACME committee, but outside evaluation would be welcome.

10. *Followup*. All responsible marriage-enrichment organizations are aware of the need to provide effective support systems, but not all are able to do much about it. Research could greatly help us here. We have already seen that the studies so far undertaken have been weak in this area, and I earnestly hope that we can soon begin to get some reliable data on this important question. The pretest and posttest comparison has already established the fact that change takes place during the retreat experience (although oddly enough, I personally have never expected this to happen, but only that the couple would enter into a serious *commitment* to change). What we now need to do is to follow up couples for periods of time after the experience and determine whether growth and change have really occurred, relating these findings to various kinds of support systems, including the faithful observance of daily sharing and of working on crises. Follow-up studies should look for continuing growth, not only in the couple's own relationship, but also in the parental and general family situation. As Gurman and Kniskern point out, evidence that marriage enrichment leads to family enrichment "would be a powerful argument for the proliferation of such programs." In my opinion, this area of followup is, in terms of research, the most urgent and important of all. We have all the evidence we need, through continuing personal contact with the couples concerned, that some of them, following the enrichment experience, undergo a quite remarkable change, which case histories could verify. But what we need to know is what happens to the other couples with whom we are unable to keep in touch over a period of years; and to whom we might have rendered better service?

11. *Failures*. An honest appraisal of what we are doing in marriage enrichment must include the question: "Are we doing any harm to people?" I have been greatly reassured by the almost total absence of complaint or criticism through the years, because I am well aware that there are people who will find

fault, if they possibly can, with any new program or project. We are probably all aware of the disturbing facts that came to light following two major studies of the encounter-group movement, due to the incompetence of unqualified leaders and to the unwise use of confrontation tactics. In marriage enrichment we have from the beginning been especially sensitive to this and have made strenuous efforts to avoid any such possibilities. I have personally begged leaders in the field to report to me any "casualties" they have become aware of, and I have carefully investigated the few that have been brought to my notice. Some reports turned out to be quite inaccurate. In the few cases where clinicians said they had picked up persons who were emotionally damaged by a marriage-enrichment event, it turned out that the leaders of that event were quite unqualified and could never have met ACME standards. In one instance, a well-known clinician, in a reported newspaper interview, suggested that marriage-enrichment events might lead to the development of triangular situations between spouses in different marriages. I wrote him a long letter, asking him for evidence; but he never replied, from which I concluded that he had no evidence.

I believe that the almost total absence of "casualties" following marriage enrichment is due to four factors: couples have to come to these events together, which means that both are seriously committed to their relationship and eager to improve it; our emphasis is entirely positive and we never use confrontation; we go out of our way to emphasize that couples in serious trouble in their marriages should not participate but should seek professional counseling; our leaders are all happily married couples, carefully selected and trained.

I must, however, add a final word under this heading. One effect of a marriage-enrichment experience is to raise, or revive, the couple's expectations of marriage. Normally this is beneficial, because it creates new hope for the relationship and produces new incentives for further growth. But in a few cases, it seems to bring only discouragement. One wife said, "When I see these happy, loving couples, it makes me realize that we have never had a real marriage at all." In a few instances, despite our most strenuous efforts to help, such couples have ended up seeking separation or divorce. We see no way of avoiding this risk. We *want* to build up high expectations, because this produces motivation for growth and change. If for a few couples the result is not hope but despair, we can only conclude that the despair was there already, but has now been intensified by the realization of the true facts that hitherto had been evaded. Such couples do not belong in marriage enrichment events, and we usually find that they have come as a desperate last resort. As one wife put it, "We've tried everything else, and we came here hoping for a miracle." Miracles do sometimes happen, but we can't guarantee them. And we can't stop saying that deeply satisfying marriages are possible for many couples, just because they seem not to be possible for a few!

Conclusion

In this chapter I have tried to stress the fact that we believe marriage enrichment to be a very promising new product, and we have plenty of evidence to support that belief. We want to offer the product to the society to which we belong, which is greatly in need of it. In order to be able to do this convincingly, we invite the help of researchers to probe and explore every aspect of our programs, in order that we may make them more and more effective and therefore have a more and more convincing story to tell.

22

ESTIMATING THE OPPOSITION

WHEN a new product is ready for the market, those who have produced it, and tested its effectiveness, must estimate its chances of being accepted.

This is where we now are. If research should, as we expect and hope, confirm our conviction that we have a new and promising answer to many of the family woes that afflict our society, how do we then proceed?

We have a twofold task. First, we must consider the forces that appear to be *opposed* to our plan, and how formidable they may prove to be. Second, we must decide what help we shall need from others outside our immediate group, and how we can rally it in support of our cause. These two objectives—to assess our prospective opponents and our prospective allies—will be considered in this chapter and the next.

We therefore begin with our opponents—or at least those who *seem* to be against us.

They appear to fall into three categories. First, the antimarriage movement, if it may be so called—those who attack the whole concept of marriage as unsound, unworkable, or malicious. Second, the guardians of the traditional marriage and family values, who see the hope of salvation only in a return to the past. Third, the advocates of the "alternative life styles," who want to introduce radical new approaches to intimate relationships, and who tend to see companionship marriage as not being significantly different from the traditional model.

In my judgment, it is this third group to which we must give most of our attention. But before doing so, let us consider the other two briefly.

The Antimarriage Campaigners

There have probably always been people who objected to marriage, even if only because it was an experience denied to them personally, or because it didn't bring them the rewards they had hoped for. There have probably always, for that matter, been people who opposed marriage as part of the social system; although under rigid regimes they probably had enough sense to keep their opinions to themselves.

In our liberated contemporary culture, in which violent attacks on all our venerable social institutions have been increasingly tolerated, it is not at all surprising that marriage, like motherhood and patriotism, has come in for its share of calumny. By way of illustration, let me borrow a few examples quoted in an earlier book authored by my wife and myself (Mace and Mace, 1974, Chapter 1).

George Bernard Shaw, the outspoken British playwright, wrote in 1908, "I could fill a hundred pages with the tale of our imbecilities and still leave much untold; but what I have set down here haphazard is enough to condemn the system which produced us. The cornerstone of that system was the family and the institution of marriage as we have it today in England."

Thomas Mann, the German novelist, wrote in 1926, "Truly one may, even without malice, easily gather the impression that today 90% of all marriages are unhappy."

Dr. Norman Haire, a radical sex reformer who lived in England at about the same time, wrote, "Any moderately intelligent person who goes about the world with his eyes open . . . must be struck by the appalling frequency of unhappiness in marriage. I can find no reason to believe that my circle of friends and acquaintances is an exceptional one, and if I am to judge by them I must conclude that a large majority of marriages are unsuccessful."

In our own time, attacks on marriage have become a form of public sport and have been increasingly vehement. A woman attorney, speaking at a conference in California, announced her subject as "Is Marriage Lunacy?" A professional marriage counselor interviewed by a reporter is quoted as saying sadly, "We know that somehow marriage stinks."

The prize example I have encountered comes from a book entitled *Marriage Is Hell* by Katharin Perutz (1972).

Our expectations of marriage have transformed it into a ghetto of lunacy where two people put their antic dispositions on to play out roles of their, and society's, devising. In the attempt at impossible union, so much indignation, individuality, egoism and pride must be compromised that, finally, the separate personality laid on the Procrustean bed is fitted to an arbitrary slot. To be married means, too often, a capitulation to sameness, an end to self-development, and unnatural death of spirit. . . . It means the end of friendships that require sacrifice, and the end of risks. It leads to self-pity and overconsumption, to a conservatism that is moral and emotional as well as political and social. After a time, it brings out crazy fears of abandonment, of not being able to cope, of change, of desertion by children, of insufficiency. It causes the premature death of mind and soul through sexual rot and ploys for power. The expectations of marriage, dreamy and filmy, become a web to imprison the self.

Generally speaking, the motives for vicious attacks like these are easily guessed at. Some of the writers may have been personally piqued, either because they themselves had been denied the opportunity to marry, or because it had turned out to be a disappointing experience (sour grapes); or because their personally chosen alternative life style had seemed to come under judgment by married persons (retaliation). Others have found that adopting a vandalistic stance by attacking a hitherto sacred institution proved to be an attention-getting device, or a means to promote a favored cause, such as the more extreme forms of women's liberation.

Most of the vehement attacks on marriage can probably be explained in these ways and need not be taken very seriously, although such abusive judgments must inevitably influence the younger generation, especially when picked up and disseminated widely in the mass media.

The more violent attacks, however, seem to be dying down. Public opinion is changing as people in responsible positions become aware that the disturbing state of family life in our culture is no laughing matter, but must be taken seriously.

The Ultraconservative Traditionalists

I have already referred to the recent resurgence of support for the traditional family. This has of course been activated by conservative groups, and especially by Christian fundamentalists. Evangelist Bill Gothard, himself unmarried, holds well-attended rallies at which "God's plan for family life" is expounded. The basic concept is the "chain of command," which resembles a military system in which those of lower rank give complete and unquestioning obedience to those above them in the hierarchy. God comes first, then the father, then the children, with the mother allied to the father but in a subservient role. The message is that if the believers will adhere strictly to this system, obeying those in authority even when they feel that the orders represent a mistaken judgment, family life will soon settle down to a state of happiness and contentment.

Similar concepts appear in books written by a number of religious writers. The best known is Larry Christenson, whose volume *The Christian Family,* first published in 1970, has become a runaway best seller. A series of publications for Christian women have appeared, with Marabel Morgan's *The Total Woman* as the frontrunner. She advocates a subtle mixture of servile submissiveness and sexual seductiveness as the sure way to win a Christian husband's favor and lay the foundations for a happy home. This approach has won considerable support from a wide circle of religiously oriented women who are weary of the struggle to become "persons in their own right." Needless to say, women's liberation has briskly challenged this slavish capitulation; but it was a male colleague of mine who summed it up neatly by saying that "the total woman is a partial person."

Ridiculing this movement, however, hardly does it justice. As I have re-marked to more liberal Christians, at least these people *care* about the sorry state of our family life and are trying to do something about it. Although the chance that they will succeed by attempting to return to the past seems remote, at least they are trying to *do* something, and they must be given credit for this.

The hierarchical family was of course the only known pattern in biblical times, as it was a recognized pattern in all the major religions and persisted without being seriously challenged until about the middle of the nineteenth century. It was accepted without question in the Old Testament and received a good deal of attention in the writings of Saint Paul. Its supporters, however, have found little justification for it in the life and teaching of Jesus, whose respect for women displayed an attitude that was nothing short of revolutionary in New Testament times.

It is difficult to imagine how this doctrine can take any lasting root in our open culture and in the libertarian and egalitarian climate of our world today. Some open opposition to marriage-enrichment concepts does exist, however, among rigid religious groups, though I suspect that the doctrinal objection to the companionship concept of marriage really provides a refuge for older cou-ples who feel threatened by the prospect of having to change the patterns of male authority and female submission to which they have grown accustomed through the years.

I do not feel, therefore, that opposition from this quarter will reach propor-tions that will do the cause of marriage enrichment any serious damage.

The Promoters of "Alternatives to Marriage"

There also exists an antimarriage movement that quite seriously considers that there are better ways in which human society can arrange for the needs of men and women to cultivate intimate relationships. In Chapters 1 and 5 of this book I have made passing reference to the so-called "alternative life styles." We must now consider these in more detail.

A considerable literature has accumulated on this subject. Indeed, the present tendency of the news media to seek out the sensational has given the subject rather more attention than it deserves. This however has had the effect of stim-ulating a number of sophisticated research projects, so that as a field for inves-tigation the alternative life styles is now reasonably well documented.

A good example of this documentation is the symposium put together by Bernard Murstein under the title *Exploring Intimate Life-Styles* (Springer, 1978). The papers were presented at a symposium assembled at Connecticut College where Murstein is professor of psychology. The participants were selected by mailing questionnaires to a number of leading marriage specialists, requesting them to furnish names of knowledgeable persons in the area concerned.

The papers provide a broad perspective on the kinds of "intimate life styles" examined in the book. They cover the following subjects:

marriage contracts and contract marriage
androgynal spousal roles
sexually open marriages
the commune movement
swinging, or comarital sex
group marriage and multilateral relations
singlehood
cohabitation
homosexuality
life styles of the future

Obviously we have here a very wide assortment of variant behavior patterns, and they can hardly be treated as a unit. Together, however, they do represent what is commonly viewed as an antimarriage movement. The people involved in this movement generally support each other, read each other's writings, and have a sense of being joined together in a common cause. They even have a journal that tries to cover the concerns of all of them (*Alternative Lifestyles,* Sage Publications).

What they are *for* is the right of all people to choose for themselves their own forms of what broadly might be called "intimate relationships"—sexual, affectional, parental, familial, communal. What they are *against* is the restrictive, legalistic, rigid marital and familial systems of the past, which they believe are now anachronistic and must be replaced.

It seems likely that these people would support my contention that the traditional marriage is in a state of decline. It is not clear, however, that they would support my further contention that a process of social adaptation is going on in which a new emergent form, the companionship marriage, is taking the place of the traditional form, and that this form represents the alternative form of marriage preferred by large numbers of today's couples. Indeed, in all the literature of this movement I have found no evidence of any clear awareness of this major cultural transition, and I can recall no reference of any kind to the predictions of Ernest Burgess and his colleagues. When the word *marriage* is used, it is rarely defined; though when the word is elaborated in any way, the implication is always that the traditional marriage is being referred to. Since no hint is given that the word *marriage* could refer to something other than, and very different from, the traditional marriage, the impression is conveyed that marriage as such is integrally and inevitably something bad that needs to be disposed of. The mood is iconoclastic, and there seems to be no hesitation about throwing away the baby with the bathwater.

In other words, the existence of the companionship marriage as a *true alternative* to the traditional marriage has never to my knowledge been recognized; although in fact, as I shall seek to demonstrate, the companionship concept probably has more in common with many of the alternative styles than it has with the traditional model. It appears, though, that the concept of an "alternative'' form *growing out of the older form,* phoenixlike, and then replacing it, is an unacceptable idea. A true alternative must apparently represent an abrupt, violent, defiant breakaway from tradition. Anything transitional is suspect.

Yet in fact, many of the alternative life styles, properly understood, are not antimarriage. They are, as I pointed out in an earlier chapter, either forms of marriage that existed in the past, and still *do* exist in some non-Western cultures, brought back in new guise; or marriages that depart from the traditional form in one or more respects considered to be important—of limited duration, sexually nonexclusive, not socially registered, not intending to involve parenthood, etc. All of the life styles in Murstein's book, except homosexuality and singlehood, could probably be covered by Westermarck's broad definition of marriage (quoted in Chapter I).

Some Comparisons and Contrasts

What emerges from this discussion is the fact that, when we review attitudes to marriage in our society today, we may conveniently identify three different groupings: those who still prefer the traditional model (now generally in a much modified form); those whose goal is the companionship form (still emerging and taking shape); and those who favor the alternative life styles (with actual commitment to one or more, but not necessarily to all of them).

The situation can be portrayed in the following diagram:

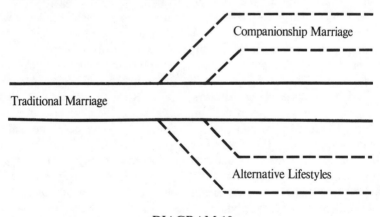

DIAGRAM 10
Marriage in Transition

The traditional marriage once reigned supreme. Then a period of confusion followed, in which the companionship marriage emerged out of the traditional form through a process of transition. At that same time, alternative life styles were being developed independently, rejecting the traditional model and ignoring the companionship form.

In Table I (Chapter 2), I made rough comparisons between a few of the characteristics of the traditional and companionship models. Now I shall make similar comparisons between some of the characteristics of the companionship model and of the alternative life styles.

First, let us look again at the ten items in the earlier table. We shall find that the alternative life styles would side quite decisively with the companionship version of all the following concepts:

1. decision making by joint consensus (Apart from a few communes with authoritarian leaders, the life styles all seem to support the egalitarian concept.)
2. fluid roles rather than fixed roles
3. flexible division of provider-homemaker functions rather than the man as provider and the woman as homemaker
4. sex initiated by either gender rather than by the man only
5. partnership rather than hierarchy
6. issues settled with reference to personal and interpersonal needs rather than to legalistic rules and principles
7. children cared for equally by men and women, rather than disciplined by men, cared for by women
8. religious roles (if any) assumed equally by men and women, not by men only
9. educational opportunities open equally to men and women, not primarily to men
10. residence decided in relation to both men's and women's vocations, not to men's only

If my assessment here is accurate, then the earlier forms of these items, rejected by the companionship marriage though central to the traditional model, would also be rejected by the life styles. At all these points both companionship marriage and the life styles have broken with tradition.

Now let us consider some areas in which the life styles have tended to go farther, in staking out new ground, than the companionship marriage. Since there is no natural order, these are listed alphabetically:

1. *Androgyny.* The life styles generally encourage fluid gender roles in special circumstances, and even, the reversal of the traditional role models. Companionship marriage would take substantially the same position.

2. *Children.* Some of the life styles tend to view parenthood as an "optional extra," and to give strong support to those who decide against it. Companionship marriage, although it does not view parenthood as a duty or obligation, tends to see it as a natural and desirable development, which expands the loving couple's inner world into a loving family circle.

3. *Cohabitation.* Some of the life styles, though not all, represent a rejection of the system of registering marriages publicly by way of identifying them as

recognized social units. Companionship marriage in general (though with a few exceptions) accepts registration as a desirable contribution to social order.

4. *Communes.* Community living and sharing has been a major emphasis for many of the life styles, though these have attempted to pioneer new forms of human community as well as to revive the practice of the extended family. Companionship marriage equally seeks to associate couples together for mutual support, as in "family clusters"; but it has not yet carried this to the extent of establishing separate communities.

5. *Divorce.* Many of the life styles accept the termination of an intimate relationship as a natural and acceptable stage in its development. Companionship marriage, although it recognizes that all couples do not have the necessary compatibility to attain relationship-in-depth, is reluctant to see a relationship terminated and encourages commitment to lifelong growth together.

6. *Homosexuality.* The life styles include the possibility of homosexual cohabitation. Companionship marriage has not included this possibility, although its principles for relational growth could clearly have wider application than to the husband-wife couple.

7. *Marriage Contracts.* Some of the life styles reject the legal contract involved in state-registered marriages, but may replace this with, or add to it, a privately negotiated contract among the persons concerned. Companionship marriage generally (but not always) accepts the state legal contract, but generally adds to it privately negotiated and flexible contracts, mainly as a means of promoting relational growth.

8. *Number of Partners.* Some of the life styles, though by no means all, include multilateral relationships—what would be called polygamy or group marriage in the old terminology. Companionship marriage, because its goal is a one-to-one in-depth relationship, is invariably monogamous.

9. *Personal Development.* All, or nearly all, of the life styles see the personal development of the individual as the primary goal, with relational development secondary. Companionship marriage sees personal development of the partners, their relational development, and their social obligations as a trio of equally important goals, to be kept in balance with each other as far as possible.

10. *Sexual Exclusivity.* Many of the life styles (though not all) see freedom to develop sexual relationships outside the one man–one woman dyad as a value to be sought or permitted. Companionship marriage generally (but not always) accepts the principle of sexual exclusivity as best serving the achievement and maintenance of loving intimacy between husband and wife.

11. *Singlehood.* Since the registration of marriages is not observed by many of the life styles, the distinction between a single and a married person is not clearly retained. The term seems, however, to apply mainly to individuals whose life style is to live alone but enter freely into a series of sexual and affectional relationships of relatively short duration. Companionship marriage, which is

couple-oriented, is concerned with singles only when they are moving into, or out of, the marriage relationship.

12. *Stability*. Many of the life styles attach no special importance to the continuance of intimate relationships over time, but see them often as phases in personal growth. Companionship marriage, while rejecting static relationships and actively fostering continual change and growth, views the continuity of the relationship over time, and commitment to this, as necessary for the full achievement of the relational potential of the couple.

I make no claim that this list is comprehensive, and my judgments are only rough estimates. However, the discussion clearly establishes the fact that companionship marriage stands in a middle position between the conservative stance of those who support the aging traditional marriage on the one hand, and the liberal, and sometimes ultraliberal, position of the supporters of the alternative life styles on the other hand. Consequently, the tendency among some conservatives (particularly couples of the older generation) is to view the companionship model with suspicion, and even to equate it with the more extreme alternatives. The tendency among liberals is likewise to see no clear distinction between the supporters of the companionship marriage and those of the traditional marriage. As we have seen, the word *marriage* covers them both, and this is taken to mean that they are both equally intractable. Since support for the life styles comes preponderantly from the younger generation, support for marriage enrichment depends heavily on the middle generation, which is neither very old nor very young.

This has its positive aspects. Marriage and family enrichment provide a bridge between the older family patterns, which are almost certainly passing away, and the comparatively new ideas, which have not yet been subjected to rigorous testing and whose durability remains unknown.

What this means is that the companionship concept offers the only really practical solution we have for the serious family troubles of our time. There is not the slightest hope that we shall revert to the hierarchical family systems of the past, though a certain amount of nostalgia for the stability they provided in our communities is understandable. On the other hand, there is no reasonable hope either that in the near future we can reorganize our society into tens of thousands of communes, give up all our registration systems for family units, or shuttle our adult population into a vast game of musical chairs with frequent changes of partnership. The implications for our society, and particularly for the children of the new generation, are too uncertain for responsible communities to risk.

It seems to me, therefore, that acceptance of the companionship concept of marriage and the family provides the via media, and therefore the practicable solution. The basic values that have undergirded family life in the past would not be lost, and yet the essential tenet of democracy—that persons must be reasonably free for growth and self-actualization, though not at the expense of relational fulfillment and the acceptance of basic social obligations—would be honored.

My hope would be, therefore, that as we put our family-enrichment concepts into operation on a large scale, we could provide solid ground over which the present generation could pass, on their journey from the irrecoverable past to the as yet unpredictable future. There would be a manageable bridge for those who will have to leave behind the finally shattered ruins of the outmoded traditional family system. There would also be enough of the new values, represented in the firm emphasis on quality relationships, to satisfy all but the most extreme devotees of radical social change. And for the vast multitude who have little comprehension of the cultural mutation in which we are involved, and who could hardly care less, there will be the possibility of happy and rewarding family relationships at a price that, once they understand what it is all about and receive the help and support they need, they can afford to pay.

The critical question remains: given a tried and tested product, and given convincing evidence that it represents the best solution to our current family crisis, can we manage to bring the detached and seemingly indifferent Establishment to a state of awareness of what needs to be done, and move its immense resources into action?

That is the question that will occupy our attention in the next chapter.

23

RALLYING EFFECTIVE SUPPORT

MAHATMA Gandhi, the Indian statesman and saint, will probably be remembered as one of the gentlest and kindest men who ever lived. Yet he was directly responsible for the death of his beloved wife. When she became seriously ill, the doctors diagnosed an infection that was spreading rapidly. Antibiotics were available, and preparations were completed for the necessary injection.

At that point, however, Gandhi intervened. He believed that the body took responsibility for its own healing, and that no alien materials from outside must be allowed to invade it. All injections were taboo. He would not give permission.

The doctors argued, friends pleaded. But Gandhi could not yield. For him, a vital principle was at stake. So, while the doctor stood by with his syringe in readiness, waiting only for Gandhi's nod of approval, the infection spread and Gandhi's wife died.

A tragic story? Yes, and all the more so because Gandhi was so tragically mistaken.

This story is a parable, a poignantly accurate parable, of something that is happening, right now, in American society. Gandhi represents the leaders of America, the people in positions of power and influence. We call them, collectively, the Establishment. They are, for the most part, responsible, sincere, and imbued with high ideals. Gandhi's wife represents the American family. It is in poor health and getting steadily worse as infection spreads. It is sorely in need of what we call a "shot in the arm." The doctors standing by are the people who have the kinds of answers that I have tried to describe in this book. The medicine has worked well wherever it has had a real chance. There is every reason to believe that, if widely applied to American families, it would be effective.

The taboo is a belief, tenaciously held by the Establishment, that family life belongs to the "private sector," a heavily protected realm where government in particular, but also other branches of the public sector, never intervene. The old saying that an Englishman's home is his castle aptly expresses the idea.

So the family gets sicker and sicker, and people even make predictions that it is dying. Yet the Establishment takes no action. The taboo holds.

In this chapter I will examine this taboo more closely, because the Establishment's adherence to principle in this matter is just as mistaken, and could be nearly as tragic, as Gandhi's pathetic firmness in refusing to give the nod that would have saved his wife's life.

Let me begin with a general description of how the taboo works in our society generally and then apply it in more specific terms to the Establishment.

Marriage Is Nobody's Business

When two young people plan to marry, others immediately become involved. The jeweler gets ready to sell them rings—for the engagement, if any, and for the wedding. The law becomes involved in checking whether they meet the necessary requirements as to age, health, relatedness, and unmarried status. The doctor arranges a blood test. There are forms to sign. The church gets busy preparing for the ceremony. The parents on both sides become involved in substantial outlays of time and money. Lists of guests must be checked over, invitations sent out. The printer is called in, and the caterer, and the florist. New clothes have to be purchased. The travel agent gets busy arranging the honeymoon trip.

When the couple plan their new home, the real estate agent becomes involved. So does the furniture and appliance vendor. When the newlyweds move in, that means new business for the grocery store, the electric power company, the purveyor of heating oil or gas, the local service station, and in due course, various repairmen.

When the first child arrives, the obstetrician is already on the scene, followed by the pediatrician. The pastor is again called in for the baptism. A new group of salesmen provide baby clothes, cot, and buggy, with the toy salesman hard on their heels. A few years later the school system prepares to receive a new student.

A whole army of people are involved when a marriage takes place. I haven't listed half of them.

But are they *involved?* They perform their duties, carry out their professional functions, deliver their goods, and take their profits. But who is concerned, really concerned, about what happens to these two people? Everyone makes great efforts to ensure the success of the *wedding,* which lasts a few hours. But nobody does anything much to ensure the success of the *marriage,* which is expected to last a lifetime. Hosts of friends congratulate the couple, wish them well, then walk discreetly away and leave them to their own devices. After that, no inquiries are made, no checkups, no offers of help. Such actions would be considered quite improper. That kind of thing just isn't done. Why? Because marriage is nobody's business.

We all understand why. We must not intrude on the privacy of young lovers, even if they are launched upon an extremely complex and difficult task with no real training, no competence in managing interpersonal relationships. We simply make the assumption that marriage requires no special skills. As Clark Vincent has expressed it, we surround it with a "myth of naturalism," which implies that human beings take to marriage as easily as ducklings take to water. It is all somehow instinctive, effortless, automatic. Of course it takes education and training to be a teacher, a carpenter, a gardener, a librarian. But *anyone* can be a husband or wife. You have to pass a test to get a license to drive a car. You simply pay cash down for a license to marry.

Even when one marriage in every two or three breaks down and ends in divorce, we persist obstinately in this line of reasoning. If planes taking off from our airports crashed at the same rate as marriages fail, there would be a public outcry and a federal investigation. But when it happens to marriage, the foundation stone of the family, which is in turn the foundation stone of human society, we simply shrug our shoulders and say, "Too bad—but what can we do about it?" If a house burns, we can rush fire engines to the spot. If there's an accident, we can call an ambulance. If a tree falls on a power wire, a trained team will be there in minutes. If your telephone goes dead, we'll have it working again in no time. We take elaborate precautions to protect you from epidemics, to keep your food and your drinking water free from impurities, to provide you with effective sanitation. We will arrange for you to have regular medical and dental checkups. But your marriage? Well, you see, that's something different. You have to understand that marriage is a personal affair. Marriage is nobody's business.

So we remain detached, apparently indifferent, pursuing the policy we adopted before marriage changed from something fairly easy to something very difficult. As the long, endless line of young men and women move into marriage, we stand aloof, letting them sink or swim. And the fact that we have never taught them to swim, although we have the knowledge to do so, makes no difference. The fact that the sea is much rougher than it was in the days when we adopted the hands-off policy makes no difference. Even the possibility that nearly every other one of them is going to sink makes no difference. We just stand by, awkwardly detached, helplessly incapable—because it has been decided that marriage is nobody's business.

The Social-Deterioration Cycle

Our refusal (for that is what it amounts to) to help and support marriage leads inevitably to a process of social disintegration, which can be portrayed in oversimplified form in the following diagram:

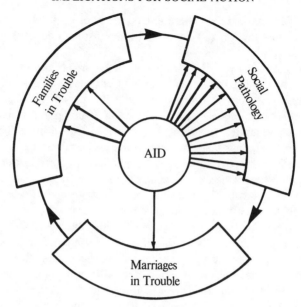

DIAGRAM 11
The Social Deterioration Cycle

At the bottom of the circle we have a marriage that is in trouble. This in turn inevitably leads to a family in trouble. A family in trouble produces disturbed and maladjusted people who create trouble out in the community, what we call social pathology. The kind of people who contribute to social pathology are difficult to get along with, and if they later marry they will be likely to create another round of marital dysfunction, family dysfunction, and yet more social pathology. So the process goes on, producing progressive social deterioration.

Lest this should not be entirely clear and convincing, let me elaborate on it a little by going through the circle backward:

Social Pathology. Our communities today are inundated with crime, delinquency, addiction, corruption, irresponsibility, social maladjustment, personality disorder—the list could go on. We are producing individuals who cannot or will not cooperate constructively in the ongoing life of society. They have bad habits, chips on their shoulders, destructive urges, predatory impulses, inordinate greed, low self-esteem, false value systems, etc.

How did these people get that way? Many reasons could be adduced. But what is really wrong is that they have somehow been deprived of what it takes to develop really healthy, mature personalities. And why is that? Were they *born* that way? Any therapist will tell you that they were injured at some point earlier in their development—deprived of emotional security, the sense of being loved and cherished, a deep confidence in their own self-worth, a code of conduct based on integrity, respect for others, respect for property, etc.

Why were they deprived? Because the family in which they were raised was unable to meet their needs. This may be oversimplified, but we are all aware, or should be, that really first-rate families don't turn out disturbed and delinquent children in any significant quantity.

Family Dysfunction. Why do families get into trouble of a kind that damages the people who belong to them? Because they develop destructive tensions in interpersonal relationships among the family members: manipulation, injustice, rejection, competitiveness, hostility, exploitation, deceitfulness, etc. How does all this get started? Obviously because the people who establish the family in the first place introduced these elements, or tolerated them, or failed to deal effectively with them when they erupted. Two warm, loving, sensitive, caring parents, united in their task, don't establish homes where the things described above go on.

Marital Dysfunction. Why do married people get into the kinds of trouble that spill out and result in conflict-ridden families? Because they have failed to achieve the kind of creative marriage relationship I have been describing again and again in this book. And why have they thus failed? Because we are all implicated in a vast evasion of the fact that marriage is a very complex undertaking for which most of us need training and guidance—in short, because marriage is nobody's business.

Surely this is clear and logical. Exceptions and elaborations could be added to every statement I have made; but I am painting a big picture with bold strokes. In such broad terms, I find the argument quite convincing, and I think it is irrefutable.

Now look at the center of the circle. What are we doing about this social-deterioration cycle?

We are trying to render aid; we have no alternative. We have in fact, across the country, developed vast programs. But at what point in the cycle are we making our major impact? I have suggested in the diagram that we are giving considerable support to programs dealing with social pathology; much less support to programs specifically directed to families; and very little support to programs dealing with marriages as such. And in the programs we operate for families and for marriages, my guess would be that practically all our efforts are going into remedial action, and virtually none into preventive action.

Let me take this discussion a step further. I would very much like an investigation to be made, by somebody capable of making it; the federal government, for example, might be ready to authorize it, or some foundation. The task would be to make the best possible estimate of the relative investment we are making, in terms of personnel employed, time spent, and money expended, in these three areas—social pathology, family dysfunction, and marital dysfunction—with comparative estimates in the field of the family and marriage between what is being done remedially and what is being done preventively.

I throw this down as a challenge, here and now. And I am even prepared to make a pure guess at what the results would look like:

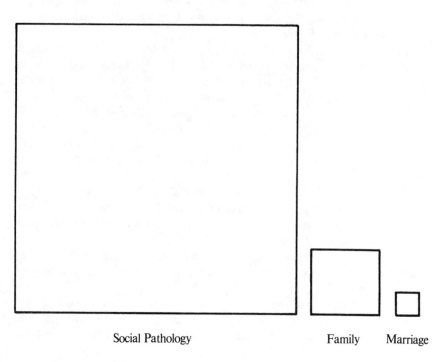

Social Pathology　　　　　　　　Family　　　Marriage

DIAGRAM 12
Proportionate Community Action (An Estimate)

Finally, we need to ask what kind of social policy this represents. It means that the thrust of our efforts to keep our communities happy and healthy is being applied most strongly at the point where the results are likely to be least effective, and being applied hardly at all where the results could be expected to be most effective. Another hypothetical diagram:

Imagine that the policy makers of the United States (the Establishment) were required corporately to appear before some major international agency to give an account of the programs they were promoting in the three areas of need we have been considering. And suppose an indictment of gross mismanagement were brought against them. What kind of verdict might a completely impartial jury bring to the court? Perhaps the most charitable would be: "guilty but insane."

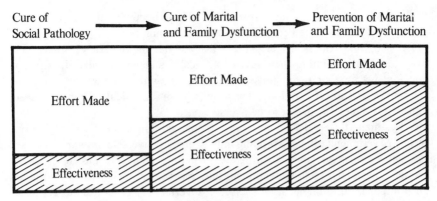

DIAGRAM 13
Effort and Effectiveness

Can the Establishment Do Better?

This kind of public policy is not new. More than a century ago, a distinguished American, who was often at variance with public policy, said what I have been saying in different words. Henry Thoreau said, "For everyone who strikes at the root of evil, there are a thousand hacking at the branches."

Another American made essentially the same point in 1915. Helen Bosanquet, in the preface to her book *The Family,* said, "It is quite remarkable how seldom the present student or reformer of society shows any recognition of the importance of the family as compared with other and more artificial institutions."

The explanation of this policy is of course clear and simple. The public sector does not intervene in the interior life of the family, because that would be an invasion of privacy. Let us examine this carefully.

I have already implied that there is an important difference between privacy, on the one hand, and what I have referred to as privatism, on the other. I value my privacy, which means that when I want to be alone I don't want intruders to interrupt me. I would also resent other people entering my home without my permission, even if they had no intention of stealing or doing damage.

Beyond that, I don't much care. If the government, or anyone else in authority, needed to have information about me, and I understood the reason, I would be quite prepared to cooperate. I try to live honestly, and have nothing I can think of to hide from legitimate or purposeful inquiry or investigation.

On the other hand, I regard privatism as unhealthy. People who have become secretive, and want to hide their inner selves from others, generally do so because they feel guilty, ashamed, or inadequate; or they have been badly hurt or deceived and can no longer trust others. These people would be far happier if they could be delivered from their "fortress mentality."

I do not find Americans in general fussy about their privacy. Some seem even to enjoy exhibiting themselves, physically and emotionally. If a person does not want publicity, as for example was true with Charles Lindbergh, he can simply ask to be left alone. Those who get a great deal of publicity seem either to welcome it, or not to be averse to it.

Why, then, this great emphasis on no intervention in family life? No one wants government officials probing into their sex lives, to be sure. Yet sex researchers seem to have no difficulty in getting people to answer the most intimate questions, so the government only has to read their reports to find out all it might need to know. In any case, if government agents tried to get information that people considered none of their business, they would not be told the truth, so they would learn nothing useful.

When I have encountered almost phobic concern about family privacy, I have responded by asking what kind of specific official action might need to be guarded against. No instance ever given has seemed to me in the least likely to happen.

I therefore suspect that the privacy plea is in fact a convenient coverup for what is really the case: that the Establishment doesn't *want* to get involved in the confusion and distress that marriages and families are going through at the present time. The "privacy" excuse has resulted, for example, in the U.S. government having no coherent family policy, which seems to me to be quite distressing. Other governments have family policies. West Germany has had a minister whose field of concern is the family (I once had a meeting with him). France and Sweden have had ministers whose portfolios include family concerns. The British government financially supports the selection and training of marriage counselors, and the country's social services are mainly family based. Yet in these other lands, all of which I know well, the governmental public policy of family support is welcomed.

Let me offer one specific instance. In 1979, the British government officially published a 146-page book entitled *Marriage Matters*. It was the report of a group of distinguished citizens who had been appointed to make a broad survey of the state of married life in the country as a whole. The report begins by describing how the Working Party, as it was called, was set up in 1975 by the Home Office, in consultation with the Department of Health and Social Security, "to assemble information relating to marital problems and the provision of helping services."

The report of this four-year investigation lists nearly a hundred organizations and individuals who gave oral or written evidence. In this document the British government submitted to the British people a full report, with a series of proposals. Here are a few comments from the concluding statement:

Marital disharmony is a major social problem, and the State should exercise a responsibility . . . for relieving private misery and exercising social concern by the provision of services . . .

Our evidence has shown us that large numbers of people seek . . . help with their marital difficulties . . . our hope is that the discussion and action arising from this document will contribute toward easing their distress and assisting their growth in love.

Could this have happened in the United States? Perhaps not. But if not, why not?

In 1980 the United States held the White House Conference on Families. I was one of the speakers at the Baltimore meeting, within an hour of its opening by President Carter. I saw how opposing political groups, aided by sensational press reports, used it as a public debating ground, trying to divert the conference from its real purpose. But the basic difficulty lay deeper: no real consensus exists today about what we mean by a "family." Consequently, the conference opened up all sorts of controversial issues, which prevented it from concentrating on its primary goals.

A better approach might have been to focus the investigation on the state of marriage, as the British did, and to set up a responsible body to investigate this thoroughly over a period of time. Of course, there are those who can argue about marriage too, but at least this would confine the inquiry to manageable dimensions. Marriage is a more definable entity, and if the emphasis is on its quality, on the factors that govern its success, and on our corporate responsibility for providing needed services, this would be a task the government might more reasonably have undertaken. It would be an issue, too, which would be relevant to the government's responsibility for the country's well-being. Although the parallel would be derided by some, it might not be wholly irrelevant to recall that the years preceding the fall of the Roman Empire were marked by the widespread disintegration of marriages.

If this country can be said to have any policy at all on marriage, it adds up to a tacit agreement to ignore the subject entirely. The huge structures of government in the United States—federal, state, and local—employ between one-fifth and one-sixth of the country's total work force. I once instituted an inquiry to ask whether, among all those millions of workers, one single person could be identified whose major or exclusive function it was to watch over the success of American marriages. All the inquiries I made received a negative response. What I was told was that the only governmental involvement in marriage lies in two areas: to make laws and to keep statistics.

Unfortunately, this attitude of indifference rubs off on other branches of the Establishment. Foundations give away vast sums of money for all kinds of excellent, and a few crazy, enterprises—not, however, to help marriage. One inquiry I made yielded the information that in a two-year period there were only four or five grants made by American foundations to organizations promoting good marriage. Three of them, adding up to a total of fifteen thousand dollars, were secured by myself to support ACME.

The business community, as far as I am aware, provides little support, even for aid to the marriages of employees, let alone for any wider projects.

It is, therefore, an accepted fact among many of us who work in the marriage field that attempting to get financial help is like trying to squeeze water out of a stone.

The mass media, if they are considered to be part of the Establishment, have a mixed record. Some women's magazines print useful material about marriage. But the more sensational press, and in the main radio and television, have done a good deal to encourage the cynical attitudes that have prevailed in recent years.

The churches are really the only section of the Establishment that have made substantial efforts to improve marriage and family life. This of course is what we would expect. Of no other branch of the Establishment, however, can anything like this be said. It is deplorable that a great nation like ours has watched marriages collapse on a scale quite unprecedented, and stood by with apparent indifference.

Many years ago, a play called *The Sleeping Clergyman* ran in London. The play was full of action; a rapid, hectic panorama of events was unfolded on the stage—drama, tragedy, humor. In one corner, as the events followed each other in rapid succession, the clergyman from whom the play derived its title sat silent in his chair—asleep, remote, uncomprehending.

Something like this is happening in America today. Marriages and families are going through a period of turbulent change and upheaval. Millions of men and women are going hopefully into marriage, struggling to succeed, giving up, getting divorced, parceling out their children, marrying again, some succeeding the second time around, more failing again. Amid this scene of chaos and confusion, the symbolic representative of the Establishment, who is not a clergyman and is not asleep, looks on with glazed eyes, indifferent, detached, uninvolved. How long will this continue?

What am I asking for? First, a little *courage*. If some of our national leaders would speak out, the climate of public opinion could quickly change. There is no need to denounce anyone—just to recognize that our family life is perhaps our most precious asset; that marriage can be a beautiful and fulfilling experience; that the responsible exercise of parenthood is a joyful task as well as a basic human obligation. If we could keep hearing this kind of message from people in high places, the cynics and detractors might realize that their abusive diatribes are not welcome and might tone down their utterances, or even fall silent. Then the youth of our land would begin to realize that men and women worthy of the greatest respect are promarriage and profamily, and that they had better take another look at the negative attitudes they have been led to adopt.

Second, I am asking for *support* for struggling programs that are trying to enable families to find what they most want: loving, creative relationships. Money is poured out in fabulous sums for all sorts of causes—good, bad, and indifferent. Isn't it time some real financial support was made available for the guidance and encouragement of families struggling desperately to be what families ought to be, and for the growth and development of truly healthy and happy marriages?

Can you imagine the electrifying effect that would surge through the nation if the federal government, which was recently wrangling about whether or not to build another nuclear aircraft carrier, solemnly decided to invest the price of such a weapon of war in an all-out program to get preventive services to American families designed and launched across the nation? That may be like asking for the moon. But after all, we *did* send men to the moon, and the American taxpayers footed the bill. Would they not at least as readily pay to see more and more truly happy families come into being, like twinkling lights illuminating the dark horizon from coast to coast?

If you think this is just idle rhetoric, read the next chapter, in which my purpose will be to describe in specific terms just how this could be done.

24
GETTING INTO ACTION

THE purpose of this final chapter is to present a program that could make possible the practical application of all that we have been discussing in the rest of the book. After some consideration, I came to the conclusion that the best way to do this would be to imagine a visit to a fairly typical American community, which might have actually established such a program five years earlier. So we shall now proceed to visit Homeville, a small town of some 120,000 inhabitants, where Peter and Judy Prescott, the joint directors of the Family Enrichment Center, are expecting us.

Visit to a Family Enrichment Center

PETER: Welcome to Homeville. I understand that you are interested in our center. As you know, my wife Judy and I run it together. She is busy now, but you'll meet her later.

VISITOR: Thank you for your welcome. I'd like to ask you some questions. First, can you explain how all this got started?

PETER: That was five years ago. But for two years before that, the citizens had been considering the project. Finally they decided to go ahead, and Judy and I were engaged to take charge.

VISITOR: May I ask what you had been doing before?

PETER: I was a pastor, but I had been trained as a family counselor, so I wasn't running a church at the time. Judy was a social worker, but doing only part-time work.

VISITOR: What motivated you to come here?

PETER: I had become more and more aware that we needed to deal with family difficulties at an earlier stage, if possible, to prevent them from ever getting serious. Judy shared my conviction about this. We began to get into marriage enrichment together, and we were trained as a leader couple and started to work as a team with couple groups. We enjoyed this more and more, and that convinced us that this was the way we wanted to go. We then went on to the full training for Family Enrichment directors and applied for this job.

VISITOR: You were hired to work together on a couple basis?

PETER: Oh yes. That's the way all Family Enrichment Centers are run. As the directors, like other staff couples, we model what we are offering to other families.

VISITOR: And you have children of your own?

PETER: A boy and a girl. They were still in high school when we started.

VISITOR: How did they feel about you both being out at work all day?

PETER: Actually we weren't. We don't both work full time. We are paid for one-and-a-half days of work at the going rate. This made it possible for one of us to be home for half of every day to take care of family duties. We don't want to set a bad example to other families with which we are working! Now that the children are away, though, the home jobs are much lighter. But we like the flexible arrangement, because a lot of our work is done in the evenings and on weekends.

VISITOR: You are both qualified professionals. Is this a requirement?

PETER: Not absolutely. It's considered important that one member of every staff couple be qualified in one of the helping professions; and the other is expected to have some knowledge of the family field. But staff couples are chosen on their personal merits, rather than on the basis of paper qualifications. Of course, we had to undergo special training, and our knowledge and skills are continually being upgraded.

VISITOR: I see. Now I'd like to ask about the center itself. You say it took a couple of years to get the project established. What was happening in that time?

PETER: I wasn't here then, of course. But I know the story pretty well. It was a matter of getting the community convinced that this was something that ought to be done.

VISITOR: And how did you go about it?

PETER: This was one of the earliest communities to take the plunge, so the issues had to be weighed pretty thoroughly. First, they had to be convinced that the idea was sound.

VISITOR: Who convinced them?

PETER: It started with a small group of couples who began an ACME chapter. This got more and more people interested. Then some highly qualified people from outside were brought in as consultants, to meet with various community groups—pastors, professionals in the family field, community leaders, businessmen, women's organizations, youth leaders, and others. A special committee was set up to do the planning and find the money.

VISITOR: That's an important point. Where did the money come from?

PETER: It wasn't easy at first. However, a number of leading citizens, when they were convinced that this was really important, pitched in. A local foundation got interested and matched their gift to pay for our building. One thing that helped was the discovery that the community was spending much more money on dealing with the *effects* of family failure than it would cost us to *prevent* family failure.

VISITOR: How did you figure that out?

PETER: They got the idea from a city in Minnesota, where all local families on welfare were investigated. It was found that lots of them needed support because of earlier broken marriages. It was also found that, at the time the marriages broke down, not one of all those families had received any kind of help from any church or any community agency. Yet they were now costing more than it would take to provide preventive family services to the whole community.

VISITOR: But that money couldn't be transferred.

PETER: That's right. But taking the long view, it was realized that prevention makes sound sense. So Homeville made the decision that a number of other communities have now made: to begin a readjustment plan that would, as soon as possible, match all remedial services to families with equal preventive services—worker for worker, dollar for dollar, hour for hour. When our city organizers figured out what this would mean, it was obvious that the amount of money that would then be available for preventive work would operate several Family Enrichment Centers! After that, the cost of opening *one* center didn't seem at all unreasonable, especially when some of the remedial services were cut back a little.

VISITOR: How did the people working in your remedial family programs react? Wasn't this rather threatening to them?

PETER: For some it was, at first. But over time, it hasn't worked that way. A few of these people are actually doing work for our center. And deep down they knew that this was the sensible thing to do. A lot of their work had been very discouraging, with people coming for help far too late. Now that we are sending them couples and families whose difficulties are not chronic, they like this kind of counseling much better, because they see results relatively quickly.

VISITOR: Does your center also do counseling?

PETER: No, not at all in the technical sense. One of our firm rules is that no clinical services of any kind are offered at the center.

VISITOR: Why is this?

PETER: There are two reasons, and both of them are very important. First, people generally feel very sensitive about "having problems" in the area of marriage and the family, and those seeking enrichment are reluctant to go for the kind of service we offer to a counseling agency where other people are going with problems. We constantly emphasize the fact that ours is an *educa-*

tional center where families meet socially, find new friends, learn about growing together, and get involved in interesting projects.

VISITOR: I'd like to hear more about how that works. But first of all, you said there was another reason.

PETER: Yes. The second reason is because one of our fundamental principles is that the center doesn't compete in any way with any other service that the community provides. We always *cooperate,* not compete. If we did counseling, we'd be competing with a number of agencies in town, and with people in private practice as well. By referring all counseling needs to them, we are helping and supporting their efforts. We do however keep a regular check on the quality of their work, and often follow up on referrals we make. So they know we expect high standards.

VISITOR: That seems a good arrangement for all concerned. Now, tell me more about your own program.

PETER: The program had begun, of course, before the center was opened. At first it was confined to marriage-enrichment retreats, miniretreats, growth groups, and support groups, with some couple-communication and parent-effectiveness programs. All this continues, of course, and will continue. Our whole program is based on the conviction that, until the parent couple have made a commitment to ongoing growth, you can't do much in the way of family enrichment. Of course that isn't possible with one-parent families, with which we work a good deal. But for all couple-based family groups, that *must* be the starting point. And in all other kinds of family relationships, we work in much the same way.

VISITOR: I can see the wisdom of that.

PETER: Before long, however, it became very clear that if you ought to start with the couple, then it would make sense to start where the couple themselves start. So the Growth in Marriage for Newlyweds program was launched.

VISITOR: What does it do?

PETER: Just what it says. The idea is to guide a couple through the early stages of their life together, so that the marriage will get off to a good start.

VISITOR: Does this mean premarital counseling?

PETER: Yes, but that isn't our main emphasis. The basic idea was to focus on the first year or year and a half of marriage. One reason for this was that most pastors try to use their contacts with couples getting married in church to give them some preparation for their future life together, and to do so in the context of their religious faith. We think this is good, and it's something that should be encouraged. So, on the principle that we don't compete with existing programs, our policy is to support and help the pastor to make the most of this pastoral opportunity.

VISITOR: That makes sense. But when does the center take over?

PETER: Actually, we are involved from the beginning. The idea is that the pastor acts as our representative, and on our behalf. In addition to whatever program he develops on his own, he tries to persuade the couple to sign up for the newlyweds service. He has forms available, and he does his best to get them to commit themselves to this, because it is both in his interest and in theirs that they should do so.

VISITOR: What does this "signing up" mean?

PETER: It enables them to avail themselves of a number of programs the center provides especially for newlyweds: couple-communication training, sexual enrichment, money management, and, later on, preparation for parenthood and parenthood enrichment. All couples enrolled for the newlyweds service receive notices about these programs and are invited to share in them. However, the real focus of the service is participation by the couple in a marriage-enrichment group.

VISITOR: What does that involve?

PETER: It can be a weekend retreat, but the usual arrangement is a six-week series held on one evening each week. We try to put together one or more groups of couples regularly each month. Six couples is the ideal number for one group. A bigger group would be divided into subgroups of about four or five couples each, with different leadership. The groups are led by ACME certified leader couples who have been specially trained for this work. They are paid a small honorarium plus expenses.

VISITOR: What is the objective here?

PETER: It was designed on the basis of research findings showing that the average couple, somewhere in their first year, reach a point where they become very receptive to the learning of new skills in such areas as communication, conflict resolution, dealing with anger, decision making, and interpersonal adjustment. The first year of marriage is the time when interaction patterns take shape, and the purpose of the enrichment program is to help the couple to develop really sound patterns. The leader couples, or facilitators, are very open in sharing their own growth struggles, and in this way they provide models that couldn't be provided with individual professional leadership.

VISITOR: It all seems to make sense. Do you find newlyweds reluctant to come?

PETER: We did at first. But now the program is well known and accepted. Couples who have been through it strongly recommend it to their friends. And high school students are told about it in advance by couples who have already experienced it.

VISITOR: Surely all this involves quite a lot of organization.

PETER: Yes. We have a special couple, John and Debora Paine, who run this program. They get to know the couples personally. And one of the features of the service is that all the couples get a friendly phone call from the center every three months during their first eighteen months of marriage, and more often where there is special need. So we keep in touch with them.

VISITOR: Do they pay anything for this?

PETER: Yes, although the fee is waived if they just don't have the money. The cost is actually split three ways between the couple, the church in which they are married, and the city—so the couple know they are receiving a gift from well-wishers.

VISITOR: This has been very helpful. But I mustn't ask too many questions about any one program. Why don't you now outline your total operation?

PETER: All right. But I don't mind spending time on the newlyweds service, because it's basic. As the years pass, it is these couples who become the nucleus around which our other programs are run—all the way up to our senior citizens' marriage-enrichment program!

VISITOR: That sounds interesting, too. But let's have the broad picture now.

PETER: Well, our purpose is to serve all families in the community, of any kind, who will accept and use our services. And the basis of all we offer is the enrichment of *all* family relationships—husband-wife, parent-child, sibling, stepparents and stepchildren, grandparents and grandchildren, uncles and aunts, even cousins.

VISITOR: I'm seeing a picture of your staff people helping family members to relate better to each other. That sounds to me very like counseling—or family therapy.

PETER: Of course there are resemblances. Our staff people know a lot about counseling. The main difference in what they do is that they spend most of their time facilitating groups, or facilitating those who are working with groups. You must understand that a good deal of our work is done by trained teams of volunteers, such as a married couple, a parent and teenaged son or daughter, a single parent, a stepparent and stepchild. We match people up—the beginners with the experienced, so that those who are well into healthy growth can model for those who are just starting.

VISITOR: I see. Then do the staff members sit in on these groups?

PETER: They may at first, to give help and support. But when volunteer teams develop skill, they can work on their own, under supervision from staff members.

VISITOR: So it's really a matter of people helping people, couples helping couples, parents helping parents?

PETER: Yes, you've got the idea. It really works, and these volunteers really enjoy it. Sometimes it's hard to know who gets the most out of it, the group members or the facilitators! And of course it's far less costly than having professionals do it all.

VISITOR: Under what circumstances do you make referrals to professionals?

PETER: That is decided by the staff member concerned. An individual, or a couple, or a whole family, may not seem to respond to the group process, and may need special attention. The staff member concerned will talk with them privately and suggest a period of counseling. If they agree, we set it all up for them; and of course they continue to be members of the center.

VISITOR: I see. Now here's another question I wanted to ask: How do you define a family?

PETER: We don't! We leave that to the people who seek us out. If they say they're a family, we accept their judgment.

VISITOR: What about minority groups?

PETER: It was hard at first to reach them, because they immediately assumed that we were a white middle-class outfit. We had to live with that for a while, until they found out how wrong they were.

VISITOR: Let me ask about your building. Was it put up especially for you?

PETER: Actually it was. The money was raised. But in some communities, they haven't been so fortunate. They have taken over existing buildings and adapted them.

VISITOR: In planning the building, what would you say were your basic needs?

PETER: When the center was started, an attempt was made to see what other kind of outfit would most closely resemble what we wanted. The decision was that the center should not resemble a clinic or a school, but be something more like a Y.M.C.A.—a friendly place in a convenient locality, with ample parking, where families and family members could come and go freely at all reasonable hours to meet their friends (the snack bar is a very important place); to attend lectures and film shows; to enjoy social gatherings; to borrow books and materials from our library; to take part in courses, weekend retreats, groups of all kinds, training programs. Families are encouraged to take out annual memberships, based on the number of persons involved and their ability to pay.

VISITOR: It sounds a bit like a recreational center. How far do you encourage this?

PETER: Only to a limited extent. We want people to come and go freely; but in accordance with our principle of not competing, we don't get into things like sports or physical fitness, which are provided elsewhere. The social gatherings we have are usually purposeful to some extent—a reunion of a couples' group, or a parent-teens group, that had already been into some pretty experiential things together. Our focus is very definitely on *learning;* but we want to avoid the formal, institutional classroom atmosphere. Comfortable chairs, for instance, make up a somewhat disproportionate item in our budget. And in all our rooms we strive to create a relaxed, homelike atmosphere. Also, we strongly encourage friendliness. If you meet someone at the center you don't know, you always say hello and greet each other. No cold shoulders or blank stares! We want the center to be a friendly place, like we want a home to be.

VISITOR: Do you provide overnight accommodations for couples taking part in weekend retreats, for example?

PETER: No, we decided against that. It wouldn't be a sound use of space at the center, so we go elsewhere for residential events.

VISITOR: By the way, how many people are on your staff?

PETER: We have built it up experimentally over the years, as we saw what our needs were. At present we have four couples, all on one and a half time, as well as the secretary and our "housemother"—a delightful widow with a warm, welcoming smile for everyone, but also with a keen sense of keeping everything in good working order.

VISITOR: Tell me more about your cooperation with other community agencies and services.

PETER: So far as management is concerned, we are under the direction of the city's United Community Services. But the affairs of the center are really settled by a committee with representatives from a very broad spectrum of community organizations—churches, the school board, youth organizations, child-care agencies, general professional organizations, as well as agencies particularly concerned with families. At first, the center was directed by our Family Service Agency, with the understanding that it would be kept quite separate, at the public level, from the clinical and counseling services. But now the base has been broadened considerably. I'm wondering, though, whether this is really answering your question.

VISITOR: It is, in part. But I would like to know also what goes on at the actual working level, as well as the administrative level.

PETER: Well, there's no standard pattern. It's very much a question of our staff making friends with people they ought to know throughout the city. Let me describe the way our spheres of primary responsibility are divided up. As I've already explained, one staff couple run the newlyweds service, which means close contact with the pastors, and some contact with youth organizations and the high schools. Another couple focus on couple-enrichment programs of all kinds, including the one for senior citizens. They of course have to be in touch with people like marriage counselors in the community, and with the churches, through which many of our programs are organized. They also cooperate with a number of progressive business firms that offer marriage-enrichment programs for their employees, which they find improves morale and reduces absenteeism. A third couple focus on parent-child enrichment programs, and with programs dealing with wider family relationships. Of course they have to work closely with all child-care agencies, with school staffs, with physicians concerned with child health, and with social workers seeking to improve home conditions and to prevent child abuse. That's the general picture. Judy and I coordinate all the center's activities; but in addition, our special responsibility is total family enrichment and family clusters.

VISITOR: Thank you. You really have given me a very clear picture of what's going on. I don't believe I have any more particular questions to ask, although I shall probably soon think of some.

Conclusion

Of course, to my knowledge, no such city as Homeville exists. The account you have just read, however, is not entirely fictional. Much of it is based on programs that have already been tried out, experimentally, in various communities. There is, in fact, nothing described in this account that could not be put into operation today in any community that had the vision, and could secure the financial support, to get going. And there is no reason why experimental programs of this kind should not be launched in a number of forward-looking communities, which could carefully evaluate their experiences in collaboration with each other. All that is needed is a change of mind and heart that will bring people in power to realize that the true wealth of a nation lies in its families, and that no price is too great to pay to give them the guidance, help, and support they need and deserve.

It must be remembered that the marriage- and family-enrichment movement is now twenty years old. And although progress was very slow in the early years, a great deal of experience has now been accumulated. Up to now, everything has had to be done on a shoestring, because people in positions of influence have taken little or no notice of those of us who have been at work in this new field; and even when an occasional opportunity for publicity has occurred, the investigator has generally been quite baffled and confused about what it was all about, and has not taken the time to probe more deeply.

Those of us who have been at the center of this movement, however, know beyond a doubt that we are dealing with something that has tremendous potential—even world-changing potential. It is becoming more and more clear to all perceptive observers that the technological revolution, which has changed our lives almost beyond recognition, can provide us with physical comforts and conveniences beyond the wildest dreams of our forefathers—yet it cannot bring us personal happiness and fulfillment in the deep and satisfying sense in which we long for it.

The final consummation of human evolution and progress will come, not by further improvement in our environment, but by the fulfillment and flowering of human personality and human relationships.

Not, however, the flowering of the individual in arrogant isolation. As a graduate student of my acquaintance put it so plainly in the title of her doctoral dissertation, "You Can't Be Human Alone." The key to human happiness and security lies in the achievement of creative relationships. In that area, we are as yet not much farther ahead than people were in the Middle Ages. But our interest is being stirred. The behavioral sciences are coming of age. The future holds great promise.

I believe that a vast improvement in human relationships represents the next great development in human history, and that now is the time to start in real earnest. And the way to begin is where all relationships begin, where life and love begin: in the family. And in the family, the natural place to start is in the nuclear husband-wife relationship. If one man and one woman come together seeking love and intimacy, and agree to share life in order to pursue that quest, and then fail, what hope can we hold out for relationships anywhere? So it is there that our critical task lies. And some of us are now satisfied that the people who fail in marriage are not in fact failures. They are victims, victims of a society that has not yet learned how to give them the skills they need, not yet shown them all the undeveloped and unclaimed potential they already possess.

The task of marriage and family enrichment is to release these hidden powers that lie beneath the surface in ordinary people, but have been stifled by the taboos and restraints that have been imposed upon them by rigid, hierarchical cultures in the past. Father Calvo, who began marriage enrichment and is now moving on to its natural implications in family enrichment, likens the power of creative love, locked up in marriages and families, to the thermonuclear energy that the physicists are now beginning to release.

What then is the outlook for marriage? We have to recognize that all people do not need marriage for their personal growth and development; that all who marry will not have the potential to succeed; that many who do have that potential will not have the motivation or the persistence to claim it; but there will nevertheless be an increasing number of couples who, for their own sakes and for their children's sakes, will be willing to learn what it takes to make a marriage all that it is capable of becoming. Those of us who have ourselves embarked on this exciting quest, and have already begun to taste the rich rewards that it can bring, know indeed that a truly loving and creative marriage is the greatest gift that human life has to offer.

To take this good news to a world in travail, and to open to countless families the door that leads to love, joy, and peace—this is our task.

EPILOGUE

THIS book has been written out of a sense of deep personal conviction, a conviction fully shared by my wife, Vera. Together we have worked, over the years and all over the world, to help to make marriage and family life richer and more satisfying experiences.

Always we have begun with ourselves. Our faith in the companionship marriage has been sustained by our own joint efforts to achieve for ourselves the kind of marriage I have described in this book. We want others to experience the joy that we have found; and we believe that this is a vital factor in bringing about that better world we all hope for.

However, many others have, behind the scenes, had a share in producing this book. With us stand a great many people who share our convictions. Among these many friends, first place must go to those who have helped us to build the ACME organization—the Association of Couples for Marriage Enrichment. Never, in any other endeavor in which we have been involved, have we found more loyal, devoted, and caring people than in ACME. They have shared with us a task that has brought its rewards, but also its difficulties and disappointments. We honor them for their selfless devotion to that task.

Among these dedicated people, I want to make special reference to Martha Jane Starr, to whom I have dedicated this book. She has not only shared the dream, but has also made it possible, in a very special way, to make the dream begin to come true.

My first contact with Martha Jane was about a quarter of a century ago. I had written an article for one of the national magazines on the importance of getting young married couples well launched in their life together. The final words in my article were: "What are we waiting for?"

Responding to that challenge, Martha Jane wrote to me from her home in

Kansas City. She invited me to let her know if I ever planned to visit her city, because she was deeply interested in what I had proposed. Not long after that, I was scheduled to take part in a Kansas City conference. We met, and talked, and out of our planning she and others developed the Family Study Center at the local university.

Later, when Kansas City was planning its bicentennial program, Martha Jane suggested that a family emphasis might be one fitting way to salute the pioneers of the American state. She asked Vera and myself if we would come and lead this program, and we did so. As we talked together, Martha Jane shared a dream she had—that Kansas City might set an example to other cities by developing some very special program to serve its families. She wondered if we would be interested in helping to achieve this. We said we would, provided the major emphasis could be on marriage and family enrichment. She was in complete agreement.

We were excited about this plan, because we saw it as an opportunity to test out enrichment programs on a community basis. For nearly three years we served as consultants to Kansas City, flying in for about a week every three months. The K. C. Mace Committee, as it was called, had an office in the city, with a project director. Martha Jane organized our visits to enable us to meet with most of the city's significant leaders. We went to churches, schools, colleges, youth organizations, women's organizations; we met with city officials, business leaders, professional leaders, and others. Everywhere we went we "told the story." An ACME chapter, the largest in the country at that time, was developed, and we trained a number of promising couples for leadership of marriage-enrichment events. Using these trainees, we were then able to launch the Growth in Marriage for Newlyweds program, in which couples were enrolled by the pastors who had presided at their weddings. Then, with strong support from the city's Family Service organization, plans were made to establish the Living Center for Family Enrichment, which is run in close cooperation with the ACME chapter, and offers a variety of preventive services to families.

In all these endeavors, Martha Jane was fully supported by her husband, John (affectionately known to his friends as "Twink"). Between us and them there grew up a strong and deep friendship, which we have come to cherish.

The description of the Homeville Family Enrichment Center is not merely a dream. In Kansas City, it *was* a dream at first; but Martha Jane has enabled it to begin to come true. The design for the Living Center for Family Enrichment was originally mine; but I was very careful, once the plan was ready to go into operation, to withdraw completely and let the local leaders develop it in their own way. All I could fairly ask was that it would be based on the promotion of marriage-enrichment and preventive services to families.

As I write this, the idea is catching on in other communities. It will take time, and a lot of experimentation, to learn how to establish and operate such centers. Nothing is yet certain. But I wanted you, the reader, to know that what I have written about in this book is not just ideas. The ideas are now being translated into action; and since Martha Jane has been the moving spirit in getting the process started in one community, it is my pleasure and privilege to dedicate the book to her.

REFERENCE LIST OF SOURCES

Adler, Felix. *Marriage and Divorce*. (Publisher unknown), 1905.

Baber, Ray E. *Marriage and the Family*. New York: McGraw-Hill, 1939.

Bach, George and Wyden P. *The Intimate Enemy*. New York: Morrow, 1969.

Bader, Edward et al. "Do Marriage Preparation Programs Really Work?" in *Journal of Marriage and Family Therapy*, April 1980.

Beck, Dorothy Fahs. "Research Findings on the Outcomes of Marriage Counseling," in *Treating Relationships* (Olson, q.v.).

Beck, Dorothy Fahs and Jones, Mary Ann. *Progress on Family Problems*. New York: Family Service Association of America, 1973.

Bernard, Jessie. "The Adjustment of Married Mates." Chapter 17 in Christensen, Harold (q.v.).

Berne, Eric. *Games People Play*. New York: Grove Press, 1964.

Blood, Robert O., Jr. *Marriage*. New York: Free Press of Glencoe, 1962.

Blood, Robert O., Jr. and Wolfe, Donald M. *Husbands and Wives*. New York: Free Press of Glencoe, 1960.

Bosanquet, Helen. *The Family*. (Publisher unknown), 1915.

Bosco, Antoinette. *Marriage Encounter*. St. Meinrad, Ind.: Abbey Press, 1972.

Bowman, Henry A. *Marriage for Moderns*. New York: McGraw-Hill, 1948, 1954, and 1960 editions.

British Home Office. *Marriage Matters*. London: Her Majesty's Stationery Office, 1979.

Burgess, Ernest W. and Locke, Harvey J. *The Family: From Institution to Companionship*. New York: American Book Company, 1945.

Burgess, Ernest W. and Wallin, Paul. *Engagement and Marriage*. New York and Philadelphia: Lippincott, 1953.

Carpenter, Edward. *Love's Coming-of-Age*. London: Mitchell Kennerley, 1911.

Christensen, Harold T., ed. *Handbook of Marriage and the Family*. Chicago: Rand-McNally, 1964.

Christenson, Larry. *The Christian Family*. St. Louis, Mo.: Bethany Fellowship, 1970.

Demarest, Don and Sexton, Jerry and Marilyn. *Marriage Encounter*. St. Paul, Minn.: Carillon Books, 1977.

Derlega, V. and Chaiken, A. *Sharing Intimacy*. Englewood Cliffs, N.J.: Prentice-Hall, 1975.

Folsom, Joseph K. *The Family and Democratic Society*. New York: John Wiley, 1943.

Foote, Nelson and Cottrell, Leonard S. *Identity and Interpersonal Competence*. Chicago: University of Chicago, 1955.

Gibran, Kahlil. *The Prophet*. London: Heinemann, 1930.

Goode, W. J. *After Divorce*. New York: Free Press, 1956.

Gordon, Thomas. *Parent Effectiveness Training*. Ridgefield, Conn.: Wyden, 1970.

Guerney, Bernard. *Relationship Enhancement*. San Francisco: Jossey-Bass, 1977.

Guldner, Claude A. "The Post-Marital: An Alternate to Pre-Marital Counseling" in *Family Coordinator*, Vol. 20, No. 2 (April 1971).

Gurman, Allen S. and Kniskern, David P. "Enriching Research on Marital Enrichment Programs" in *Journal of Marriage and Family Counseling*, Vol. 3, No. 2, (April 1977).

Haire, Norman. *Hymen: The Future of Marriage*. London: Kegan Paul, 1927.

Hine, James. *What Comes After You Say "I Love You"?* Palo Alto, Calif.: Pacific Books, 1980.

Hof, Larry and Miller, William R. *Marriage Enrichment: Philosophy, Process, and Program*. Bowie, Md.: Brady, 1981.

Hopkins, LaDonna and Paul, and Mace, David and Vera. *Toward Better Marriages*. Winston-Salem, N.C.: ACME, 1978.

Jourard, Sidney. "Reinventing Marriage: The Perspective of a Psychologist," in Otto, 1970 (q.v.).

Jourard, Sidney. *The Transparent Self*. New York: Van Nostrand, 1964.

Karlsson, Georg. *Adaptability and Communication in Marriage*. Uppsala: Almquist and Wicksells, 1951.

Kirkpatrick, Clifford. *The Family as Process and Institution*. New York: Ronald Press, 1963.

Kunkel, Fritz. *What Do You Advise?* New York: Washburn, 1946.

Landis, Judson. *Building a Successful Marriage*. Englewood Cliffs, N.J.: Prentice-Hall, 1953.

Lederer, William J. and Jackson, Don D. *The Mirages of Marriage*. New York: Norton, 1968.

Leslie, Gerald. *The Family in Social Context*. New York: Oxford University Press, 1967.

Levinger, George and Rauch, Harold L. *Close Relationships*. Amherst, Mass.: University of Massachusetts, 1977.

Lewis, J. M., et al. *No Single Thread*. New York: Brunner-Mazel, 1976.

Lindsey, Ben B. *The Companionate Marriage*. New York: Boni and Liveright, 1927.

Mace, David R. *Marriage Counselling*. London: Churchill, 1948.

———. *Marriage: The Art of Lasting Love*. Garden City, N.Y.: Doubleday, 1952.

———. *Marriage as Vocation*. Philadelphia: Friends General Conference, 1969.

———. "Marriage and Family Enrichment—A New Field?" in *Family Coordinator*, July 1979.

———. *Love and Anger in Marriage*. Grand Rapids, Mich.: Zondervan, 1982.

Mace, David and Vera. *Marriage Enrichment Retreats*. Philadelphia: Friends General Conference, 1972.

———. *We Can Have Better Marriages*. Nashville: Abingdon, 1974.

———. *Marriage Enrichment in the Church*. Nashville: Broadman, 1976.

———. *How to Have a Happy Marriage*. Nashville: Abingdon, 1977.

Magoun, Alexander. *Love and Marriage*. New York: Harper, 1948.

Mann, Thomas, in Keyserling, H., ed. *The Book of Marriage*. New York: Harcourt, Brace, 1926.

Miller, Sherod, et al. *Straight Talk*. New York: Rawson, Wade, 1981.

Morgan, Marabel. *The Total Woman*. Old Tappan, N.J.: Fleming Revell, 1973.

Murstein, Bernard, ed. *Exploring Intimate Life Styles*. New York: Springer, 1978.

Oden, Thomas. *Game Free: Guide to the Meaning of Intimacy*. New York: Harper, 1974.

Olson, David H. L. *Treating Relationships*. Lake Mills, Iowa: Graphic, 1976.

O'Neill, George and Nena. *Open Marriage*. New York and Philadelphia: Lippincott, 1972.

Otto, Herbert. *The Family in Search of a Future*. New York: Appleton-Century-Crofts, 1970.

Otto, Herbert. *Marriage and Family Enrichment: New Perspectives and Programs*. Nashville: Abingdon, 1976.

Perutz, Kathrin. *Marriage Is Hell*. New York: Morrow, 1972.

Peterson, James A. *Education for Marriage*. New York: Scribner, 1964.

Sawin, Margaret M. *Family Enrichment with Family Clusters*. Valley Forge, Pa.: Judson Press, 1979.

Sell, Kenneth and Shoffner, Sarah. *Enriching Relationships: A Guide to Marriage and Family Enrichment Literature*. Salisbury, NC: Catawba College, 1980.

Sharrar, Robert G. "Legionnaires' Disease: Stalking a Killer Epidemic" in *Yearbook of Science and the Future, Encyclopedia Brittanica*, 1979.

Shaw, George Bernard. *The Prefaces*. London: Constable, 1934.

Stinnett, Nicholas. "In Search of Families" in Stinnett et al., *Building Family Strengths*. Lincoln, NE: University of Nebraska, 1979.

Suttie, Ian D. *The Origins of Love and Hate*. London: Julian Press, 1952.

Terman, Lewis, et al. *Psychological Factors in Marital Happiness*. New York: McGraw-Hill, 1938.

Vincent, Clark. *Sexual and Marital Health*. New York: McGraw-Hill, 1973.

Watzlawick, P., et al. *Pragmatics of Human Communication*. New York: Norton, 1967.

Westermarck, Edward. *The History of Human Marriage*, 3 vol. London: Macmillan, 1925 (first published 1891).

Winch, Robert F. *Mate-Selection*. New York: Harper, 1958.

Zimmerman, Carle C. and Cervantes, Lucius F. *Marriage and the Family*. Chicago: Henry Regnery (now Contemporary Books), 1956.

Appendix One

ABOUT ACME

A DESCRIPTION of how the Association of Couples for Marriage Enrichment, Inc. started, and an account of its early development, were given in Chapter 13. The purpose of this Appendix is to add some further details.

Our goal in establishing ACME has never wavered. It was, and is, to create an international organization that will unite married couples in support of the marriage relationship. This is summarized in the slogan "To Work for Better Marriages, Beginning with Our Own."

This objective is somewhat expanded in the ACME brochure. It lists the following purposes:

1. support and help each other in seeking growth and enrichment in our own marriages
2. promote and support effective community services to foster successful marriages
3. improve public acceptance and understanding of marriage as a relationship capable of nurturing personal growth and mutual fulfillment

Although the title ACME is an acronym based on the name of the organization, it is also a Greek word meaning "the point of utmost attainment," the summit or peak of a mountain. This concept very appropriately expresses the goal.

ACME exists for the sole purpose of promoting better marriages, and all income is used to promote this cause. Membership is open to all married couples, and to couples about to marry. Associate membership is also available to individuals who support the cause; they may participate in all activities that are not exclusively couple-oriented.

Those interested in membership should secure a copy of the brochure from the ACME office. Dues are twenty dollars a year.

All members and associate members receive the monthly newsletter *Marriage Enrichment,* which contains news items, book reviews, and information about national enrichment events and training workshops.

ACME is a nonsectarian, nonprofit organization with national officers, regional vice-presidents, state and provincial representatives, and directors-at-large. All offices are held by couples. The strength of the organization is in its chapters. Member couples in a community may form a chapter, and the ACME office will provide resource material to help. Chapters sponsor programs for marriage enrichment: lectures, films, workshops, support groups, courses in couple communication, growth groups, retreats, and conferences. Opportunity for meeting other ACME members exists at state or privincial, regional, national, and international conferences.

ACME plays a coordinating role in CAMEO, the Council of Affiliated Marriage Enrichment Organizations, which fosters cooperation among national organizations that work together to promote the cause of better marriages. A list of these member organizations is given in Appendix 2.

One of ACME's services to the cause of marriage enrichment has been the establishment of standards for the selection, training, and certification of leader couples for marriage-enrichment events. Details of these standards are given in Appendix 3.

ACME began in the United States and Canada, and is now international. It has helped to establish affiliated organizations in Britain, in Australia, and in South Africa; and it has members in a number of other countries. Its outreach has touched the lives of thousands of couples.

You are cordially invited to join in the support of this vital cause. For further information, get in touch with ACME's administrative directors, Alice and Hampton Morgan, at the North American Office, 459 South Church Street, P.O. Box 10596, Winston-Salem, NC 27108 (telephone: 919-724-1526).

Appendix Two

MEMBER ORGANIZATIONS OF THE COUNCIL OF AFFILIATED MARRIAGE ENRICHMENT ORGANIZATIONS (CAMEO)

Aid Association for Lutherans
Appleton, WI 54919

Association of Couples for Marriage Enrichment, Inc.
P.O. Box 10596
Winston-Salem, NC 27108

Christian Church (Disciples of Christ)
P.O. Box 1986
Indianapolis, IN 46206

Church of the Brethren
1451 Dundee Avenue
Elgin, IL 60120

Church of God
Board of Christian Education
P.O. Box 2458
Anderson, IL 46011

Ecumenical Family Ministries
8 Cobalt Street
Copper Cliff, Canada

Family Service Association of America
44 E. 23rd Street
New York, NY 10010

Friends General Conference
1520 Race Street
Philadelphia, PA 19102

General Conference of Seventh-Day Adventists
6840 Eastern Avenue, NW
Washington, DC 20012

General Council Assemblies of God
1445 Boonville Avenue
Springfield, MO 65802

Interpersonal Communication Program
1925 Nicollet Avenue
Minneapolis, MN 55403

International Marriage Encounter, Inc.
955 Lake Drive
St. Paul, MN 55120

The Living Center for Family Enrichment
3515 Broadway, Suite 203
Kansas City, MO 64111

Lutheran Church—Missouri Synod
3558 S. Jefferson Avenue
St. Louis, MO 63118

Marriage-Family Encounter, Inc.
P.O. Box 20756
Bloomington, MN 55420

National Council of Churches
475 Riverside Drive (Room 711)
New York, NY 10115

National Marriage Encounter
7241 N. Whippoorwill Lane
Peoria, IL 61614

National Presbyterian Mariners
Box 1270
League City, TX 77573

Reformed Church in America
Western Regional Center
Orange City, IA 51041

United Methodist Church
Marriage Enrichment Program
P.O. Box 840
Nashville, TN 37202

U. S. Army Chaplain Board
Myer Hall
Fort Monmouth, NJ 07703

Worldwide Marriage Encounter
3711 Long Beach Avenue
Long Beach, CA 90807

These are by no means the only organizations that are organizing marriage-enrichment programs in the United States. They are, however, the ones that have linked up with each other in a cooperative enterprise and have thus recognized the value and importance of united action.

Further information can be obtained from the administrative directors of ACME, who also serve as secretary and treasurer of CAMEO.

Appendix Three

CERTIFICATION OF LEADER COUPLES FOR RETREATS AND GROWTH GROUPS

SOON after ACME was launched, it became clear that standards would have to be set for the training of couples to lead marriage-enrichment events. So a committee was appointed to establish and maintain standards for selection, training, and certification. The couples who have served on this committee through the years brought to their task an outstanding degree of skill and dedication. Thanks to their efforts, the ACME training process has, in the view of all who have experienced it, been of exceptionally high quality. Today, ACME certification is required by many of the CAMEO organizations; and where such organizations have developed their own training programs, these have usually been modeled on the ACME standards. These standards are also accepted in other countries.

One point must be made clear at the outset. ACME requires no specified model for marriage-enrichment events. Rather, it has laid down conditions to define what it regards as an acceptable program. They are:

1. The event should be led by one or more qualified married couples, whose leadership reflects an interacting, participatory style.
2. The method should be basically experiential and dynamic, as oposed to didactic and purely intellectual.
3. There should be occasion for both couple interaction within the context of the group and private couple dialogue.
4. Use may be made of structured experiential exercises, either to initiate dialogue or in response to it.
5. Group size should be composed on a ratio of one leader couple for each four to eight participant couples.
6. Participant couples should have some voice in determining the agenda for the event.
7. Planned session time should cover at least fifteen hours, preferably in a residential retreat setting or sequential weekly meetings.

Obviously where requirements are not very demanding, training standards can be eased. For example, the Marriage Encounter does not permit couple group interaction, thereby maintaining the intermarital taboo. This means that members of the leadership team will not be required to deal with the kinds of crises that occasionally occur in group interaction. Also, models which rely mainly on the use of a printed manual, on didactic material or simple exercises, likewise would not require any significant amount of leadership training.

ACME, however, insists that its leaders should be able, if and when necessary, to facilitate couple group interaction. From the beginning it has kept a close watch on what its leader couples were doing, and has required evidence that their skills be proved by a record of successful performance.

A number of professionals go through the ACME training process even when they are already highly qualified as therapists. They are invariably impressed by the high standards.

Selection Requirements

Quite apart from skills to be learned, a couple who seek ACME certification must be judged to possess certain personal qualities which have been found, by long experience, to be necessary for really effective leadership. They are:

1. The couple are committed to marital growth and are currently working effectively on their own marriage.
2. The couple are able to function well as a team, cooperating smoothly and not competing or getting in each other's way.
3. The couple can communicate a warm and caring attitude to other couples in the group.
4. The couple are ready to share their own experiences, to be open and to make themselves vulnerable if necessary, in order to help other couples.
5. The couple are sensitive to the others in the group, and perceptively aware of what is going on.
6. All prospective leader couples should have some basic knowledge about human development, marital interaction, and group process.

How do we evaluate a couple in terms of their possession of these qualities? There is only one way. They must be *observed in action*. To make this possible, they are required to participate in two separate marriage-enrichment events that meet ACME standards and are led by certified ACME leader couples. They are personally observed while taking part in marriage-enrichment experiences, for a total period of thirty hours, by different leader couples, involving four persons in all. Unless these four persons are agreed that the couple possess the necessary qualities, no further progress can be made toward certification. If the two observing couples disagree, the matter can be settled by participation in a third qualifying event.

There is nothing automatic about measuring up to these standards. A number of dedicated ACME couples have failed to meet this requirement, although possessing many gifts in other areas. For the most part, they have sensibly concluded that it is better to drop out at the start than to go on and risk doing a poor job of leadership.

Even if a couple meet selection requirements, another test follows later. Before completing full certification, they must lead or co-lead five marriage-enrichment events and submit the names and addresses of all the participants. These latter are then sent a questionnaire in which they assess the quality of leadership of the trainee couple. If any questions are raised that need investigation, and there is evidence of ineffective leadership, certification can be denied by the committee. And even after certification, any evidence of poor leadership can call for disciplinary action. In one case, for example, a leader couple caused trouble by disclosing, to fellow members of their church, certain sensitive information about a couple who had been under their leadership.

It is doubtful whether, even in the training of members of the helping professions, more effective safeguards are required than this. ACME's view is simply that leading marriage-enrichment events is a sensitive and responsible task, and that we cannot afford to train persons who do not possess the necessary personal qualities.

Training Workshops

A couple seeking certification would begin by signing up for a basic training workshop. Ideally they should already have met selection requirements. In fact, however, many couples have not yet done so; but they are aware that certification will be out of their reach until they do.

The workshop is residential and intensive, covering about forty hours of supervised activities. Not more than eight trainees may participate unless two trainer couples share the leadership, in which case the upper limit is sixteen. The event begins with a retreat specially designed as a learning experience, in which a sense of community is built up. Reports on this may count toward selection. Following the retreat, the trainees are exposed to a variety of leadership styles, given a basic grasp of marriage-enrichment theory, and taught to make effective and appropriate use of exercises. They then do practice leadership in subgroups, under observation by the trainers. Finally, and also in subgroups, each trainee couple must engage in a one-hour open dialogue in which they examine their own marriage and particularly their areas of vulnerability, in depth. The purpose of this is to enable them to be ready to share any area of their own relationship if this could be a means of helping others. It is an experience always approached with apprehension, but invariably viewed afterward as liberating and highly rewarding.

Completion of basic training, and meeting the selection requirements, can lead to Provisional Certification by ACME. Then, not less than a year later, and after leading or co-leading at least two events that meet ACME requirements, the couple may come back for Advanced Training—again a residential experience, involving some thirty supervised hours. This is more flexibly planned to meet the specific needs of the particular trainee group. Again, however, it is intensive.

When both basic and advanced training have been completed, and the required five events led, with satisfactory reports from the participants, the couple may be granted Full Certification, which is renewable every three years if all requirements have been met.

This brief summary should indicate clearly that ACME tries to do a responsible job in the selection and training of its leader couples. Full details of the process are contained in the document entitled "Standards for the Training and Certification of Leader Couples," obtainable on request from the ACME office.

INDEX

261